SHAKESPEARE SURVEY

ADVISORY BOARD

SHAKESPEARE SURVEY

AN ANNUAL SURVEY OF
SHAKESPEARIAN STUDY AND PRODUCTION

24

EDITED BY
KENNETH MUIR

CAMBRIDGE
AT THE UNIVERSITY PRESS
1971

Published by the Syndics of the Cambridge University Press
Bentley House, 200 Euston Road, London NW1 2DB
American Branch: 32 East 57th Street, New York, N.Y. 10022

© Cambridge University Press 1971

Library of Congress Catalogue Card Number: 49–1639

ISBN: 0 521 08204 8

Shakespeare Survey was first published in 1948. For the first eighteen volumes it was edited by Allardyce Nicoll under the sponsorship of the University of Birmingham, the University of Manchester, the Royal Shakespeare Theatre and the Shakespeare Birthplace Trust

Printed in Great Britain
at the University Printing House, Cambridge
(Brooke Crutchley, University Printer)

EDITOR'S NOTE

The first six papers in the present volume were read at the International Shakespeare Conference at Stratford-upon-Avon in September 1970.

As previously announced, the central theme of *Shakespeare Survey* 25, now in the press, will be 'Shakespeare's Problem Plays'. Number 26 will include some papers from the 1972 conference on the theme of 'Shakespeare's Jacobean Tragedies'. Contributions on that or on other subjects, which should not normally exceed 5,000 words, should reach the Editor (Department of English Literature, University of Liverpool, P.O. Box 147, Liverpool L69 3BX) by 1 September 1972. Contributors are asked to provide brief summaries of their articles.

K.M.

CONTRIBUTORS

J. J. ANDERSON, *Lecturer in English Language, University of Manchester*

ANNE BARTON, *Fellow of Girton College, Cambridge*

J. P. BROCKBANK, *Professor of English Literature, University of York*

JOHN RUSSELL BROWN, *Professor of Drama and Theatre Art, University of Birmingham*

INGA-STINA EWBANK, *Senior Lecturer in English Literature, University of Liverpool*

J. D. GOLDER, *Lecturer in French, University of Bristol*

ROBERT HAPGOOD, *Professor of English Literature, University of New Hampshire*

TERENCE HAWKES, *Senior Lecturer in English Literature, University College, Cardiff*

DAVID KAULA, *Professor of English Literature, University of Western Ontario*

KATHLEEN E. McLUSKIE, *Lecturer in English Literature, University of Kent*

KENNETH MUIR, *Professor of English Literature, University of Liverpool*

RICHARD PROUDFOOT, *Lecturer in English Literature, King's College, University of London*

JOAN REES, *Lecturer in English Literature, University of Birmingham*

NORMAN SANDERS, *Professor of English Literature, University of Tennessee*

LEAH SCRAGG, *Lecturer in English Literature, University of Manchester*

PETER THOMSON, *Lecturer in Drama, University of Manchester*

CHARLES VANDERSEE, *Professor of English Literature, University of Virginia*

CONTENTS

PLATES

Plate I (A–C) is reproduced by permission of the Comédie-Française; Plates II–VI are reproduced by permission of the Governors of the Royal Shakespeare Theatre; and Plates VII and VIII are reproduced by permission of the Governors of the National Theatre

viii

HEARING SHAKESPEARE: SOUND AND MEANING IN 'ANTONY AND CLEOPATRA'

ROBERT HAPGOOD

Shakespeare the theater poet was certainly writing his lines to be heard – as spoken by actors with appropriate intonation, pace, rhythm and volume. Yet when one seeks to hear *Antony and Cleopatra* in one's mind's ear one finds remarkably little help from commentators. Bradley and Wilson Knight have several fine paragraphs each on the overall tone of the play.[1] Granville-Barker has a valuable page on the range of tones that Cleopatra deploys.[2] Now and again a critical interpreter will follow the changing tones and rhythms of a scene or episode. Editors occasionally suggest the manner in which they think a word or speech should be spoken. But the upshot of this commentary is incidental and fragmentary. Nowhere in print is there a sustained effort to hear the whole play.

Why this neglect? One reason is that the commentators' interest has been elsewhere. In their search for Shakespeare's meanings, scholars have focused either on the very small areas of glossing words and phrases or on the very large areas of tracing themes which extend through the whole play. It is quite possible, though risky, to deal with these matters tonelessly, not 'hearing' the lines at all but merely gathering their bare gist. It is in the middle-sized areas of meaning – of speeches and groups of speeches – that matters of tone are most important. These too have been relatively neglected. This is true even of 'close readings' which proceed sequentially through the play.[3] Although they have more to say

than most about the sound of *Antony and Cleopatra*, their point of view is ultimately the same as that of other critical interpretations: they are more concerned with looking back over the play and stating what it all adds up to than with following the moment-by-moment process through which its meanings unfold.

Scholars may also have felt that hearing the lines is too elementary a matter to call for much comment, something that an intelligent reader can do for himself, or for which he can resort to a popularized 'Reader's Shakespeare' narrative or study-guide.[4] Perhaps that is why remarks about verbal sound effects are often

[1] A. C. Bradley, *Oxford Lectures on Poetry* (London, 1926), pp. 283–7; G. Wilson Knight, *The Imperial Theme* (1931; rpt London, 1936), pp. 200–5.

[2] Harley Granville-Barker, *Prefaces to Shakespeare* (1930; Princeton, 1946), I, 438–9.

[3] Specifically, Derek Traversi, *Shakespeare: The Roman Plays* (Stanford, 1936); and A. P. Riemer, *A Reading of Shakespeare's Antony and Cleopatra* (Sydney, 1958).

[4] Such as Babette Deutsch, *The Reader's Shakespeare* (New York, 1946); Marchette Chute, *Stories From Shakespeare* (New York, 1956); *Antony and Cleopatra: Notes* (Cliff's Notes, Lincoln, Neb., 1960); William Walsh, *Shakespeare's Antony and Cleopatra* (Monarch Notes, New York, 1966). These are scarcely more than plot summaries, their comments on tone being sometimes mistaken, often arbitrary or eccentric, always cursory. The Cliff's Notes study-guide is particularly debased, making the play sound like a scandal sheet. Unfortunately, Charles and Mary Lamb (who often have fascinating remarks about tone) did not include *Antony and Cleopatra* among their *Tales From Shakespeare*.

summary and arbitrary. How are we to hear Caesar's 'Poor Antony'? Traversi pronounces it 'an offhand and contemptuous statement of pity'; Kittredge, 'an expression rather of pity and regret than of scorn'.[1] Either tone is defensible but neither is defended. Surely the whole truth requires some discussion of alternatives and the bases for the commentator's preference?

For in fact such questions of tone are anything but obvious and easy. Even our closest readers have made gross errors, especially in hearing Cleopatra. From many examples, I cite two. Traversi completely misses her irony in the first scene when she repeatedly pretends to urge Antony to hear the messengers from Rome; everything indicates that she intends just the opposite, but Traversi supposes that she 'is determined to force the messengers upon her unwilling lover' (p. 82). Wilson Knight misses her mockery in observing 'How this Herculean Roman does become/The carriage of his chafe'. Without qualification, he groups this 'lovely phrase' with 'those stressed and highly-coloured phrases which continually emphasize Antony's nobility in war' (p. 211).

The truth is that fully hearing a Shakespeare play is a highly sophisticated undertaking. There are certain external aids. We do not, of course, have Shavian captions preceding the speeches with explicit directions for their delivery. But characters do at times comment directly on their own manner of speech and that of others. The use of pronouns is often a barometer of tone, as with the royal plural or the intimate or condescending *thou*.[2] The use of an epithet of address often sets the tone of a whole speech.[3] The reactions of other characters to a speech are often indicative. But these provide only the sketchiest guide-lines. A full imaginative hearing of a play depends on one's whole understanding of it, and vice versa. Like character and structure, the sound of the lines is one of those integers of interpretation with which the study of a play both begins and ends. As such – I say it one last time – the matter deserves much more attention than it has received.

The best current guides to the sound of *Antony and Cleopatra* are not in print but on recordings. Here is yet another neglected area. Although the latest Schwann catalog lists over one hundred separate Shakespeare recordings currently available, these have scarcely been noticed in learned journals, let alone thoroughly reviewed.[4] They invite a wide variety of scholarly activities. We ought to have complete archives of the Shakespeare recordings, including all of the rare early ones; a history of their production; and a complete and up-to-date discography. We should be taping important productions. We should have studies of the changing stage conventions for speaking the lines[5] and a theoretical literature on the nature of 'the recorded play' as a distinct art-

[1] Traversi, *Roman Plays*, p. 156; *The Tragedy of Antony and Cleopatra*, ed. G. L. Kittredge, rev. I. Ribner (Waltham, 1966), p. 98.

[2] Sister St Geraldine Byrne, *Shakespeare's Use of the Pronoun of Address* (Washington, D.C., 1936) provides a compilation of instances that is useful but incomplete and insufficiently detailed and subtle.

[3] In *The Development of Shakespeare's Imagery* (London, 1951), p. 167, Wolfgang Clemen collects the epithets applied to Cleopatra as a deft way of showing the many facets of her personality. These epithets tell even more, however, about the tone and attitude of the speaker using them.

[4] Honorable exceptions include J. Dover Wilson, 'The Marlowe Society Records', *Review of English Literature*, v (1964), 115–19 and a series of reviews beginning in 1960 of 'Poetry and Drama on Records' by Margaret Willey in *English*.

[5] Pioneer efforts in this direction are a tape-recording by Frederick C. Packard, Jr, *Styles in Shakespearian Acting from 1890–1950* (Creative Associates, Boston, n.d.) and a series of BBC broadcasts in 1968–9 by Richard Bebb on such topics as 'Acting Then and Now', 'The Voice of John Gielgud', 'Gielgud's Hamlet'. Both Packard and Bebb illustrate their observations with rare, early recordings.

form.[1] Above all, we need a series of studies which take the recordings seriously as a body of interpretation, especially capitalizing on what they can tell us about the sound of the plays.

There is some urgency about these projects. The early recordings grow more rare and expensive by the year. Productions worth remembering pass by without a record.[2] And our own ears change. For communicative sound is not only something spoken; it is something understandingly *heard*. And as the necessary rapport between speaker and listener fades, it becomes increasingly difficult for this communication to take place. Old recordings, even to the initiated, can sound merely quaint and artificial. My undergraduates enjoy Richard Burton on record, but they simply cannot hear the expressiveness of John Gielgud. To them he is no more than an elocutionist.

That is one reason that the job of hearing Shakespeare cannot simply be left to the recording artist. Words in print are a more durable medium than the perishable rapport between an actor and his auditor. Another is that directors and actors in rehearsal obviously have less time than scholars do, to analyze and research and ponder. Furthermore, the performer's purposes are limited and practical: what he wants is a manner of speech that he has it in him to render convincingly, that suits his conception of his role generally, and that fits into the whole production.[3] The scholar can range much more widely, surveying the tones that various actors have used for a given speech and scouting out further valid possibilities. The two activities are thus parallel but distinct. And they ought to be mutually helpful.

I should like now to try to hear *Antony and Cleopatra*, using as aids excerpts from the only two complete recordings of the play.[4] I will begin by recalling some sounds that seem to me characteristic of the whole play and then comment in detail on a few episodes.

I

One's first impression of *Antony and Cleopatra* is of size and breadth, of extreme contrasts boldly juxtaposed; and these features are as evident in the sounds of the play as in every other aspect. In pace, the play can idle with bored Cleopatra:

Cleopatra. Charmian!
Charmian. Madam?
Cleopatra. Ha, ha!
   Give me to drink mandragora.
Charmian.   Why, madam?
Cleopatra. That I might sleep out this great gap of time
   My Antony is away.   (I, v, 1–6)[5]

[1] Interesting comments on such matters are included in a set of statements by Peter Wood, Howard Sackler, and Peter Orr (often quoting George Rylands) concerning 'Theater on Record', *Plays and Players* (January 1964), pp. 16–18.

[2] Of the most recent important productions of *Antony and Cleopatra*, neither the Zoe Caldwell–Christopher Plummer production at Ontario nor the Margaret Leighton–John Clements production at Chichester was taped.

[3] The same limitations apply to the practice of 'oral interpretation', where the governing emphasis is on techniques for effective performance rather than on analysis of the author's intentions as to tone.

[4] When given as a talk at the International Shakespeare Conference at the Shakespeare Institute, Stratford-upon Avon, in September 1970, the various verbal sound-effects under discussion were illustrated by excerpts from the two complete recorded versions of the play: *Antony and Cleopatra* (Phonodisc, directed by George Rylands, Argo, Lond A 4427 (5746–9), 1963), with Irene Worth as Cleopatra, Richard Johnson as Antony, and Robert Eddison as Caesar; and *Antony and Cleopatra* (Phonodisc, directed by Howard Sackler, Shakespeare Recording Society, SRS 235, 1963), with Pamela Brown as Cleopatra and Anthony Quayle as Antony. Except where noted, all excerpts used were from the Argo (Marlowe Society) recording. A reader who has access to these recordings may wish to play the relevant passages for himself. But the discussion here is, I believe, intelligible without them.

[5] All line references are to the new Arden edition of *Antony and Cleopatra*, ed. M. R. Ridley (London, 1968).

It was Kittredge who suggested Cleopatra's 'Yawn of ennui' at 'Ha, ha'. Is there a play on 'gap' as 'gape' in 'great gap of time'? Then, in contrast to this idleness, the next scene brings on resolute Pompey and others 'in war-like manner'.

In volume, the play can shift from the silence of Octavia, so submissive that she whispers her farewells to her brother and says no more for the rest of that scene, to the outspoken imperiousness of Cleopatra in the next scene:

Cleopatra. Where is the fellow?
Alexas.   Half afeard to come.
Cleopatra. Go to, go to...
      Come thou near.
Messenger. Most gracious majesty!
Cleopatra.   Didst thou behold
   Octavia?
Messenger.   Ay, dread queen.

(III, iii, 1–3, 7–9)

In tone there are all sorts of polarities juxtaposed. Cleopatra defines one of them in her dream of Antony:

                        his voice was propertied
As all the tuned spheres, and that to friends;
But when he meant to quail, and shake the orb,
He was as rattling thunder.

(V, ii, 83–6)

Notice how Irene Worth's voice subtly reflects the tone-qualities her words extoll, becoming musically iambic with 'As all the tuned spheres' and then capitalizing on the onomatopoeia of 'rattling thunder'.

The point of view of the speakers ranges from the drily ironic detachment of Enobarbus to the utter subjectivity of Cleopatra persuading herself that Octavia is 'dull of tongue, and dwarfish'. Caesar combines the two attitudes in a single speech:

If they had swallow'd poison, 'twould appear
By external swelling: but she looks like sleep,
As she would catch another Antony
In her strong toil of grace.

(V, ii, 343–6)

Here his diagnosis that there is no 'external swelling' is so objective as to sound clinical; yet it gives way to a pair of similes that show a surprising empathy.

Where Cleopatra is concerned, the dialogue is full of *double entendres*:

Agrippa.   Royal wench!
   She made great Caesar lay his sword to bed;
   He plough'd her, and she cropp'd.

(II, ii, 226–8)

Such earthy innuendo contrasts with the awe of the soldiers who hear unearthly 'Music i' the air': and the two tones meet when the eerie prophecies of the Soothsayer are interrupted by the trifling bawdy of Cleopatra's *ménage*:

Soothsayer. Your fortunes are alike.
Iras. But how, but how? Give me particulars.
Soothsayer. I have said.
Iras. Am I not an inch of fortune better than she?
Charmian. Well, if you were but an inch of fortune
   better than I, where would you choose it?
Iras. Not in my husband's nose.

(I, ii, 52–8)

Yet the impression of all-inclusive scope – of a grand passion being acted out within a global, in fact cosmic, scene – can be misleading. For one thing, the extreme tones are not sustained: the scenes are very numerous and relatively short, and so are the individual speeches.[1] Nor do the extremes go as deep as in other tragedies. Antony becomes angry to the point of madness, but we do not hear the raging madness of Lear. He is frequently sententious and has some acute psychological perceptions; but we do not hear the metaphysical speculations of Hamlet. He expresses shame but little guilt: he is not a Macbeth. Like many of the other characters, he explodes into scorn and hatred; but nowhere in the play do we hear the confirmed malignity of Aaron or Iago.

In fact, most of the verbal sound-effects in *Antony and Cleopatra* fall within quite a limited

[1] Mark Van Doren, *Shakespeare* (New York, 1939), p. 269.

range. These are sophisticated people. Their talk is intense but controlled, and always self-conscious. It is almost always calculated – rarely is speech a simple expression of feeling or observation. Often it is forced, as when reluctant messengers bring bad news. And often the listeners do not want to listen. For these people are constantly engaged in exploiting speech, trying to use it as a way of imposing their wills on a recalcitrant world – whether to transform the world or merely make it appear better to others and themselves.

When in soliloquy or confidence a feeling is directly expressed, its tonal coloring is likely to be complex, often ambivalent. Even so ostensibly carefree a scene as when Cleopatra plays 'squire' and helps Eros arm Antony must be heard with contradictory undertones; for at its end she needs to be led to her chamber, wishing that Caesar and Antony might clash 'in single fight': 'Then Antony – ; but now – Well on' (IV, iv, 38).

This is not the stuff of grand opera – as Samuel Barber was to learn.[1] Nor will these situations sustain the spectacularly visual productions with which the play has regularly failed during the past century. The immense scope of the background is certainly there in Shakespeare's text, but it may be time to try a different sort of immediate context for the action, something less grand. For most of the tones we hear in *Antony and Cleopatra* are those that might be overheard through the walls of the luxury apartment next door. The three principals are locked in a strange triangle. They are engaged in a constant struggle for sovereignty – less for rule of the world, one often feels, than for personal primacy over one another. Scene after scene is given over to their accusations of infidelity, vows of loyalty, pleas for pardon, and words of reconciliation. Even when they are not in direct confrontation, these patterns are developed through messengers and invocations.

Not that the play verges on domestic tragedy. It comes closer to drawing-room tragedy – such as *Uncle Vanya* or *Rosmersholm* or *Dance of Death* or *Heartbreak House*. Yet it is more public than these. It is Shakespeare's most persistently *courtly* tragedy. Other Shakespeare tragedies leave the court for the wilds of the heath or the intimacies of the private chamber or the inner landscape of the soliloquy. In *Antony and Cleopatra*, even the battle scenes tend to begin and end in the royal palace. It is the small scene at court – where we are in the 'presence' of one or two of the principals, where a few 'others' are almost always involved or looking on, where the tones are always personal but rarely intimate – that is the defining context for these wars of the heart.

Down deep, *Antony and Cleopatra* is perhaps closest to John Ford's *The Broken Heart*. The feelings and words of Shakespeare's characters are, of course, much less subdued than those of Ford's characters – with Shakespeare there is no room for doubt that the powerful feelings being controlled are truly there. Yet beneath its flamboyance, *Antony and Cleopatra* is like *The Broken Heart* in making a sensitive yet rigorous incision into 'the very heart of loss', both plays being centrally concerned with doomed love, the prolonged con-

[1] There is a privately made tape of the NBC broadcast of the first performance of Barber's opera *Antony and Cleopatra* (16 September 1966) in the Harvard Music Library. To listen to it is to hear the complexity of Shakespeare's tones simplified to conventionally operatic ones: at Antony's departure, it is Cleopatra's few lyric moments that dominate ('Eternity was in our lips', 'You and I must part'); at his return, the 'If it be love indeed' passage (transposed from the beginning) is rendered simply as soaring love music; there is no undercurrent of regret in the episode in which Cleopatra helps to arm Antony. The choppy first part of the opera suggests the incidental music of a movie sound-track; only in the brooding latter part does the music find its integrity, with its minor-keyed laments by Antony, Cleopatra, Enobarbus, and Caesar. Caesar's mourning 'I have followed thee to this' is especially powerful.

sequences of betrayal, the gradual draining away of the life-blood ability to master one's self and the world, the stoic endurance of heart-ache.

Of course, Shakespeare makes it clear that the hearts of his principals do not break. The hearts of Enobarbus and Iras break; Charmian wishes that hers would; and Antony implores his heart to crack its frail case. But there is a valiancy about the heart of the two lovers that not only withstands misfortune but makes their deaths something much more affirmative than the spartan wedding of 'the Broken Heart' to 'the Lifeless Trunk'. Ultimately, as Gide – who translated *Antony and Cleopatra* – observed: 'all is conquest; there is no submission'.[1] The finales in Shakespeare and Ford thus differ fundamentally; but the emotional milieu from which they issue seems to me very much the same.

II

Let us try to hear the first scene.

Philo's opening speech illustrates one of the play's most important tonal polarities: rhapsodic praise for Antony as he was versus acrid dispraise for Antony as he is:

> his captain's heart,
> Which in the scuffles of great fights hath burst
> The buckles on his breast, reneges all temper,
> And is become the bellows and the fan
> To cool a gipsy's lust. (6–10)

There is also an argumentative tone heightening Philo's language. Responding to whatever Demetrius has been saying in Antony's defense offstage, he is making a point, and to that extent the apparent choric authority of his judgments is limited by his tone.

I should like to dwell a bit on the first exchange between Antony and Cleopatra:

Cleopatra. If it be love indeed, tell me how much.
Antony. There's beggary in the love that can be reckon'd.
Cleopatra. I'll set a bourn how far to be belov'd.
Antony. Then must thou needs find out new heaven, new earth. (14–17)

This is not just conventional love talk. The sheer fact that the lovers are self-consciously talking about their love is in character; as Coleridge remarked, their passion 'is supported and reinforced by voluntary stimulus and sought-for associations, instead of blossoming out of spontaneous emotion.'[2] Their tone is light. Instead of the supercharged exchange of home-truths in classical stichomythia, their give-and-take has the quality of quick-witted fencing, of repartee – yet it is by no means inconsequential. This is the kind of idle but meaningful banter through which a relationship can feel free to define itself.

As usual in the first part of the play, the initiative is with Cleopatra, and she is making herself engaging by her self-defined method of contrariness. King Lear simply wants his daughters to tell him how much they love him. Cleopatra needs reassurance, too; but she asks Antony to 'tell me how much' because she knows that such quantifying will provoke his natural expansiveness.

Antony's response (that 'There's beggary in the love that can be reckon'd') shows considerable poise. Note how his 'reckon'd' plays on Cleopatra's 'tell'. This is the first of the play's numerous (yet unstudied) economic metaphors. Cleopatra's riposte seems to me very witty indeed. Her offer to 'set a bourn how far to be belov'd' completely shifts her ground, no longer questioning Antony's love and its extent but assuming it and seeking to set its limits! 'Bourn' may suggest a very distant boundary – as if to invite the answer: 'How deep is the ocean?' Or perhaps she is thinking of a self-limited intimacy, as in the marriage contract of Millamant and Mirabell. Or perhaps she would stipulate that Antony should not

[1] Philip Roddman, 'André Gide on Shakespeare', *Shakespeare Encomium*, ed. Anne Paolucci (New York, 1964), p. 80.
[2] *Coleridge on Shakespeare*, ed. Terence Hawkes (Harmondsworth, 1969), p. 269.

love to the extent of losing his imperial power. Certainly, her speech is highly provocative to Antony's expansiveness, with its limiting words: 'set', 'bourn', 'how far'. And it achieves the desired result, for Antony's reply makes a splendid vault to the visionary ('new heaven, new earth'), plus a new intimacy: whereas before their talk had been about abstract 'love', Antony now uses a warm 'thou'.

When the Attendant interrupts, deferring the key words 'from Rome' until last (whether for emphasis or from fear or both), Antony is terse – as he can be when irritated. But he does ask to hear a summary. Cleopatra immediately intercedes to prevent this; playing on contraries, she defers the news by insisting – at length – upon hearing it (19–32)!

The impulses behind Cleopatra's outburst are complex. In part, her words are simply expressive. Her psychic metabolism is much faster than most – she often interrupts, her fears breaking forth uncontrollably. One sometimes wonders what Antony 'sees' in Cleopatra, beyond her sexual attractions. Part of her appeal to him is shown here: their love matters so much to her that she compulsively ventilates every last aspect of every crisis.

At the same time she is manipulating Antony, appealing to his pride and will, trying to make him blush at any shame he may feel toward Fulvia and Caesar. In a strange way she becomes the voice of the worst Roman thoughts she can imagine. Is it an accident that all of the words she uses for the message have Latin roots – mandate, dismission, process? Certainly, she becomes as shrill as Fulvia. She strikes a response from Antony with 'Perform't, or else we damn thee', imagining that Caesar is assuming the royal 'we' and employing the insulting 'thee' toward Antony, as toward an inferior. At first she does no more than urge Antony 'to hear the messengers', but as she becomes sure of her ground, she

then goes further and calls them in herself. As before, this produces the desired response (33–9). Again vaulting to a spacious extreme, Antony not only thrusts aside Caesar and Fulvia but all Rome and its empire. To me his first clause ('Let Rome in Tiber melt, and the wide arch/Of the rang'd empire fall') rings true, hyperbolic as it is. But an element of play-acting immediately enters, for he not only makes the physical gesture of rapport ('do thus'), but holds it as a pose and expounds it. And his extravagant protestation of devotion turns into a rather easy rhetorical challenge to the world. He deserves Cleopatra's oxymoron 'excellent falsehood'. Shortly she will urge him to play another scene of 'excellent dissembling'.

No one is more suspicious of dissembling than she is, being such a dissembler herself. Whether or not 'Why did he marry Fulvia, and not love her?' is heard as an aside, it shows an extreme self-consciousness, an ability to see herself as a role-player: 'I'll seem the fool I am not'. For her way of holding Antony is very like that which Falstaff uses to beguile Prince Hal from his responsibilities. They both assume a series of diverting roles, 'becoming' whatever they think will 'eye well' to their loved one. But what is most attractive about Cleopatra to Antony he sums up when he follows her 'Antony will be himself', with 'But stirr'd by Cleopatra'. 'Stir' here meaning 'arouse sexually', 'inspire', and 'provoke'. Shakespeare elsewhere uses the word in these senses, and they all apply here; for in all these ways, Cleopatra enlarges Antony's potency, releases his bounteousness to new limits. He is most 'himself' when joined with her.

Having stirred Antony to truly imaginative utterance, Cleopatra relaxes; and he subsides into grandiose conventionalities. He takes her final joking challenge to 'Hear the ambassadors' (humorously elevating their status) as the occasion to make yet another vault. In a speech filled with absolutes (44–55), he goes beyond rejecting the Roman empire to exclude the whole world – to be 'all alone' with her and hear 'No messenger but thine'. Yet his language is now abstract; there is something 'warmed over' about his invitation to do what Cleopatra desired last night; the poetry is gone. I find the same pattern in the forthcoming departure scene, where Antony rises to a fresh and concrete declaration of his fealty, swearing 'By the fire/That quickens Nilus' slime' (I, iii, 69–70) but ends with a pat couplet:

> That thou, residing here, goes yet with me;
> And I, hence fleeting, here remain with thee.
>
> (104–5)

The pattern is there, too, in Antony's death scene, where 'I am dying, Egypt, dying' (IV, xv, 18) gives way to a final speech which is full of the Roman conventionalities Shakespeare found in Plutarch (50–9).

How 'wrangling' should Cleopatra be? To me, both recordings seem timid about her tone, softening it. There is a great deal of playfulness throughout this episode. But I find Pamela Brown and Anthony Quayle on the Shakespeare Recording Society version too playful. I do not hear any insecurity in their voices: this Antony is totally devoted and this Cleopatra seems to have no doubt about it; yet in the next scene Antony will be leaving.

On the Marlowe Society recording, Richard Johnson is less the glib and ardent lover than is Quayle. He has a more independent existence. It may be that, as Samuel Barber decided, Antony's baritone should incline more to the bass than to the tenor. Irene Worth is less gay than Pamela Brown, but she might let more anxiety show through; and she might be more disagreeable, too. Antony after all speaks of 'conference harsh'. For the most part, Miss Worth is caressing Antony with her voice, not challenging him. And Antony finds a dare irresistible, whether from Cleopatra or Caesar. Although he can stand only so much of it, he loves her in part because she chides him, not merely in spite of it.

Since Strindberg, it should be easier for us to recognize mutual hatred as part of what holds these two together. In one of his *Open Letters to the Intimate Theater*, Strindberg in fact has a thoroughly characteristic commentary on *Antony and Cleopatra*. In his view, Cleopatra is Antony's 'dear fury', sharing with him a 'mixture of will to power, hate, contempt, cruel sensual pleasure, the need to debase [each other], faithlessness, in a word – enmity; and in the midst of the hatred both of them are whipped by the demon fear-of-losing (jealousy)'.[1] As he hears the first scene, Cleopatra comes on furious and continues her 'raging as usual' throughout! One need not go this far to see a kinship between Shakespeare's play and such post-Strindberg plays as *Long Day's Journey into Night* and *Who's Afraid of Virginia Woolf?*, where hatred is seen as an aspect of love and quarreling as a form of love talk.

III

Antony's first encounter with Caesar is reminiscent of his first encounters with Cleopatra. Although Caesar and Cleopatra are customarily contrasted, they have some striking resemblances, especially in their relationships with Antony. Both are engaged in a loving rivalry with him. They have seen Antony's visage in his mind and are deeply attached to it; in parallel scenes they have in their own ways just celebrated Antony at length: she envying the 'happy horse' that bears the weight of Antony (I, v, 21); he recalling the hardy soldier who 'didst drink/The stale of horses' (I, iv, 61–2). Yet they are both possessive of Antony (both hate Fulvia); and they both want to dominate him utterly. Cleopatra envies Antony his 'inches' and takes his potent sword away

[1] *Open Letters to the Intimate Theater*, trans. Walter Johnson (Seattle, n.d.), p. 275.

from him, metaphorically as well as actually. And if Caesar completely had his way he would not only subjugate his 'mate in empire' but turn his men and Cleopatra against him, and then scorn them.

To Antony and others his two loving rivals have uncanny powers, especially over him: Cleopatra is literally 'enchanting' and Caesar is 'beguiling', with a daemon that takes mysterious precedence over his. They live at a faster pace than does Antony. Verbally, this is shown in Cleopatra's constant interruptions and Caesar's laconic impatience with verbiage (as with Pompey, II, vi, 32). They seem more intelligent than he, cunning past men's thought, especially in their manipulation of appearances. Given to role-playing, as they are, they are both ever conscious of decorum.

The present scene (II, ii) is an exercise in role-playing. Although it takes the form of a quarrel over the past, it is really a struggle for primacy in the present. Both men want to patch up an alliance against Pompey. The question is, on what terms? Antony's poise is being tested. He must maintain his own honor without seriously insulting Caesar's, a subject about which Caesar is very touchy indeed. Everything, thus, depends on Antony's tone.

The opening interchange sets out the two extremes available to Antony: Lepidus' way of appeasing 'soft and gentle speech' versus Enobarbus' way of bravado, speaking 'as loud as Mars'. Note that both men not only advocate a tone but themselves illustrate it.

Everything that follows can be heard as part of the war of nerves. Are the adversaries truly concerned with other affairs or merely making a show of preoccupation? The neatness of the parallel between their exchanges suggests the latter. Is the business of sitting down merely a polite formality, or does it reflect the struggle for precedence? Since Antony is at this point trying to take the offensive, I hear him resisting Caesar's attempt to play the host (Caesar has presumed to welcome Antony to Rome) and himself taking over that role, prevailing on Caesar to 'sit'.

The next exchange shows Antony trying to hold the initiative, but with Octavius countering skillfully, speaking very cautiously and precisely, and taking it away from him. For instance, Octavius' rejoinder to Antony's charge (30–5), deliberately answers Antony's first line first, his second line second, with a rhetorical play on being 'laugh'd at' (a constant fear of Caesar's). Is there a genuine expression of feeling in 'with you/Chiefly i' the world'? Only gradually does Caesar edge into his first charge against Antony, his language at this point being full of conditionals like 'if' and 'might'. Caesar then continues to make a series of increasingly personal and direct charges, each time extracting an apology or excuse from Antony and then moving abruptly on to the next. Although Antony is awkward (contrast the clarity of his speech when he is on the offensive with the obscurity of his defenses), he does manage to keep both his head and his dignity, going to neither Enobarbus' nor Lepidus' extremes. The relation of 'brothers' is then fabricated. Query: Who married Antony? Octavia? Or Octavius?

Although Antony can hold up his end in the complicated games that Cleopatra and Caesar play, he is not 'good at them'. They do not seem his natural idiom. His instinct is to break through to something simpler and more physical: to 'do thus'. Part of what is appealing about Antony is that Shakespeare repeatedly shows his warm and expansive nature having to deal with impossibly demanding people on their own grounds.

The points that his loving rivals score off Antony in these early encounters are small, but – like banderillas – they begin and portend his eventual diminution. Like Othello, Antony has added a great love to his greatness as a general. As the play begins this combination is threatening to fall apart, and we see Antony trying to fight a holding-action. In fact, however, we can also see that these scenes begin the retreat in which the man who had everything will eventually lose it all. Although he can cope with his loving rivals individually, together they are too much for him; and – as they betray him – he gradually loses his ascendancy over them.

The resulting structure of Antony's tragedy is unique in Shakespeare: his fall on fortune's wheel being not precipitous but by degrees, each stage in his descent being precisely graduated. The effect resembles that of the long, long fall of the hero of a naturalistic novel, little by little losing status and hope, the difference being that Antony's losses do not diminish his essential self. Even as his judgment and sense of identity dissolve, he remains large-hearted, open-hearted, tender-hearted, stout-hearted. Like Othello, his heroism shows itself most in the tone and quality of his response to suffering, in the great-hearted way in which he meets his ordeal.

IV

The Battle of Actium, of course, marks the point of decision in Antony's downfall, and with it there is a major tonal shift. The time of playful, idle talk and preliminary sparring is now in the past. The early blend of truth and falsity – of half-meant accusations and half-meant reassurances – crystallizes either to outright lies or to truly and deeply felt speech that is close to action. In the first part of the play, Cleopatra's outburst at the news of Antony's marriage to Octavia stands out, for its directness of expression and closeness to action (she hales the messenger up and down and draws a knife). In the latter part, Antony's parallel outburst against Thidias seems very much in the general idiom. In this part, it is Antony who has been betrayed and who sets the tone of the relationships; it is he who does the accusing and seeks the pleas for pardon or vows of devotion. Although he is still self-conscious (at the height of his rage he prays to Alcides to teach him to rage), his speech is much more simple and direct than that of Cleopatra or Caesar, less calculating, more expressive and sincere.

In the Thidias episode (III, xiii) Antony is striking back in all directions. Thidias is a 'Jack' not only in the sense of 'low-bred servant' but of a stand-in, or, as the *OED* puts it, something 'which in some way takes the place of a lad or man'. He serves Antony as a whipping-boy for all those who have betrayed him – Caesar, Cleopatra, his men, and himself.

The Shakespeare Recording Society version of this episode is particularly interesting. Whether deliberately or not, there is a quality of play-acting in Anthony Quayle's carefully modulated climaxes that to my ear seems right. In part, of course, Antony is putting on a show meant to be impressive to Cleopatra and – by report – to Caesar. But in contrast to the pseudo-events that they stage, his tirade seems to come less from policy than from need. It is a compulsive acting out of his frustrated desire for active retaliation (in the person of Thidias he wants to make the 'boy' Caesar cry and beg pardon) and a necessary preparation for the worked-up rallying of his courage with which the scene ends, as he resolves to be 'treble-sinewed, hearted, breath'd,/And fight maliciously'.

V

Cleopatra's final speech (v, ii, 279–312) recalls and completes the main modes and tendencies of speech in the play. For example, the disparity of lying and telling true has been pushed to new extremes after Antony's death, as Dolabella repeatedly and ever more clearly betrays the reality beneath Caesar's false magnanimity toward Cleopatra. She has responded with false submissiveness toward Caesar. Now she goes beyond dissembling into visionary fiction, not only dreaming of an Emperor Antony (v, ii, 76–92) but imagining him alive in Elysium and calling her to join him. In a way that recalls but transcends the combination of truth and falsity in the half-meant speech with which the play begins, her fiction has a strange validity, since it is joined to the real act of dying. Truly, this is 'lying in the way of honesty'.

Everything is distilled and presented in quintessence. The farewells and greetings (to which so much of the dialogue has been given) are now abbreviated. The constant dispraise becomes an asp's imagined mockery of 'great Caesar ass,/Unpolicied!' (Do the sibilants here invite the hint of a hiss?)

In pace, Cleopatra's speech has a lingering quality amid a felt need for haste; in volume, the chief effect is of extreme quiet. Both of these effects are pointed by the Countryman's prologue. In contrast to Cleopatra's presumably whispered instructions to Charmian (191), he is preceded by 'A Noise within' (232); and for the only time Cleopatra is out-talked, as in very short speeches she tries to send him on his voluble way.

The effect of quietness is especially striking. Although commentators do not mention this quietness, both recordings present it thus. It is, of course, easier to render a hushed effect on record than on stage; yet there, too, the whole speech could have the muted yet intense quality of a stage whisper. Again the effect recalls the 'idleness' of the beginning of the play, but with a difference: one being the uneasy calm before the storm, the other the peace after it. There is much, in fact, that is totally silent in this speech: Antony's praise of Cleopatra's noble act and his mockery of the luck of Caesar; Cleopatra's unfinished contempt of the vile world, which Charmian must finish for her; Iras's silent departure, thereby telling 'the world/It is not worth leave-taking'.

The last is another of 'the silent griefs which cut the heart-strings' as in *The Broken Heart*. The whole speech anticipates the 'moment of stillness' that Clifford Leech has discerned in Ford's plays.[1] Yet Cleopatra's death is much more positive than that of Ford's Calantha. It is also more positive than any of her own living moments. Although she has a twinge of jealous fear about losing Antony's kiss to Iras that recalls her constant fearfulness until now, there is in general a new assurance and resolution in her tone, and a new hopefulness about the future. Her words are now, for once, joined to decisive action. It is, to be sure, a typically passive sort of action (she must stir the asp to 'do his kind' even as she stirred Antony to 'be himself'). When the time comes, she does not so much die as vanish – like fire and air. There is a moment of self-rebuke ('This proves me base') but no longer any need for pardon; she feels sure that her act is right and will win Antony's praise. Instead of the forced vivacity of the first scene, her dying speech has a strange carefreeness about it; she is 'gay' as Yeats in 'Lapis Lazuli' felt Hamlet and Lear to be gay, with a 'Gaiety transfiguring all that dread'.

The trance-like 'moment of stillness' is sustained through Charmian's farewell and then abruptly broken by the Guard, who comes 'rustling in' (319; thus subtly had Shakespeare imagined the contrasting sound-effect) and demands in a voice that Charmian hushes: 'Where's the queen?' In contrast to the free and fluid rhythms of Cleopatra, Caesar then enters, *marching* – regulated and regulating. In the tones of rational inquiry, he determines the probable cause of Cleopatra's visionary death

[1] *John Ford* (London, 1964), pp. 30–7. In *John Ford and the Drama of His Time* (London, 1957), Leech makes a few brief but suggestive comparisons between *Antony and Cleopatra* and Ford's plays, particularly mentioning the scene of Hercules' desertion as resembling Ford's method of providing 'A point of rest, of static contemplation' (p. 72).

and decrees a conventionally 'solemn show' to mark the lovers' funeral.

I seem now to hear my skeptical listener saying to himself: We have been trying to 'hear Shakespeare' in the sense of hearing the tones and undertones of the characters. But what about hearing Shakespeare himself? – the overtones that indicate his own attitudes? Is he as rhapsodic about the love of Antony and Cleopatra as Harold S. Wilson? Or as satiric as Brents Stirling? Or as ambivalent as Norman Rabkin?[1] This is, I would agree, a question to be asked; but not a question to be answered definitively.

It is a mistake, to begin with, to try to lock Shakespeare's protean genius into a single tone or attitude, especially concerning 'his most prismatic play', as Gide described it (p. 80). At various moments his dialogue seems to me as warm and bounteous in its verbal generosity as Antony, as regretfully unsparing in its treatment of Antony as Caesar, as determinedly sardonic in its candour as Enobarbus.

It is characteristic of Shakespeare's chameleon style that it takes on the quality of the world it depicts. In this play he seems as self-conscious about his use of language as are his characters. Behind Enobarbus' highly wrought description of Cleopatra's barge I sense the theater poet making Plutarch's purple passage still purpler. And there is something calculating about the way he plants time-bombs of exact prophecy among the banter in the soothsaying episode.

Not that he totally loses his identity in his created world. Like his characters his imagination is obviously stirred by the lovers, but he never seems as carried away as they, either in admiration or vituperation. Behind their extravagances he always reveals a heightening incitement – disillusionment, grief, or masturbatory fantasizing. Toward his dissembling characters this arch-dissembler is careful never to be taken in and seems to take sly satisfaction in letting the overtones of their own lying words tell the awkward truth, as when in III, xiii Caesar's ambassador offers to take Cleopatra 'under his shroud' (71), and she hears in Caesar's words 'the doom of Egypt' (78).

Even so, Shakespeare seems to be sharing essentially the same experience that his characters do, joining into the state of mind and feeling that distinguishes their relations, and rendering it in their unique idiom. It is almost as if he were a character in his own play. And he invites his audience to follow suit, to enter into the imagined world of his play. That is the overtone that I hear most clearly from Shakespeare the theater poet of *Antony and Cleopatra*: a tone of invitation – as full of flickering enticements as that of Cleopatra herself.

[1] Harold S. Wilson, *On the Design of Shakespearian Tragedy* (Toronto, 1957), pp. 158–82; Brents Stirling, *Unity in Shakespearian Tragedy* (New York, 1957), pp. 157–92; Norman Rabkin, *Shakespeare and the Common Understanding* (New York, 1967), pp. 184–91.

'MORE PREGNANTLY THAN WORDS': SOME USES AND LIMITATIONS OF VISUAL SYMBOLISM

INGA-STINA EWBANK

When the Painter in *Timon of Athens* puts the Poet in his place by pointing out that not only is his message 'common' but it also needs another medium —

A thousand moral paintings I can show
That shall demonstrate these quick blows of Fortune's
More pregnantly than words —

(1, i, 93–5)

then, obviously, neither interlocutor is concerned with the idea of a 'theatre poet'. Despite his fine lines on the nature of poetic inspiration, the Poet thinks of poetry mainly as something which gives outward form to an inner moral. And his narrow definition of style as a garment is so tied up with his sycophantic use of poetry that both can be punctured by the disillusioned Timon, in an even more relentless reminder of the limits of language:

Poet.   I am rapt, and cannot cover
   The monstrous bulk of this ingratitude
   With any size of words.
Timon. Let it go naked: men may see't the better.

(v, i, 62–5)

The presentation poem in the opening scene would at best make a scenario for a masque. The whole abortive quarrel between Poet and Painter may seem more relevant as an anticipation of the Ben Jonson–Inigo Jones controversy than as an entry-point into a discussion of words versus 'show' in Shakespeare. For everyone knows that the dichotomy between what is said and what is shown on stage in a Shakespeare play is an unreal one; and that

verbal and visual unity is a characteristic of Shakespearian drama.

Yet, there is a sense in which the Painter is worth listening to in 1970, for we are perhaps now in an era of *visual* theatre never equalled since the days of the masque. I, for one, have often recently come away from a performance with the impression that it is by visual means — costumes, décor, choreography, even dumb-shows — that the producer has tried to 'demonstrate' the matter of the play, 'more pregnantly' than by words; indeed that the stage picture, like Hamlet's actors, must 'tell all' — whether it means miming Leontes's dark imaginings or cutting Macbeth's lines in favour of a ballet of writhing shapes.[1]

Some of the questions I have been turning over for this paper crystallised a few weeks ago as I saw a performance of the National Theatre's *Hedda Gabler*, where Ingmar Bergman, producer and film-maker, has been at work on the text of Ibsen, who thought himself a poet. This *Hedda Gabler* starts with a dumb-show in which we learn that the trouble with Hedda is that she is caught in the trap symbolised by her pregnancy; and, casting aside the author's stage directions, it proceeds to set its action in a red, womb-shaped area where the characters act out their (mainly sexual) obsessions and repressions. The 'vine-

[1] I have in mind the Royal Shakespeare Company's 1969 production of *The Winter's Tale* and Steven Birkoff's version of *Macbeth* which opened at the Place, London, in August 1970.

leaves' of Ibsen's text are discarded, but phrases like 'enter through the back-door' are given meanings which most of us, in our naïveté, had never guessed at. It is an exciting theatrical venture; but it is also often at war with the text of the play – and sometimes fatally so. The moment when Mrs Elvsted produces the manuscript notes for Løvborg's prophetic 'History of Civilization', which she happens to be carrying about with her, is an awkward one even in a straightforward production: its symbolical load very nearly overtaxes the realistic convention. In the National Theatre version of the play – so centred on babies, literal and metaphorical, lost and found – it is clearly central: here is the babe that, carried by Mrs Elvsted, will replace the one that Hedda burnt, as relentlessly alive and as much of a trap as the one in Hedda's womb. Because the producer has, visually, writ so large what Ibsen hints at in undertones, our imaginations are peculiarly alerted and expectant – and so, when Mrs Elvsted takes out of her Victorian handbag a few thin sheets which at most could be the draft of a British Council pamphlet, the symbolical structure comes, anti-climactically, tumbling down.

The obvious point to crystallise out of this sort of theatrical experience is how much more fortunate Shakespeare was when *he* wanted to write about a couple whose vital energies turned destructive and sterile; and when his vision of such an action took the shape of babies born and unborn, murdered or living on into an endless future. He had available a verbal poetry which makes us see, in our imaginations, more than is or ever could be shown on stage; but he also had a theatre which could show, to our outer eye, more than man can find words to express. On the one hand he could put 'pity, like a naked new-born babe' into Macbeth's language; and, on the other, he could put on stage apparitions of '*a Bloody Child*' and '*a Child Crowned, with a tree*

in his hand', to speak more pregnantly than words about the fortunes of Macbeth.

But a second point crystallises, too. In a production which is to serve the play, rather than the producer's idea of what the play is about, we must be allowed to feel that some moments are more visual, or more verbal, than others. In speaking of a visual and verbal unity, in Shakespeare or any other dramatist, we must not be so intimidated by our own critical terminology as to assume that visual and verbal effects are always mutually interchangeable. When Mrs Elvsted brings out her embryonic manuscript, one wishes that one were listening to a radio play. This may be a fault in *Hedda Gabler*, but there is no fault in *Macbeth* when the last fifty-five lines of act I, scene vii, form a kind of *Hörspiel* where the language does all. The structure and the grammar of the dialogue become a living image of how Macbeth's will feeds upon Lady Macbeth's, until he can speak the final few lines with what is virtually her voice:

> I am settled, and bend up
> Each corporal agent to this terrible feat.
> Away, and mock the time with fairest show;
> False face must hide what the false heart doth know.

Irving, we know, gave those lines to Lady Macbeth and so spoilt the effect of what Shakespeare makes us *hear*. But it is only by *seeing* the apparitions, with Macbeth, in act IV, scene i, that we fully experience the way he has been trapped by his own actions. And there are moments when the stage picture does and should tell all, like the wordless reunion of Leontes and Hermione, where the by-standers speak only stage directions (and we know what Garrick made out of Shakespeare's miraculous scene when he tried to fill in the deficient text).

Perhaps, then, it would be tempting to arrange Shakespeare's plays on some kind of continuous scale, recording the relative pregnancy of words and visual effects. Perhaps one might even chart a 'development', beginning with an early stage where words often have the task of accompanying and commenting on pageant or emblematic effects. Certainly in scenes like the one gathered around the stage direction '*Enter a* Son *that hath kill'd his Father, at one door; and a* Father *that hath kill'd his Son, at another door*' the drama is working like a 'moral painting': with the advantage that issues are sharply defined, and yet also with the disadvantage that the stage image has become a symbol of a general condition, without having passed through a particular experience. Against this, one might set '*Enter* Lear, *with* Cordelia *dead in his arms*' and say that here we are at the opposite end of the scale: a dramatic experience so painfully realised in its particularity that there is no language adequate to deal with it, except a howl. In another way, visual effects sometimes replace dramatic poetry in the Romances, where the sense of wonder tends to derive from scenes or moments of what some would call 'pure theatre'. And in between these two limits one might chart a stage where words and visual impact are married, but with the word as a dominant partner. Here, one might say, the great tragedies show that, while visual symbolism may define a mood and outline a relationship, it is only in language that the inner lives of characters can be penetrated and analysed and their interactions with other characters explored. Act I, scene ii, in *Hamlet* might form an illustration, for as the court enters and Hamlet remains apart in his 'inky cloak' we have as clear an emblem of a state of opposition as we could wish for. But, as Hamlet reminds his mother and us, none of the visual signs can truly denote 'that within' (and that which the play is really about) – that has to be done by the clash of words in his stichomythic interchanges with Claudius and Gertrude and by the verbal imagery in his soliloquy.

But, of course, such a chart is as easy to pull apart as it is to put together. Try, for example, to fit *Richard II* into visual–verbal categories, and they will crumble before a play, richer than most in pageantry, where the emblematic situations are inextricably part of the rhetoric and the character analysis of Richard, and where yet also that very rhetoric is subjected to the whole play's examination of the relationship between words and reality. Or try to fit *Timon of Athens* into a pattern of chronological development: no play is more like a 'moral painting' in its whole structure, and Professor Bradbrook has recently shown, most suggestively, how this play's relationship with pageantry and entertainments may be right at the centre of its intention and its source of strength.[1]

Maybe, then, it is less neat but more fruitful to see in individual Shakespeare plays a kind of purposeful dialectic between what is seen and what is said; between the power of words, on the one hand, and their impotence before a visually presented reality, on the other. We might take courage from the fact that such a dialectic takes place, more explicitly, within another kind of Shakespearian poetry. The very 'poetic' of the *Sonnets* combines a tremendous belief in the power of language to render and preserve the identity of the beloved with a similarly strong humbleness about the possibilities of showing, through words, 'That you

[1] M. C. Bradbrook, *Shakespeare the Craftsman. The Clark Lectures 1968* (London, 1969). There is also an illuminating examination of this aspect of *Timon of Athens* in W. Moelwyn Merchant, *Shakespeare and the Artist* (London, 1959), chap. 10 ('*Timon of Athens* and the Visual Conceit'). Professor Merchant emphasises how, in scenes like the masque and the false feast, 'the theme is treated, not poetically but almost wholly in terms of significant mimetic action; it is not dramatic poetry but "pure theatre", a situation not so rare in Shakespeare's plays as our exclusively "literary" approach to the text would tend to indicate'; and he also relates the Painter/Poet quarrel to the *Paragone* controversy about the quality of insight into reality inherent in the visual, as against verbal, arts.

are you' (Sonnet 84).[1] We might even find a
paradigm for the interplay of eye and ear by
putting together the closing couplets of two
sonnets printed consecutively in 1609. First,
Sonnet 23 where – with far more urgency than
the conventional sonneteer's claim that his
lady's beauty is beyond the power of poetry
to express – the poet's emotion overruns the
limits of language. It is surely no mere coincidence that the sonnet starts from the image
of the 'unperfect actor on the stage', nor that
the couplet anticipates the final scene of *The
Winter's Tale*:

> O, learn to read what silent love hath writ!
> To hear with eyes belongs to love's fine wit.

Then, the Hamlet-like questioning of visual
evidence in Sonnet 24:

> Yet eyes this cunning want to grace their art:
> They draw but what they see, know not the heart.

This is not the place to get involved with the
thematic ramifications of the eyes/heart or
appearance/reality opposition, or with the
greater sincerity of the first sonnet versus the
playfulness of the second. I merely want to
suggest that the two couplets, taken together,
may prepare us for the kind of teasing of our
imaginative responses – 'what you see is the
real thing'/'what you hear is the real thing' –
which takes place in, and is essential to, some
Shakespearian scenes.

I am thinking, for example, of the persuasion
scene in *Coriolanus*, where the crucial moment
– the dramatic *peripeteia* – happens in one of
Shakespeare's most famous stage directions:
'*Holds her by the hand, silent*'; and where
yet that moment has been arrived at through a
peculiarly keen interplay between what is seen
and what is heard. Closely as he follows
Plutarch's description of the scene, Shakespeare
has constructed out of it a visual and verbal
dynamism which is irresistible to Coriolanus
and strangely haunting to us, the audience.

Volumnia starts with a kind of stage direction:

> Should we be silent and not speak, our raiment
> And state of bodies would bewray what life
> We have led since thy exile;   (v, iii, 94–6)

but, like Hamlet, she has 'that within which
passes show' and which can only be expressed
in words. Coriolanus knows the overpowering
force of the visual impact, as he tries to turn
away from the scene before him:

> Not of a woman's tenderness to be
> Requires nor child nor woman's face to see;
>   (129–30)

but the last straw to break him is made up of
the words through which Volumnia threatens
to deprive him of every identity,

> Come, let us go.
> This fellow had a Volscian to his mother;
> His wife is in Corioli, and his child
> Like him by chance,   (177–80)

and, worse, the untold horrors of the words
she has not yet spoken:

> I am hush'd until our city be afire,
> And then I'll speak a little.
>   [*He holds her by the hand, silent.*

Who is the more powerful persuader, all told,
the wife in her 'gracious silence' or the mother
who knows exactly what words will produce
the desired effect in the son? And yet Volumnia,
too, knows the potency of visual images – both
imagined ones, as she conjures up the two
alternatives which the future appears to hold,

> either thou
> Must as a foreign recreant be led
> With manacles through our streets, or else
> Triumphantly tread on thy country's ruin,
> And bear the palm for having bravely shed
> Thy wife and children's blood,   (113–18)

[1] There is a particularly helpful discussion of the
'poetic' of the *Sonnets* in Joan Grundy, 'Shakespeare's
Sonnets and the Elizabethan Sonneteers', *Shakespeare
Survey 15* (Cambridge, 1962), pp. 41–9, to which I
am indebted.

and actual ones, as she stage-manages the kneelings which make up the 'unnatural scene' and as her language functions merely to present and interpret a dumb-show:

> Nay, behold's!
> This boy, that cannot tell what he would have
> But kneels and holds up hands for fellowship,
> Does reason our petition with more strength
> Than thou has to deny't. (173–7)

Coriolanus does not – and the rest of the play makes us feel that he could and would not – analyse his 'silent' decision; and it is apt that the only words he can find to articulate what that decision means and does to him are merely devices to evoke a tableau of even greater dimension:

> O mother, mother!
> What have you done? Behold, the heavens do ope,
> The gods look down, and this unnatural scene
> They laugh at. (182–5)

To know Coriolanus here, we must indeed 'hear with eyes'; and yet that knowledge must always – more than in the case of any other Shakespearian hero – be tempered by the awareness that eyes 'draw but what they see, know not the heart'.

Clearly many of the adapters of *Coriolanus* have felt that in this scene Shakespeare had not got the most out of his stage tableau, nor out of the rhetorical possibilities of the dialogue. When, for example, John Philip Kemble, in his 1806 version of *Coriolanus; or, The Roman Matron*, reaches Volumnia's climactic verbal thrust, he shuns Shakespeare's 'silent' moment and switches instead to the text of James Thomson's tragedy of *Coriolanus* – so that twenty lines after Volumnia's unbearable words Coriolanus can still ask his wife and mother, in curiously irrelevant diction, to

Come, and complete my happiness at Antium.[1]

Kemble gives fifteen gushing lines to Virgilia, the 'gracious silence', and eventually makes Coriolanus collapse, before Volumnia's drawn and suicidal dagger, with a

> Ha!
> What dost thou mean?

So by filling in words where they are not wanted, and 'show' where it is not wanted, Kemble not only ruins Shakespeare's dynamic build-up of an 'unnatural scene' but also drains away the mystery at the heart of the tragedy of this inarticulate hero.

Finally, it seems to me that two passages from act IV, scene vi, of *King Lear* demonstrate Shakespeare's most poignant use of a visual–verbal dialectic. Everyone knows that this is a play about seeing and not seeing, about true and false values; but perhaps we do not always appreciate how much the dramatic technique of the play depends on the pitting of seeing against not seeing, speaking against not speaking. The first passage is Edgar's speech evoking the dizzy height of the non-existent rock from which Gloucester is about to throw himself – spoken to one on whom all visual symbolism would be wasted, one who is soon to say that he sees 'feelingly' and to be told, by the mad Lear, to 'Look with thine ears'. Apparently, here, the spoken word is all-powerful:

Come on, sir; here's the place. Stand still. How fearful
And dizzy 'tis to cast one's eyes so low!
The crows and choughs that wing the midway air
Show scarce so gross as beetles. Half-way down
Hangs one that gathers samphire – dreadful trade!
Methinks he seems no bigger than his head.
The fishermen that walk upon the beach
Appear like mice; and yond tall anchoring bark
Diminish'd to her cock; her cock, a buoy

[1] *Shakespeare's Coriolanus; or, The Roman Matron, A Historical Play, Adapted to the Stage, with Additions from Thomson*, by J. P. Kemble (London, 1806), p. 59. In his 1789 acting version of the same play, Kemble omitted Volumnia's climactic lines ('This fellow had a Volscian to his mother...'), which makes the switch to Thomson just a little less incongruous. See the Cornmarket Press reprints of the two Kemble versions (London, 1970).

Almost too small for sight. The murmuring surge
That on th' unnumb'red idle pebble chafes
Cannot be heard so high. I'll look no more;
Lest my brain turn, and the deficient sight
Topple down headlong. (11–24)

Unless, like Dr Johnson, we think that the circumstantial detail of Edgar's verbal painting 'stops the mind in the rapidity of its descent through emptiness and horror',[1] we are likely to feel that it creates and makes real to us a scene which yet our eyes tell us does not exist. We both are and are not in Gloucester's position, and the ultimate effect of this pitting of eye against ear is a strong and perhaps paradoxical sense both of man's control of reality and his tenuous hold on it.

One hundred and twenty lines later Edgar is again telling us, the audience, about what is real; but now, faced with the encounter between the blind Gloucester and the mad Lear, he speaks a different language:

I would not take this from report. It is,
And my heart breaks at it. (141–2)

His lines are both a tragic version of 'If this were played upon a stage now, I could condemn it as an improbable fiction' and a dramatic version of the insistence in Sonnet 84 that the whole point of writing is to show 'That you are you'. Apparently, we are faced with a reality so overpowering that language is utterly defeated. Edgar can speak only what he feels, and what he feels needs no other expression than the most ultimate stage direction: 'it is'.

In many ways, this 'it is' is the greatest line of Shakespeare, the theatre poet. But, of course, it would not be so if it did not occur in a context where – as in the Dover Cliff speech – Shakespeare has stirred and sustained our imaginations by both visual and verbal means. What *is* is not only Gloucester kissing the hand of his King but also Lear's words that that hand 'smells of mortality'; not only a stage image of two shattered old men but a stage dialogue such as:

Lear. I remember thine eyes well enough. Dost thou squiny at me? No, do thy worst, blind Cupid; I'll not love. Read thou this challenge; mark but the penning of it.
Gloucester. Were all thy letters suns, I could not see one. (136–40)

If we were to try to say how this theatre poetry works, we would have to admit that it is both by asserting the pregnancy of words and yet also by creating on stage an image more pregnant than words. A thousand moral paintings could not do that.

[1] See the convenient anthology of reactions to this speech in the Furness *Variorum* edition of *King Lear* (Philadelphia, 1880), pp. 266–8, which in itself forms a history of English poetic tastes.

© INGA-STINA EWBANK 1971

SHAKESPEARE AND THE LIMITS
OF LANGUAGE

ANNE BARTON

It's strange that words are so inadequate.
And yet we go on trying to compel them to our service
Though all words fail us, even falsify our meaning.[1]

These lines, from the last scene of T. S. Eliot's play *The Elder Statesman*, express an attitude towards language characteristic of our own moment of historical time. We live in a period marked by its profound mistrust of words. How this distrust has arisen, and what the role may have been of the mass media and of the revolution in philosophy instituted by Wittgenstein in producing it, is not my concern here. I would merely suggest that when Eliot, in another work, described his own craft of poetry as 'a raid on the inarticulate, with shabby equipment, always deteriorating',[2] he spoke not merely for himself as an artist but for a modern society which has become obsessed with the limitations and inadequacies of speech.

Certainly the contemporary theatre reflects this obsession. For Beckett, for Pinter, for Albee and Ionesco, dialogue has become not so much a medium of understanding, the means through which human beings reveal themselves to one another, as a measure of the hopelessness of any attempt to communicate. Words measure the gap between individuals: they do not bridge it. Every man is an island in a sense slightly different from the one John Donne had in mind, but this fact is no longer a source of suspect spiritual pride. In it, we find our own particular despair. The characters of *Waiting for Godot*, of Pinter's two plays *Landscape* and *Silence*, of *Who's Afraid of Virginia Woolf?* or

of Ionesco's *Exit the King* talk and talk and talk. At the end of it all, language arrives at self-contradiction. It is there to reinforce and make more poignant a human isolation which cannot even be regarded as tragic.

Arguably, this way of handling dramatic dialogue, a style in which the unsaid looms larger than what is actually spoken, in which characters talk at but not really to one another, stems from the plays of Chekhov. It is there at least, in the pathetic cross-purposes, the endless but futile discussions among people placed in the attitudes of conversation whose words and thoughts never meet, that modern dramatists (or many of them) have found the source of a technique. This technique seems strikingly un-Shakespearian. In her book *Themes and Conventions of Elizabethan Tragedy*, M. C. Bradbrook has emphasised that a faith in words was characteristic of Shakespeare and his contemporaries:

The essential structure of Elizabethan drama lies not in the narrative or the characters but in the words. The greatest poets are also the greatest dramatists. Through their unique interest in word play and word patterns of all kinds the Elizabethans were especially fitted to build their drama on words.[3]

It would seem, then, that we stand today at an opposite extreme from the Elizabethans with respect to the trust we are willing to place

[1] From a typescript of the play. Eliot retained only the first of these lines.
[2] T. S. Eliot, *Four Quartets* (London, 1944), p. 22.
[3] Cambridge, 1960, p. 5.

in words. This, indeed, is one of the points made by George Steiner in the introduction to his collection of essays, *Language and Silence*. According to him, Shakespeare is divided from us now less by questions of the so-called Elizabethan world picture, Tudor orthodoxy or religious and moral conservatism, than by his unfaltering belief in language: a belief which we, in the twentieth century, can no longer share.[1]

The plays of Shakespeare do indeed stand as the most complete testimony there has ever been to the efficacy of language, to what words can make. They deny and refute the reductivist attitude towards language and the imagination later promulgated by Hobbes, an attitude from which much modern thinking derives. Nevertheless, they are concerned at times to criticise the means of their own success. Certainly the word in Shakespeare is not allowed an unexamined triumph. At the heart of his drama lies an ambiguity of attitude towards the transformations effected by language which links him, surprisingly, with the outlook characteristic of our own theatre. Although his plays celebrate words, exploit their capacities fully, they also include and foreshadow something of the twentieth-century distrust. I should like to look at some of the plays in which linguistic doubt seems most important. I shall be concerned in all of them with questions of the relationship between words and deeds, between speech and silence, and with the adequacy (or otherwise) of verbal formulation to the events and emotions upon which it operates. Even for the dramatist who depended most heavily upon it, there were certain limits to language. Shakespeare confronted these limits squarely. They are never, in fact, far away from his tragic vision of life, nor from his understanding of his own art.

It may be useful to begin by considering an Elizabethan play which does not recognise these limits: a play which actually embodies the attitude towards language which Steiner would attribute to Shakespeare. In Marlowe's *Tamburlaine*, words can do almost anything:

> Brother Cosroe, I find myself aggriev'd:
> Yet insufficient to express the same,
> For it requires a great and thundering speech:
> Good brother, tell the cause unto my lords;
> I know you have a better wit than I.

This is the weak and contemptible King Mycetes, in the opening moment of part I. The very first lines of *Tamburlaine* indicate that this is a play in which an inability to command words will be identified with political failure. Mycetes cannot express himself adequately, and we are asked to accept this fact as evidence of his unfitness to rule. He himself recognises the importance of eloquence. Feebly, he asks his brother to make the speech the king himself should make. He sends Theridamas out to capture Tamburlaine with the significant judgement: 'thy words are swords' (I, i, 74). But Theridamas is no match, linguistically, for Tamburlaine. After about five minutes of rhetoric he and his thousand horse belong to Tamburlaine and no longer to Mycetes. That this purely verbal winning over of Mycetes's captain got Marlowe out of the awkwardness of a staged battle is true. The important thing is the degree to which victory in these linguistic terms is characteristic of the play generally. It seems right and proper that Tamburlaine's conquest, offstage, of Bajazeth and his army should be represented by Zenocrate's purely verbal triumph over Bajazeth's queen.

Tamburlaine himself may be a brute, a beast, a murderer. The fact remains that before the verbal splendour of 'Now walk the angels on the walls of heaven/To entertain divine Zenocrate', or the promise that 'Thorough the streets, with troops of conquer'd kings/I'll ride

[1] London, 1967, pp. 44–5.

in golden armour like the sun', the antipathy towards the speaker which we ought to feel simply collapses. As readers, or members of a theatre audience, we are scarcely more successful than Theridamas or Zenocrate at resisting the appeal of Tamburlaine's rhetoric. If we were, there would be no play. Over and over again Marlowe persuades us that words are self-sufficient: not the servants of reality, but reality's masters. So, when Tamburlaine betrays Cosroe, he does so, as it seems, purely because of the effect upon him of a verbal formula: 'Your majesty shall shortly have your wish,/And ride in triumph through Persepolis'. This is what one of Cosroe's followers, most unfortunately, says to his master. Tamburlaine overhears him and the results are fatal:

> And ride in triumph through Persepolis!
> Is it not brave to be a king, Techelles!
> Usumcasane and Theridamas,
> Is it not passing brave to be a king,
> And ride in triumph through Persepolis?
>
> (II, v, 50–4)

Words, the emotional force of a chance phrase, generate a real and consequential political ambition. And one feels, I think, that had the name only been different – had it been Leeds (say) or Slough that was offered as the scene of triumph, instead of that many-syllabled splendour Persepolis, the streets might have been paved with diamonds and Cosroe would still have been safe, the course of history different.

In the special context of this play, Tamburlaine is absolutely right when he refuses to accept the crown of Persia as the shamefaced gift of Mycetes, who has been trying in his terror to bury it on the field of battle. A crown accepted in such a hugger-mugger fashion, with no onlookers and no opportunity for a great and thundering speech, would be a crown devalued, indeed meaningless.

> Nature, that framed us of four elements
> Warring within our breast for regiment,

> Doth teach us all to have aspiring minds;
> Our souls whose faculties can comprehend
> The wondrous architecture of the world
> And measure every wandering planet's course,
> Still climbing after knowledge infinite,
> And always moving as the restless spheres,
> Wills us to wear ourselves and never rest,
> Until we reach the ripest fruit of all,
> That perfect bliss and sole felicity,
> The sweet fruition of an earthly crown.
>
> (II, vii, 18–29)

These are the words with which Tamburlaine eventually consents to become king of Persia. As he speaks them, the crown itself – that circlet of mock-gold which is a mere stage property, the embarrassing object Mycetes tried to conceal – becomes what Tamburlaine says it is. It alters its identity, grows great before our eyes. Words do not simply interpret events and emotions. They *create* reality in the act of defining it. There has never perhaps been a play which so greatly magnified the power of language. It is true that at the end Death cannot be persuaded away by rhetoric. Tamburlaine may talk about setting black streamers in the firmament to signify the slaughter of the gods. His words have no power to bring back Zenocrate, or avert his own fate. In the course of the action they have, however, been able to do virtually everything else: to conquer kingdoms, persuade enemies and even to turn the whole world and its moral values upside-down.

That scene in which Tamburlaine and Mycetes stand on the field of battle with the crown of Persia suspended between them can usefully be compared with the deposition scene in Shakespeare's *Richard II*. Here again is a situation in which one claimant to the crown is a master of language, of words in all their shapes and colours, while the other is basically matter-of-fact. But the balance of political power here lies with the silent Bolingbroke, not with Richard's verbal dexterity. It is the weak king in Shakespeare who insists upon inventing a rite, a ceremony which may invest the crown, and the transference of royal power, with meaning. Richard, not Bolingbroke, gropes towards the invention of a litany, fumbles for words which will make this moment of time significant. Bolingbroke submits up to a point –

Here, cousin, seize the crown.
On this side my hand, and on that side thine.
Now is this golden crown like a deep well
That owes two buckets, filling one another:
The emptier ever dancing in the air,
The other down, unseen, and full of water.
That bucket down and full of tears am I,
Drinking my griefs, whilst you mount up on high...
                                        (IV, i, 181–9)

– but his submission is oddly qualified. Bolingbroke is willing to participate in the game to the extent of reaching out his hand, silently, at Richard's request, to seize the crown. Verbally, he will not co-operate at all. 'I thought you had been willing to resign': this blunt inquiry is all the response he will vouchsafe to Richard's imaginative enactment of the situation, and it serves to tear through and destroy the validity of metaphor.

Essentially, the situation here is the reverse of the one in *Tamburlaine*. Shakespeare's man of power, Bolingbroke, simply does not believe in the transforming power of language. Terse, impersonal and reticent, he trusts to cold fact, avoids eloquence. Not for nothing does Richard call him the 'silent king' (IV, i, 290). It is Bolingbroke's defeated rival who indulges in dazzling word-games, only to find that language breaks against a reality which it is powerless to alter. After his return from Ireland, Richard's chief activity is that of attempting to change the nature of things as they are by means of words. His success is doubtful. Certainly he plays with words in a vacuum as Tamburlaine had not. The world in this play is very far from being the docile servant of Richard's imagination, springing to life at his

touch. Rather, he is checked at every turn, made to feel the difference between words and those unalterable facts – like the stone walls of his prison – against which imagination breaks.

On the surface, no two Shakespearian characters could seem more dissimilar than Richard and Falstaff. And yet I would suggest that it is through Falstaff that the attitude towards language associated with Richard is extended into the two parts of *Henry IV*. After all, Falstaff's one aim, his tireless activity, is to transform the facts of a world of time and harsh reality into more attractive entities. The distinguishing feature of his wit is its extraordinary ability to make things look like something they are not, to re-create reality in Falstaffian terms:

Let not us that are squires of the night's body be called thieves of the day's beauty; let us be Diana's foresters, gentlemen of the shade, minions of the moon; and let men say we be men of good government, being governed, as the sea is, by our noble and chaste mistress the moon, under whose countenance we steal.   (I, ii, 23–8)

As an example of how to avoid the plain and consequential word 'thief', how to employ language to metamorphose fact, this speech from *1 Henry IV* could hardly be bettered. It is a kind of transformation at which Falstaff is an adept. He tries it again, with remarkable success, in his account of what really happened at Gadshill. Just as the Prince and Poins think they have him trapped at last, Falstaff metamorphoses things as they really were on that occasion into a fictional encounter between a true prince in disguise and a valiant but extremely discerning lion. To this conjuring trick with words, they have no effective rejoinder.

A little later, in the Boar's Head Tavern play scene, Falstaff employs the same technique, but this time the sense of strain is evident and disturbing. By the sheer force of wit, he tries to alter the disreputable facts of his own character and appearance, to pass himself off as 'sweet

Jack Falstaff, kind Jack Falstaff, true Jack Falstaff, valiant Jack Falstaff'. But not for nothing is Hal Bolingbroke's son. The Prince is no more taken in by Falstaff's rhetoric here than his father had been by Richard's poetry, or by old Gaunt's persuasions that a man may sweeten the rigours of banishment through the exercise of imagination. Just as fast as Falstaff transforms things into what they are not, Hal turns them back again. 'This chair', Falstaff announces, 'shall be my state, this dagger my sceptre, and this cushion my crown.' But the Prince will have none of it. 'Thy state is taken for a join'd-stool, thy golden sceptre for a leaden dagger, and thy precious rich crown for a pitiful bald crown' (II, iv, 366–71). The man of fact announces firmly that he is not fooled, that reality resists linguistic metamorphosis. Hal's own attitude is typified by his final response to Falstaff's elaborate pleas that he should not be turned away in the golden time to come: 'I do. I will', four bare, stripped monosyllables that are precisely equivalent to fact.

In the end Falstaff, like King Richard, is defeated. Or at least on one level he is. There is a sense in which both these characters do indeed create something of value out of words, taking with them into oblivion more sympathy than we can accord to their victorious opposites. The fact remains that they are losers, and losers in precisely those areas of life where Tamburlaine, whose linguistic attitudes they share, had been triumphant. It is tempting to believe that Shakespeare recognised and deliberately reminded his audience of the gulf dividing his tragical histories from Marlowe's *Tamburlaine* when he allowed Henry V, the night before Agincourt, to encounter Ancient Pistol. The two men can barely communicate. Pistol, for the most part, spouts verse. Henry's laconic replies are couched in prose. 'As good a gentleman as the Emperor', as he puts it, Pistol creates an imaginary sovereignty for himself by linguistic means. He is Shakespeare's mis-chievous parody of Tamburlaine: gorgeous, assertive, an ego magnified. With Pistol, the high, astounding terms of Marlowe's hero appear once again on the stage, but they break and become absurd in a world which refuses to accommodate itself now to Pistol's overblown imagination. Impersonal, terse and matter-of-fact, Henry himself seems almost colourless beside Pistol, but his is the sovereignty in which we believe. Pistol, like Falstaff, is only a king in jest: a character composing lines for himself in a play of his own devising. When Henry leaves Pistol, still secure in his cocoon of grandiloquence, and moves on to encounter Williams and Bates, the last of three linked Shakespearian meetings comes to its end. Richard and Bolingbroke, Falstaff and Prince Hal, Pistol and Henry V. One meeting was tragic, one comic, and one a mixture of both, but in all of them the issues were fundamentally the same. Imagination against fact, words against political realism, the personal against the unmoving mask of kingship. Our sympathies may be drawn towards the former qualities; it is the latter which win out. Not until *Antony and Cleopatra* will King Richard, and with him Falstaff (even in a sense, Ancient Pistol) at last come out on top.

The history play was by no means the only dramatic form in which Shakespeare explored the relation between speech and silence, imagination and fact. *Love's Labour's Lost* stands out among the comedies as a play overtly about language, filled with verbal games, with parody and word patterns, firing off its linguistic rockets in all directions. Yet this, paradoxically, is a play which ends with the defeat of the word. After Berowne and his companions have painfully forsworn 'Taffeta phrases, silken terms precise' (v, ii, 406), after they have admitted that the language of love has become so contaminated that it can no longer exact belief, they face an impasse. Words have got them into their dilemma, but words are incapable of getting them out again. Only through an acceptance of silence, that year of residence in a forlorn and naked hermitage, can the King, Dumain and Longaville persuade the women that their love is genuine and not merely an idle game. As for Berowne, the penance enforced upon him by Rosaline, to 'jest a twelvemonth in an hospital' will be, in effect, a demonstration of the way language breaks before the reality of pain and death (v, ii, 859).

Although *Love's Labour's Lost* is the most striking example of a Shakespearian comedy concerned to examine the nature of its own medium, it is by no means the only one. Touchstone and Feste, Elbow, Dogberry and Lavatch are all corrupters of words. Their mistakings are in some cases wilful, in others involuntary, but all of them – the wise fools and the dull – use puns, quibbles and plain misunderstanding to open a rift between words and the things they signify. 'To see this age!', Feste says admiringly to Viola in *Twelfth Night*. 'A sentence is but a chev'ril glove to a good wit. How quickly the wrong side may be turn'd outward... words are grown so false I am loath to prove reason with them' (III, I, 10–24). He is, of course, only half serious. In general, the positive side of language is uppermost in the comedies, *Love's Labour's Lost* excepted. It is in the tragedies (as one might expect) that words are exposed to a scrutiny not only intense but, in the case of *King Lear*, distinctly unfriendly.

This scepticism becomes apparent in the first scene of the play:

Sir, I love you more than word can wield the matter;
Dearer than eyesight, space, and liberty;
Beyond what can be valued, rich or rare;
No less than life, with grace, health, beauty, honour;
As much as child e'er lov'd, or father found;
A love that makes breath poor, and speech unable:
Beyond all manner of so much I love you.

(I, i, 54–60)

This is how Goneril fawns on her father. She insists that language is inadequate to express the depth of her love. Where her predecessor in the old anonymous play of *King Leir* had offered, melodramatically, to kill herself at once if her father wished, to leap into the sea or marry a slave if this would please him, Shakespeare's Goneril contents herself with saying, at some length, that she can't say how much she loves the king.

Something very like Goneril's technique here is familiar from Elizabethan sonnet sequences. The lover's assertion, carried through fourteen carefully-wrought lines, that the worth of the beloved passes the power of language to express is a common enough device. Sidney could spend a whole sonnet informing his reader that nothing but the simple naming of Stella was worthwhile. Drayton, in the twenty-eighth Sonnet of *Idea*, asserted that his lady's graces were more than 'my wond'ring utterance can unfold', but promptly went on to unfold them. It is, after all, a stock rhetorical device, like the claims made by Greek and Latin orators in their court pleas: 'I could not begin to describe to you this man's iniquities' – followed inevitably by several thousand words describing them in detail. Goneril's graceful, fluent protestation of the inadequacy of language belongs to a recognised literary tradition. And her sister Regan underscores it.

One begins to see something of the true and agonising nature of Cordelia's problem. 'What shall Cordelia speak? Love, and be silent', is her response to Goneril (I, i, 61). 'My love's more ponderous than my tongue', she says when Regan has finished speaking (I, i, 76–7). The irony lies in the fact that both these broken statements only echo what her sisters have so fulsomely been saying: 'I love you more than word can wield the matter'. In Cordelia's case, the declaration of the inadequacy of language happens to express a true state of feeling. Her love for her father does indeed make her breath poor and speech unable; it is not a mere rhetorical flourish. But how can one tell the difference between sincerity and pretence, especially when both employ the same disclaimers? Cordelia's sisters have usurped, falsely, her own genuine excuse. All she can do at this point is to state plainly what they have offered with embellishments, conscious that this plainness must appear ungracious. Their professions have contaminated the truth of her own situation. When Cordelia says, 'Unhappy that I am, I cannot heave/My heart into my mouth', she is being honest (I, i, 90–1). But she has already been anticipated in this very protestation by Goneril. For her at the beginning of the tragedy, as for the lovers at the end of *Love's Labour's Lost*, actions provide the only test. Words have lost all significance. 'And your large speeches may your deeds approve,/That good effects may spring from words of love', as Kent says bitterly when he has heard the love-trial through (I, i, 184–5).

Winifred Nowottny has pointed out that Lear himself is a character who must consistently 'use language not as the adequate register of his experience, but as evidence that his experience is beyond language's scope'.[1] This judgement seems to me true, and also applicable to other characters besides Lear. Over and over again, in the vital moments of the play, it is stated explicitly that language has failed. In scene iv of act II, Lear is about to exchange the comforts of Gloucester's house for the heath and the storm. He speaks what will be his last words to Goneril and Regan in the play:

> No, you unnatural hags,
> I will have such revenges on you both
> That all the world shall – I will do such things –
> What they are, yet I know not; but they shall be
> The terrors of the earth.   (II, iv, 276–81)

The breaks in his utterance here, the disjointed phrases, are not due entirely to climbing sorrow and the madness it portends. The fact is that the old king cannot find words adequate to his anger, cannot give his intentions a linguistic shape that is worthy of them. There is no vocabulary for what he feels. There will not be one in scene vii of act IV either, when he wakes to find himself clad in fresh garments, and tended by Cordelia. 'I know not', he falters, 'what to say' (54). The words he does find in the scene are so slow, so halting and simple as almost to constitute a language invented on the spot; full of monosyllables and terms so stripped and bare that they seem talismanic: 'You do me wrong to take me out o' th' grave' (45). Not even in the world of this play can such a line be regarded as normal speech. Nor is Cordelia much more articulate here than she had been during the love trial at the beginning, or in scene iii of this same act, when Kent received an account of her behaviour at hearing of her father's misfortunes. 'Made she no verbal question?' Kent asked the gentleman giving the report, and he was told:

> Faith, once or twice she heav'd the name of father
> Pantingly forth, as if it press'd her heart;
> Cried 'Sisters! Sisters! Shame of ladies! Sisters!
> Kent! Father! Sisters! What, i' th' storm, i' th' night?'
>   (IV, iii, 25–8)

Once again it is a broken, a dislocated speech that is offered. All Cordelia can do is to repeat proper and generic names, tangible things which weigh like coins in the hand, without verbs to link them, without sentence structure.

Edgar too discovers the limits of language:

> O gods! Who is't can say 'I am at the worst?'
> I am worse than e'er I was...
> And worse I may be yet. The worst is not
> So long as we can say, 'This is the worst'.
>   (IV, i, 26–9)

This is what he says in the moment that he recognises his father coming towards him, blind and poorly led. He returns to the idea later on

[1] In 'Some Aspects of the Style of *King Lear*', *Shakespeare Survey 13* (Cambridge, 1960), p. 53.

in the act, in the midst of the encounter between Gloucester and the mad Lear. Of Lear's appearance in this scene, one of Cordelia's attendants says that it is 'A sight most pitiful in the meanest wretch,/Past speaking of in a king' (IV, vi, 206–7). Witness to the appalling interchange between his blind father and Lear, Edgar says simply: 'I would not take this from report. It is,/And my heart breaks at it' (IV, vi, 141–2). Once again, events have outrun language, have rendered it inadequate. Situations overwhelm words.

'It is': to those two words, the barest possible indication of existence, much of what happens in *King Lear* must be reduced. So, at the end, Albany will be unable to find a word that can describe Goneril accurately. 'Thou worse than any name', he calls her (v, iii, 156). Not, I think, by accident are repeated words so characteristic of this tragedy. The last two acts are filled with frenzied repetitions, some of them hammered upon as many as six times in the course of a single line: 'Kill', 'Now', 'Howl', 'Never', the monosyllable 'No'. One comes to feel that these words are being broken on the anvil in an effort to determine whether or not there is anything inside. It is a common psychological experience that if you look at or repeat a single word long enough, concentrate upon it in isolation, it ceases to be a familiar part of speech. Instead, it will take on a bizarre, essentially mysterious quality of its own, like a word in some arcane and alien tongue. Something of this kind happens as a result of the *Lear* repetitions. If only one could crack these words: words of relationship, of basic existence, simple verbs, perhaps they would reveal a new and elemental set of terms within big enough to cope. So, Lear's fivetimes-repeated 'Never' in the last scene is like an assault on the irrevocable nature of death, an assault in which the word itself seems to crack and bend under the strain.

Caroline Spurgeon has stated that the dominant image of *King Lear* is that of a body on the rack: stretched and twisted, wrenched in agony.[1] This is something which happens to words in the play, as well as to characters. Language itself is tormented and broken. It is uttered much of the time by people who confess themselves to be incapable of expressing what they feel, who are halting and dumb before the enormity of occurrences. It is true that Oswald and Cornwall, Goneril and Regan display a certain kind of linguistic efficiency. But it is oddly lifeless. Language in this tragedy is really fluent, is various and highly coloured, only on the lips of madmen or of fools. They are the custodians of verbal excellence, but the nature of their office gives one pause.

Edgar in his role as Bedlam beggar, Lear in his insanity and the Fool (who is partially deranged) all make an assault upon the normal conventions of language. A near neighbourhood to nonsense is characteristic of all three. When, in their heightened state of consciousness, they are most eloquent, they are also only one step away from entire incomprehensibility. The Fool takes refuge in scraps from forgotten ballads – 'Whoop Jug, I love thee' – and in riddles which have no point. He deals in chaotic prophecy, or in aphorisms which can be understood only if you reverse all the terms in them. As poor Tom, Edgar's speech is voluble, copious and unstructured. His sentences move forward by fits and starts, following remote chains of association, connections dimly grasped in a dark, devil-haunted world. Like the Fool, he is a truth-teller, but it is a truth continually lapsing into gibberish. Lear too, fantastically crowned with flowers, invents a kind of wild language with which to penetrate the veil of appearances. Both he and Edgar rely heavily on mere sounds in their utterance: they imitate the wind blowing through the hawthorn, the whistling of an arrow, hunting horns, the wordless babble of an infant, or

[1] *Shakespeare's Imagery* (Cambridge, 1935), p. 339.

inarticulate cries. Their most terrifying generali-sations about the gods, or human life, are likely to trail off in some such fashion. They are fond, too – and this is something they share with the Fool – of nonsense words: 'Fie, foh and fum', 'nonny', 'alow'. Non-words of this kind are a familiar feature of ballad refrains and nursery rhymes. Used, however, as a sub-stitute for normal speech, as the place towards which language tends when hard-pressed, they become sinister and disturbing. They remind us that structured language, as opposed to the simple capacity to make a noise, not only dis-tinguishes the rational human being from the idiot. It also separates man from the other members of the animal kingdom. In *King Lear*, this distinction between man and beast is of vital importance precisely because it comes so close to being lost.

I am not trying to suggest that in the end *Lear* leaves us with the conviction that man is on a level with the beast. This is a dark tragedy, but not quite that dark. Although one may feel that a distinction made as much as it is in terms of man's capacity for complex and excruciating suffering, suffering out-reaching that of the animal, is a distinction dearly bought. The failure or distortion of language evident throughout the play is, however, linked closely with its discussion of man's relation to the animal: his equivalence or superiority. These are inter-locking strands in the tragedy, and they are anything but cheering. Truth and love in this world are tongue-tied and silent. The glib and the verbally adroit, the Edmunds, Oswalds and Regans, are deeply suspect. Only madness and folly are truly articulate, and their speech hovers continually on the edge of the meaningless, the place where words dissolve into pure noise or inarticulate cries. At the very end, entering with Cordelia dead in his arms, Lear will find that the howl of an animal is the only possible response to the situation. As for the gods, so often invoked, accused and ques-tioned in this tragedy, their usual reponse is silence. When they do speak at all, they do so in the form of thunder: an undistinguishable blur of sound which will not resolve itself into words, let alone into doctrine.

If *Richard II* is a play whose protagonist tries desperately to transform fact through lin-guistic means, and *King Lear* a tragedy in which words seem to undergo a general attack, *Coriolanus* by contrast presents a Roman world of rhetoric and persuasion in which the hero alone resists the value placed on verbal formulations. To a surprising extent, the tragedy of Coriol-anus is worked out in terms of the hero's attitude towards words. A hatred not merely of flattery but even of a just recital of his own exploits is absolutely characteristic of this man. Cominius speaks more truly than he knows when he tells Coriolanus after the surrender of Corioli that 'if I should tell thee o'er this thy day's work/Thou't not believe thy deeds' (I, ix, 1–2). Later, Coriolanus will insist upon leaving the Senate until the oration in praise of his valour has ended:

Oft,

When blows have made me stay, I fled from words...
I had rather have one scratch my head i' th' sun
When the alarum were struck than idly sit
To hear my nothings monster'd.
(II, ii, 69–75)

This word *monster'd* means something more than just 'exaggerated'. It suggests distortion, a grotesque and degrading alteration. And here, in truth, lies the heart of the matter. Essentially, Coriolanus fears and despises words. They are, for him, serviceable commodities, but notably inferior to the deeds and actions they describe. The terrible consideration is that, even so, they should be able to violate the integrity of events. You transform facts by speaking of them, and this Coriolanus simply cannot bear. Action is simple while it is taking place, while the sword strikes, while the body of the enemy is still toppling to the earth. It is only afterwards that moments of this kind become complicated and uncertain. That they should do so is the direct result of their subjection to words, the fact that events live only by way of verbal description. In a very real sense, language assaults the purity of action.

Hence the ghastly appropriateness of the means by which Coriolanus is destroyed. The consulship of Rome, which his mother and his friends desire for him, is an office which must not only be won by words, it places these words in a relation to actions past which is calculated to outrage Coriolanus' very nature. 'It then remains/That you do speak to the people' (II, ii, 133). The man who could not bear to hear his friends violate his exploits by speaking of them must now consent to carry out the desecration himself, before a crowd of people he despises. From this point on, the people of Rome are characterised almost obsessively as 'voices'. 'Sir', says Sicinius, 'the people must have their voices' (II, ii, 137–8). The word comes to hammer through the play: 'If he do require our voices, we ought not to deny him...if he show us his wounds and tell us his deeds, we are to put our tongues into those wounds and speak for them' (II, iii, 1–7). Talkers and not doers like Coriolanus, the people of Rome place their trust in words over deeds. A voice cannot wield a sword, does not fight off invading Volscians. The exile of Coriolanus is made even bitterer by the fact that it constitutes a victory of language over action. By the 'voice of slaves', the hero is 'whoop'd out of Rome' (IV, v, 77–8).

In the end, words destroy this man utterly. Back in Corioli, Aufidius has only to use language to distort what actually happened in the scene between Coriolanus and the women and his purpose is achieved:

> at his nurse's tears
> He whin'd and roar'd away your victory,
> That pages blush'd at him, and men of heart
> Look'd wond'ring each at others.
>
> (v, vi, 97–100)

It is an extreme example of the violation of action – here, of that eloquent moment of silence in which Coriolanus had taken Volumnia's hand – by dishonest speech. Reality is monstered by language in the way Coriolanus most fears and detests. Predictably, he revolts, and is hacked down by the swords of the conspirators. Afterwards, Aufidius repents. But there is a terrible irony in the words he speaks over the body of his fallen enemy: 'Yet he shall have a noble memory' (v, vi, 154). Language in the end, stories, elegies and accounts, are to be the keepers of Coriolanus' fame: indeed of all of Coriolanus that survives. He detested the praises of his friends, the monstering of action by words. He is now given over utterly into the power of language.

Beyond *Coriolanus* lies the world of the last plays. Unlike M. M. Mahood, whose book *Shakespeare's Word-Play* I have otherwise found extremely illuminating, I cannot see the final romances as embodying a renewed faith in words after the scepticism of the tragedies. If anything, they seem to me to foreshadow, at a number of points, those techniques with dialogue employed by the post-Chekhov theatre. In act IV of *Pericles*, Marina walks on the sea-beach with Leonine, a murderer. This is what they say to one another in the moments before Leonine tries to kill his companion.

> *Marina.* Is this wind westerly that blows?
> *Leonine.* South-west.
> *Marina.* When I was born, the wind was north.
> *Leonine.* Was't so?
> *Marina.* My father, as nurse says, did never fear,
> But cried 'Good seamen!' to the sailors,
> galling
> His kingly hands hauling ropes;
> And, clasping to the mast, endur'd a sea
> That almost burst the deck.
> *Leonine.* When was this?
> *Marina.* When I was born.
> Never was waves nor wind more violent;
> And from the ladder-tackle washes off

A canvas-climber. 'Ha!' says one 'wolt
                         out?'
And with a dropping industry they skip
From stern to stern; the boatswain
                      whistles, and
The master calls, and trebles their con-
                      fusion.

Leonine. Come, say your prayers.
Marina. What mean you?   (IV, i, 52–67)

These two people may be placed, formally, in the attitude of conversation. Until Leonine draws out his dagger with unmistakable intent, neither one is really listening to the other. Arbitrarily sealed off in separate worlds, they talk at but not really to each other.

It is true that there are a number of examples in the early and mature comedies of characters like Feste and Touchstone, Dogberry and Elbow who either wilfully or out of ignorance misunderstand one another. Anger could transport Hotspur into a frenzy which baffled Northumberland's attempt to talk to him. Mistaken identity, concealed facts in the intrigue, can also produce dialogue at cross-purposes in these earlier plays as it does in the first meeting between Olivia and Sebastian in *Twelfth Night*, or in the terrible misunderstanding in *The Comedy of Errors* when Antipholus of Syracuse tries to make love to a woman who, for her part, believes that he is already married to her own sister.

Leonine and Marina labour under no delusion born from mistaken identity. Neither one is hysterical, nor are they trying to overwhelm each other through any linguistic sleight of hand. They are simply not listening to any voice but the one which sounds within their own minds. Although parallels can be suggested from earlier plays, dubious verbal encounters such as the one involving Margaret and Suffolk at the end of *1 Henry VI* (v, iii, 60–109), the special quality of the last plays as a group and, particularly, the simplification of character upon which Shakespeare was now

insisting lends to these linguistic mis-meetings a new and more central significance. Words define the gap between individuals; they do not bridge it. Certainly Marina stumbles through most of her scenes, up to the point of her recognition of King Pericles, as a creature apart for whom the speech of her associates registers dimly, if at all.

Bawd. Pray you, come hither awhile. You have fortunes coming upon you. Mark me: you must seem to do that fearfully which you commit willingly; to despise profit where you have most gain. To weep that you live as ye do makes pity in your lovers; seldom but that pity begets you a good opinion, and that opinion a mere profit.
Marina. I understand you not.   (IV, ii, 116–23)

From the moment of her first appearance, bearing flowers to strew a grave, and speaking a lament which takes no cognizance of the other characters on the stage, Marina is a figure strangely sealed off from other people.

At the end of *Pericles*, when Marina at last finds her father, this sealed-off quality moves into the centre of the stage, becoming the subject of action as well as a feature of dialogue. King Pericles, as Helicanus says, has not spoken to anyone for three months. Even more radically than his daughter, he has cut himself off from that world of speech which binds human beings together. On board the Tyrian galley, father and child deal for a time in obliquities and broken language:

Pericles. My fortunes – parentage – good
                         parentage –
        To equal mine! Was it not thus? What
                         say you?
Marina. I said, my lord, if you did know my
                      parentage
        You would not do me violence.
Pericles. I do think so. Pray you turn your eyes
                      upon me.
        You are like something that – What
                  countrywoman?
        Here of these shores?
Marina. No, nor of any shores.

> Yet I was mortally brought forth, and am
> No other than I appear.
>
> *Pericles.* I am great with woe, and shall deliver
>
>   weeping...
>
> Where do you live?
>
> *Marina.* Where I am but a stranger.
>
>   (v, i, 96–113)

Question and answer circle like hawks about a quarry around the hidden, essential fact of their relationship to each other. Once this fact is out, Marina and Pericles leave their respective private worlds for an entire mutual awareness. Words and eyes meet as they have not done before in this play. The enormous emotional force of this recognition scene seems to depend upon our sense of release, of giddy joy, at the re-establishment of communication, a vindication that had come to seem impossible, of words.

In subsequent plays, the barriers dissolve less easily. In *The Tempest*, in fact, they never disappear. At the end as at the beginning, characters remain isolated. They are disposed about the stage singly, like Prospero or Caliban, or else in strangely inviolable groups. When Prospero taught Caliban language, the only profit his pupil gained was the ability to curse his master. Obviously, this is an extreme and distorted view of the value of speech. Yet it remains true of this play as a whole that words catch up and express the separateness of characters more than any mutual understanding. This isolation persists up to the very end. The eyes of Prospero and Antonio, of Miranda and Sebastian, Gonzalo and Ariel, Ferdinand and Caliban will never meet: neither on the island, nor back in Naples, or Milan. These are parallels which require infinity to conjoin them. The play itself offers us nothing closer to infinity than Prospero himself and a magic which he rejects at the end as rough and insufficient. This distrust of dialogue in *The Tempest*, the insistence upon the difficulty of communication, foreshadows the techniques of the modern theatre. Not even Prospero, the magician—dramatist who orders this play-world, can bring about a true coherence of minds. He stands among characters sealed off in private worlds of experience, worlds which language is powerless to unite. It seems at least possible that *The Tempest* was Shakespeare's last play because in it he had reached a point in his investigation of the capabilities of words beyond which he could not proceed.

© Anne Barton 1971

REVENGE, RETRIBUTION, AND RECONCILIATION

JOAN REES

There is a poem of D. H. Lawrence's called 'The Work of Creation',* in which he speaks of the creative process as it is experienced by God and also by the artist:

The mystery of creation is the divine urge of creation,
but it is a great strange urge, it is not a Mind.
Even an artist knows that his work was never in his
                                                    mind,
he could never have *thought* it before it happened.
A strange ache possessed him, and he entered the
                                                    struggle,
and out of the struggle with his material, in the
                                        spell of the urge
his work took place, it came to pass, it stood up and
                                        saluted his mind.

God is a great urge, wonderful, mysterious,
                                        magnificent
but he knows nothing beforehand. His urge takes
                                    shape in flesh, and lo!
it is creation! God looks himself on it in wonder, for
                                        the first time.
Lo! there is a creature, formed! How strange!
Let me think about it! Let me form an idea!

I quote this poem because it seems to me that the point Lawrence makes about the creative imagination is particularly worth stressing in relation to Shakespeare. Shakespeare criticism, as we all know, is a highly sophisticated business and a good deal of learning and ingenuity, not to speak of baring of the soul, goes into the interpretation of the plays. The tendency of these studies, whether by intention or not, often seems to be to encourage the notion that Shakespeare worked in each play according to a pre-formed and carefully articulated intellectual scheme which study can identify. This seems to me to be a false position. To derive the creative act primarily from a conceptualising power is to turn the situation back to front. Instead of 'ideas' about the finished work, therefore, whether historical, philosophical, or any other, I propose in this paper to consider briefly a few plays at the 'pre-idea' stage, that is the point at which Shakespeare is still struggling with his material – before it came to pass, and stood up, and saluted his mind. His handling of plot material seems to provide an opportunity for doing this, and I take as my point of departure the common observation that there are very few basic stories in the world. If this is so, as it appears to be, it should be a matter of some interest to observe how a busy dramatist searches for and tries out the possibilities inherent in these few stories, what sort of problems and opportunities his researches reveal, and how he seeks to deal with them. I shall talk about one kind of story: that which has its origin in a crime or dastardly act and which pursues the consequences of this act.

  * We are grateful to the following for permission to quote copyright material: William Heinemann Ltd, Laurence Pollinger Ltd and the Estate of the late Mrs Frieda Lawrence for 'The Work of Creation' by D. H. Lawrence from *The Collected Poems of D. H. Lawrence*; 'The Work of Creation', from *The Complete Poems of D. H. Lawrence*, volume II, edited by Vivian de Sola Pinto and F. Warren Roberts, Copyright 1933 by Frieda Lawrence. All Rights Reserved. Reprinted by permission of the Viking Press Inc.

There appear to be three possible kinds of development of this basic story. One is the revenge plot: a central figure has imposed upon him, or undertakes, the duty of avenging the sinful act which has been committed. *Hamlet* is the prime example of this kind of plot in the Shakespeare canon. As plot material, revenge has obvious advantages. The initial crime provides a strong opening, the vengeance taken provides a strong close. The problem of the dramatist working on this material concerns the middle, the filling of the interval between the occasion of revenge and the execution of it. Kyd, who was clever at these things, went some way towards solving the problem by starting his *Spanish Tragedy* twice, once with the situation of Don Andrea, and again with the murder of Horatio. Shakespeare delays the start of *his* revenge plot until the end of the first act when we first hear that a crime has been committed and Hamlet assumes the burden of revenge. In act I, scene v, with the Ghost's instructions to Hamlet and Hamlet's acceptance of them, Shakespeare lays down a programme of the action to be developed in the rest of the play. Such programmes, provided by curses, instructions as here, prophecies, or statement of intent as in Prince Hal's soliloquy near the beginning of *1 Henry IV*, are a device often used by Shakespeare to keep the story-line firm while he avails himself of whatever exploitable opportunity the material may be made to yield. In *Hamlet* he explores by subtle and various means the consequences of the interview with the Ghost as they affect Claudius, the Queen, Ophelia, and Hamlet himself. As he handles it, this turns out to be somewhat intellectual material, involving psychological discrimination and contrast but not much physical action. Hamlet's soliloquies may be described as a device of the dramatist developed in response to this narrative deficiency. They compensate for the lack of lively episode, of the sort with which Kyd fills the middle of

his play, by producing, through their intensity, the illusion of action at the time of speaking, and, by their promise of action, as Hamlet rushes off at last resolved to do something, they keep the audience in a state of expectation and suspense.

A second possible development of the basic story is the retribution plot. Retribution is closely connected with revenge but not identical with it. Personal revenge may make a part of it but the retribution plot has as its core the assumption that the sheer momentum of evil will create in time its own punishment, that the career of the wrong-doer is a violation of some ultimately inexorable law, and cannot, in the nature of things, triumph. Two of Shakespeare's plays, in particular, are founded on the retribution plot, *Richard III* and *Macbeth*. This kind of material has similar advantages to those which the revenge plot offers, in that it provides strong situations and a strong resolution, but, whereas when revenge is the motive, attention is focused on the avenger, when the plot hinges on retribution, attention is directed to the evil-doer. The retribution plot is not subject, consequently, to the implicit disadvantage of the revenge plot, that an interval has to be filled between the occasion of vengeance and the fulfilling of it. In the retribution plot, the evil-doer has the initiative and may be allowed to retain it until the last moment, wading further and further in sin until the final scene or two. *Richard III* and *Macbeth* both follow this pattern but in *Macbeth* the threads are drawn much more tightly together. In the earlier play we may find, in spite of the programme of prophecies and curses, that retribution comes in the end as a dramatic finale imposed on the action when we have all had a good time watching Richard manipulate events for the greater part of the play. In *Macbeth*, the collapse of Lady Macbeth's mind and her suicide indicate the torment that Macbeth endures and underline the fact that retribution in this play springs from and accompanies the action at every stage, from beginning to end.

The reconciliation plot is the third possible development of the basic story of a crime and its consequences. While retribution has elements in common with revenge, reconciliation as a state of mind disavows revenge, and the reconcilation plot would seem to have no connection with the revenge plot except by opposition. As dramatic material, however, reconciliation shares with revenge the problem of the middle. Like revenge, it may provide strong dramatic material at the start, but there is the interval between initial estrangement and final reconciliation to be filled. Since estrangement implies separation, there is also dispersal of characters to be reckoned with, and how to bring them together again in a way that suggests peace and harmony and yet is not so restful that it loses interest is another problem posed by the material. The dramatic opportunities offered by the reconciliation plot are in general much more limited than those offered by revenge or retribution. The crisis comes early, and the plot does not offer obvious opportunity for a variety of episodes as retribution does. *Cymbeline* and *The Winter's Tale* exemplify two treatments of the problems that arise in the handling of this difficult material.

Since the estrangement of Posthumus and Imogen in *Cymbeline* stems from a deliberate lie, the undoing of the damage is not necessarily a very difficult matter but Shakespeare assembles an extraordinary collection of narrative lines to keep his story going and to produce a complicated final revelation and reunion. It is as though, recognising the difficulty of sustaining a reconciliation plot for a whole play's length, he took care to stack up a great deal of episodic material so as to be in no difficulty in keeping things going and maintaining interest. Indeed, he over-provides, the character of the Queen, interestingly sketched at the beginning of the play, being among the casualties of an over-crowded scene.

The accumulation of supplementary material in *Cymbeline* enables Shakespeare to give a 'purer' treatment of the reconciliation plot in this play than anywhere else. For, as we look more closely at the reconciliation material, it becomes evident that, far from being at the opposite pole from revenge material, in fact the reconciliation plot includes within itself a revenge potential. This potential is recognised in *Cymbeline*, but Shakespeare refrains from developing it. At the end of act II, Posthumus is in the grip of a mad and violent jealousy, but, though he orders the murder of Imogen, the audience is assured at once that Pisanio will not carry it out. The revenge potential of the story is consequently minimised, and when Posthumus appears again, at the beginning of act v, he has already repented of his anger. Although he still believes Imogen guilty, he renounces vengeance. How and when the change occurred in him we are not told, for Posthumus's bloody intentions are only one element in the narrative tissue and scarcely more important than others.

The situation is different when we turn to *The Winter's Tale*. In that play, Leontes appears, not only to himself but to the audience, to have actually executed a terrible revenge, and we are shown the moment when delusion falls from him and he realises what he has done and the life of remorse to which he has condemned himself. The first three acts of *The Winter's Tale* constitute, in fact, a fully-fledged revenge story, full of strong dramatic situations and contrasts, and treating the revenge situation and its destructive passions much more fully than *Cymbeline* does. *The Tempest*, it may be noted in passing, also exploits the revenge potential of the reconciliation theme and does it in a way different from that of either of the other two plays. Though *The Tempest* is ultimately resolved as a reconciliation plot, the action is directed to building up a situation which could lead to either reconciliation or revenge, and there is no certainty till towards the end which it is going to be.

These explorations of the revenge, retribution and reconciliation developments of the basic story provide, I suggest, glimpses of Shakespeare at work, and we may especially note how, after *Cymbeline*, his treatment of the reconciliation plot becomes less 'pure', as though he had found it dramatically intractable. In place of the proliferation of stories clustering round the central core, by which he seeks to maintain interest in *Cymbeline*, he uses revenge in *The Winter's Tale* to provide striking dramatic effect. The problem of the middle he solves as a dramatist in full and confident enjoyment of his powers by the wonderful bravura scene of the sheep-shearing in act IV. The narrative function of the scene is to establish the love of Florizel and Perdita and to send them and Camillo to Sicily: the richness of the treatment is a measure of the superlative creative skill of Shakespeare at this stage of his career.

By the time he came to the last scenes of *Cymbeline*, Shakespeare could have had no worries about material, for there is an abundance of threads to tie up or cut short. The first four acts of *The Winter's Tale*, on the other hand, project no inevitable ending except the reunion of Leontes and Perdita and of Leontes and Polixenes through the love of their children. The meeting and recognition of Leontes and Perdita could have made a moving episode but the culminating scene was not written – or if it was, and Simon Forman saw it at that performance at The Globe in 1611 when the statue scene seems so oddly to have left no impression on him, Shakespeare thereafter discarded it and chose instead to subordinate the expected climax to the quite unexpected resuscitation of Hermione. The

statue scene being written, we respond to it as we can and may, but how did Shakespeare come to write it? If we believe that he worked out his plays from an 'idea' and that he wished to exemplify in *The Winter's Tale* the operation of Divine Grace, or the healing and vivifying power of love, or some other such concept, we may wish to argue that the resurrection of Hermione was in his mind from the start. But if we envisage instead a dramatist working at a certain body of plot material we may see it, not as a pre-conceived 'idea', but as a splendid response to the demands and limitations of the material as they are revealed in the working. A *coup de théâtre* is needed at the end of *The Winter's Tale* to stop the audience putting its things together and beginning to move off while Leontes and Perdita make their no doubt beautiful but expected speeches; and so Shakespeare created the statue scene, like the sheep-shearing, one of the marvels of *The Winter's Tale*.

Reconciliation is difficult material to animate dramatically and Shakespeare had found problems with it in *King Lear* also. The structure of *King Lear* has similarities to that of *The Winter's Tale*. Like the later play, it begins with a complete story very rapidly and economically executed. By the end of act III the original impulses of both the Lear and Gloucester stories have been worked out. Misconceptions have been corrected and the lessons of experience have been understood and accepted. All that remains is for the old men to be reunited with their good children and for the bad children to be punished. The last acts of *King Lear* constitute a working of the reconciliation and retribution plots, the two being conducted simultaneously. As in the other plays, the retribution material lends itself much more readily to varied dramatic treatment than the reconciliation material does, but, with some evidence of difficulty, Shakespeare manages to hold back the reunion of Lear and

Cordelia till the end of act IV. He still has some business to finish in the retribution plot, but it would be unthinkable for attention finally to be directed anywhere else than on the main characters. The expected reconciliation of Gloucester and Edgar is achieved offstage and reported, as the expected reunion of Leontes and Perdita is. What is there for Lear and Cordelia to do? A *coup de théâtre* is needed at the end to pull attention sharply to where it should rightly be, on Lear and his enormous sufferings, just as it is needed at the end of *The Winter's Tale* to prevent the play merely fading away.

The *coup de théâtre* in *Lear* is a shocking death. In *The Winter's Tale* it is a miraculous coming-to-life; Hermione's revival affirms triumphantly the movement to reconciliation in *The Winter's Tale* from act III, scene iii onwards, but the ending of *King Lear* is ambiguous. There is a strong movement in the later stages of the play towards reconciliation, but the death of Cordelia seems to counter it. It frustrates the expected resolution of the play's discords and leaves all its questions open.

To suggest that Shakespeare wrote this most discussed of scenes because of a limitation in the plot material he was working with may seem a kind of heresy; and, of course, even if the suggestion could be supported by external evidence, this would in no way affect the scene's capacity to arouse strong reactions and stimulate our minds and emotions. Nevertheless, it seems to me that, for *King Lear* as for other plays, this approach via the exploration of story material may provide a useful method of analysis. Lawrence's 'The Work of Creation', quoted at the beginning of this paper, pointed to the distinction between the plays as works which Shakespeare evolved and wrote down line by line and scene by scene and the 'ideas' of the critics, scholars, and others which are generated by the finished product. Interpretative criticism, description, that is, of the 'ideas' which the plays produce, is one kind of tribute we make to what Shakespeare has achieved: poetry, as Keats wrote, 'should strike the Reader as a wording of his own highest thoughts'. But there is always the danger for the literary critic that he will begin to equate his own highest thoughts with the 'meaning' of the poet. To study the relation of the complete play to the story element which it contains and which, more often than not, it transcends, may be one way of reminding ourselves and others that the exuberant vitality of the great creative urge is what Shakespeare's plays above all exemplify for the delight and enrichment of our lives.

© JOAN REES 1971

SHAKESPEARE THE PROFESSIONAL

KENNETH MUIR

A conference on the theme of Shakespeare, theatre poet, encourages the reiteration of commonplaces: and, if my argument is familiar, two sentences which, according to Boswell, were deleted from *The Vicar of Wakefield*, may serve as an apology. 'When I was a young man, being anxious to distinguish myself, I was perpetually starting new propositions. But I soon gave this over, for I found that generally what was new was false.'[1]

Shakespeare's greatness as a poet has never been in doubt in English-speaking countries; the critics and actors have always paid lip-service to his greatness as a dramatist. Yet it is only during the last hundred years that we have known enough about the conventions of the Elizabethan theatre to judge Shakespeare's technical competence. Early this century, Robert Bridges, reacting against Bradley, wrote his famous attack on Shakespeare's carelessness and incompetence. He had the excuse that Victorian productions, however brilliantly acted, were merely adaptations. This was brought home to me very forcibly by Sir Donald Wolfit's production of *Cymbeline* in which he made precisely the same cuts as Irving had done half a century earlier. As a result the last act was completely unintelligible to those who had not read the play. Memories of the Irving production seduced Bernard Shaw into rewriting the last act for a production at the Stratford Memorial Theatre; but when he re-read Shakespeare's fifth act he frankly confessed that it was better than his own.

Actor-managers in the nineteenth century, despite their avowed bardolatry, believed they could improve on his plays and therefore assumed that he was not really a competent dramatist. Part of the trouble, but only part, was the difficulty of adapting the plays for a different kind of stage. One early production of *As You Like It* at Stratford, to judge from the prompt book, divided the play into three acts, the first ending with the line

So this is the forest of Arden!

The curtain fell and rose again on a tableau of Rosalind, Celia and Touchstone, shading their eyes as they gazed into the distance. Even worse than this, the Arden scenes were all run together, instead of alternating with the court scenes.

It is not surprising that when Thomas Hardy was asked to contribute to a Shakespeare memorial in the shape of a national theatre, he replied that he did not think

that Shakespeare appertains particularly to the theatrical world nowadays, if ever he did. His distinction as a minister of the theatre is infinitesimal beside his distinction as a poet, man of letters, and seer of life, and that his expression of himself was cast in the form of words for actors and not in the form of books to be read was an accident of his social circumstances that he himself despised.[2]

---

[1] *Life of Samuel Johnson*, ed. G. B. Hill (Oxford, 1934), III, 376.
[2] Florence E. Hardy, *Life of Thomas Hardy* (London, 1962), p. 341.

Hardy went on to hazard a guess that Shakespeare's plays 'would cease altogether to be acted some day, and be simply studied'.

There was some slight excuse for Hardy's anti-theatrical bias in 1908 and we are told that when he did go to see Shakespeare performed his eyes were riveted not to the stage but to the text of the play. It is, moreover, arguable, even if the *Sonnets* are not autobiographical, that Shakespeare was sometimes uneasy in his profession. He confesses that he has made himself 'a motley to the view'; and even if this is only metaphorical, in the next sonnet (111) he blames Fortune

> That did not better for my life provide
> Than public means which public manners breed.
> Thence comes it that my name receives a brand,
> And almost thence my nature is subdued
> To what it works in, like the dyer's hand.

The two sonnets together suggest that Shakespeare was thinking of his profession as an actor rather than his work as a dramatist, though in both capacities he could be described as making 'old offences of affections new'. In any case, if the *Sonnets* were not wholly fictional, he was involved in a situation where he was bound to feel socially inferior.

But the feelings expressed in these sonnets were probably momentary and there was perhaps an element of that self-dramatisation for which Othello has been wrongly blamed. Shakespeare must have been aware that his dramatic, as well as non-dramatic, verse would outlive the monuments of princes. All the poets he depicted in his plays were foolish, ineffective or time-serving, but no one would deduce from that that he had a low opinion of his own profession as poet, so one would expect similar ironies in his references to his other profession as actor. For Shakespeare had the advantage, shared by few dramatic poets, of being intimately concerned with every aspect of the theatre; as shareholder, actor, dramatist and perhaps even as director, he was entirely professional. Racine had an intimate acquaintance with the theatre – or at least with actresses – but he was no actor. Ibsen had worked in the theatre, but not while he was writing his masterpieces. Strindberg, likewise, had little experience of acting, although he wrote detailed instructions to the company which performed his plays. Chekhov's leading lady became his wife; but he declared that fiction was a lawful wife, while drama was 'a showy, noisy, impertinent and tiresome mistress' and the theatre 'a serpent that sucks your blood'.[1] Shaw had been the greatest of all dramatic critics; he had affairs, like Racine, with a number of actresses; and he directed a number of his own plays. But of the great dramatists, only Molière and Shakespeare were professional in every sense of the word.

There are, of course, dangers involved. The actor, particularly the actor in a repertory theatre, knows what tricks will enable him to get by; his work is often hurried and makeshift; he aims sometimes at immediate applause rather than the praise of the judicious. And, as Hamlet implies, though not necessarily with the poet's concurrence, the judicious will always be in a minority.

The actor–dramatist, writing for a stable company, is apt to rely on the talents of his fellow actors to bring to life imperfectly realised characters; he will be tempted to repeat effects which have paid off before; he will, for example, disguise yet another heroine as a boy; and he will certainly rely on his knowledge that the audience simply won't notice minor discrepancies and improbabilities. He will, in other words, be writing for the present and not for posterity. But those who write for posterity have never reached their audience.

It was considerations like these which led

[1] *Life and Letters of Anton Tchekhov*, trans. and ed. S. S. Koteliansky and Philip Tomlinson (London, 1925), pp. 36, 38.

Robert Bridges to denounce Shakespeare's audience whose low standards and bad taste prevented the greatest of poets from becoming a great artist. Bridges was doubtless reacting against bardolatry, but he seems to have been ignorant of the real nature of Shakespeare's audience, and, much more seriously, of the conventions of the Elizabethan theatre. If one examines the attempts of the best nineteenth-century poets to write plays, one will take leave to doubt whether the absence of an audience is conducive to the production of great drama, and whether it is a disadvantage to write for a particular theatre and a particular company. *The Borderers*, *The Cenci*, and the plays of Tennyson, Browning and Bridges were never clapper-clawed by the palms of the vulgar, yet many of them sacrifice character to situation in ways which the better Elizabethan dramatists would have avoided. The advantages of being a professional theatre poet can be seen from the failures of these amateurs. But perhaps the most telling example is afforded by the great poet of our day, whose dramatic experiments extended over thirty years from *Sweeney Agonistes* to *The Elder Statesman* and whose interest in the problems of the dramatist can be seen in his dialogue on dramatic poetry at the beginning of his career and his lecture on poetry and drama near the end. Mr Martin Browne's recent book,[1] with its lavish quotations from early drafts of Eliot's plays, reveals only too clearly that in some respects he remained an amateur who leaned heavily on Browne's advice. The last and weakest of the plays, *The Elder Statesman*, underwent some radical revisions. Between the performances at the Edinburgh festival and its opening in London some weeks later, many changes were made. Actors found it difficult to speak some lines naturally, and these were altered or cut. Eliot was dissatisfied with the reactions of the audience and he felt that some passages were too 'poetical'. These were eliminated. The

final scene between the young lovers had gone badly and Eliot reduced it to a third of its length. What is more significant, he transferred words spoken by the man to the woman. This is surely an indication that the characters had never come alive.

Eliot was a poet who had invaded the professional theatre rather late in life – at about the age when Shakespeare retired to Stratford – and despite his prestige as a poet, as a dramatist he never left off his L plates. He did not know instinctively what lines would be effective in the theatre; he found it difficult to vary his style to suit different characters; and too many of his characters are either caricatures or mouthpieces for himself. He was not writing for a particular company, so he did not know how effective his speeches would be in the mouths of the actors who were afterwards chosen to speak them.

Shakespeare, of course, acquired his mastery only by degrees. In his earliest plays the characters are differentiated not by how they say it, but only by what they say. Often indeed, they are not distinguished at all. Here, for example, are three speeches from *Henry VI*:

(i) Why stand we like soft-hearted women here,
     Wailing our losses, whiles the foe doth rage,
     And look upon, as if the tragedy
     Were play'd in jest by counterfeiting actors?
     Here on my knee I vow to God above
     I'll never pause again, never stand still,
     Till either death hath clos'd these eyes of mine
     Or fortune given me measure of revenge.

(ii) I will stir up in England some black storm
     Shall blow ten thousand souls to heaven or hell;
     And this fell tempest shall not cease to rage
     Until the golden circuit on my head,
     Like to the glorious sun's transparent beams,
     Do calm the fury of this mad-bred flaw.

(iii) I cannot weep, for all my body's moisture
     Scarce serves to quench my furnace-burning
                             heart;

[1] E. Martin Browne, *The Making of T. S. Eliot's Plays* (Cambridge, 1969).

Nor can my tongue unload my heart's great
                    burden,
For self-same wind that I should speak withal
Is kindling coals that fires all my breast,
And burns me up with flame that tears would
                    quench.
To weep is to make less the depth of grief –
Tears then for babes; blows and revenge for me!

These three speeches are by York, Gloucester and Warwick, but it would be difficult to say which was which.

By the time he wrote *Romeo and Juliet* Shakespeare was able to differentiate between the speech of Mercutio, Capulet and the Nurse, besides that of the lovers: but in the years that followed (as Granville-Barker pointed out) the most vital characters speak mainly in prose – Shylock, Falstaff, Rosalind, Beatrice. Prose, of course, is nearer to the colloquial than verse is likely to be; but no one who has read Brian Vickers's book[1] will imagine that Shakespeare eschewed rhetoric when writing prose. Indeed Kenneth Hudson has shown[2] that Shakespeare's prose was never as close to the ordinary talk of the time as Middleton's, Dekker's, or even Jonson's. By the time Shakespeare had finished *2 Henry IV*, the verse itself had acquired a new flexibility and subtlety, so that one could say, with pardonable exaggeration, that Shakespeare taught himself to write his mature dramatic verse by experimenting with dramatic prose.[3]

Alleyn and Burbage were both praised for their naturalness; but it is clear that between 1587 and 1597 the style of acting became increasingly subtle. It is unnecessary to discuss whether the change was caused by the fact that the better dramatists had begun to write in a more colloquial style, or whether the dramatists were driven by the actors to write parts in which their new techniques could be manifested – unnecessary both because the question cannot be resolved, and because Shakespeare, as I have emphasised, was an actor as well as a playwright, an actor before he was a playwright.

The new verse style reached its early perfection in *Hamlet*. I need only recall a few of its characteristics. The style varies according to the character and even according to the situation. The formal oration by Claudius in the second scene with its suavely balanced phrases differs radically from the speech in which he attempts to pray and likewise from the deviousness of his temptation of Laertes, though all three are acceptable as the utterances of the same man. Hamlet's speech goes through numerous mutations: courtly formality, savage parody of Laertes, parody of Osric, antic disposition with Polonius, ratiocination on the drunkenness of the court or on the Senecal man, literary and dramatic criticism in the scenes with the players, and, lastly, the four major soliloquies, all different. Superficially, indeed, the first and the third are concerned with the temptation of suicide, and the second and the fourth with self-reproaches because his task is still unfulfilled; but the differences are equally obvious. Yet behind all these manifestations is a coherent personality, not Everyman, as C. S. Lewis perversely argued. One other example may be given – the Ghost. As Bernard Shaw said 'the weird music of' the Ghost's 'long speech which should be the spectral wail of a soul's bitter wrong crying from one world to another in the extremity of its torment', should not be given to 'the most squaretoed member of the company'.

The second point about the style of *Hamlet* is equally important. There are nearly 3,000 lines of verse in the play and over 1,000 lines of prose. But, unless one's attention is called

[1] *The Artistry of Shakespeare's Prose* (London, 1968).

[2] *Shakespeare Survey 23* (Cambridge, 1970), pp. 39–48.

[3] One can observe something of the same kind in Marlowe, though in a more condensed form: his most flexible dramatic verse – Faustus's last speech – comes just after the wonderful prose in the scene with the scholars.

to it, one is unlikely to notice which medium is being used at any particular moment. Eliot expressed the hope that the audience would not be aware during a performance of one of his later plays that it was written in verse, and he avoided the alternation of verse and prose because he thought the audience would thereby become more conscious of the verse. Shakespeare, being himself without this kind of embarrassment, does not embarrass us. We forget we are listening to poetry: we seem rather to be listening to men and women talking. The different levels of reality provided by the Dido play and 'The Mouse-trap' make Hamlet's intervening soliloquies seem perfectly natural speech.

Another aspect of Shakespeare's professionalism is his use of imagery. Critics have differed about the extent to which he knew what he was doing. That he deliberately inserted a score of sickness images into *Hamlet* strains one's credulity; but that he was completely unconscious of them strains it more. Nor is it possible to accept Pasternak's view, which he advanced after translating the play, that the repetition of such images was due to carelessness or haste. It may be worth while to suggest that the main groups of images take their origin in plot and situation. The war imagery, for example – which most critics have tended to overlook – arose naturally from the military operations of Fortinbras, as well as from the struggle between Hamlet and his uncle. What Richard Altick calls 'the odour of corruption' could have been suggested by the dead bodies and skulls, as well as by the thing which is rotten in the state of Denmark, the rank smell of sin; and since Shakespeare in many of his plays had associated disorder in the state with sickness and sickness with sin, it is not surprising that it should pervade the world of Elsinore. The sickness images, of course, if considered in their contexts, apply to the guilt of Claudius and Gertrude, and only once to

Hamlet himself.[1] The poisoning of Gertrude, Laertes, Gonzago, Hamlet and his father naturally spills over into the imagery of the play. The theatrical imagery arises naturally from the scenes connected with 'The Mouse-trap' and even the imagery related to cosmetics springs from the hypocrisy of Claudius (who himself refers to the harlot's cheek), from the frailty of women, which sets a blister on 'the fair forehead of an innocent love', and perhaps from the reiterated idea that Fortune is a strumpet – for Hamlet, as critics have suggested, moves from this idea to an acceptance of the fact that he is guided by Providence.

It does not greatly matter where Shakespeare derived his images, whether from his sources or from his imagination setting to work on the sources. As Professor Bradbrook suggested long ago, the breast-feeding images in *Macbeth* may have been prompted by the account given in the *Chronicles* of the way in which Scottish women preferred to nurse their own babies; or it may rather be prompted by the subject proposed for debate before James I, whether a man's character was influenced by his nurse's milk – or, indeed, by a combination of the two.

Shakespeare was professional, too, in his method of composing his plays. All the evidence would seem to show that he hunted for plots rather than for themes. He would not have decided to write a play about Justice and Mercy, or about Jealousy, or Ingratitude or Ambition; but he would read *Promos and Cassandra* or the old play of *King Leir* and decide how best to dramatise the material, what theme he could extract from it. It is possible to deduce why Shakespeare made the alterations he did – why he linked the Lear story with that of the Paphlagonian King, why he rejected the marriage of Promos and Cassandra, and substituted Mariana for Isabella. Reading the story of Disdemona and the Moorish captain, he would

[1] See 'Imagery and Symbolism in *Hamlet*', *Études Anglaises*, XVII (1964), 352 ff.

see the need for raising the status of the Moor, for eliminating the months of happiness before the voyage to Cyprus, for altering the motive of the villain, for making the Moor alone responsible for the murder of Desdemona, and for making him commit suicide when he learns that Desdemona is innocent. But these changes alone would not turn the sordid *novella* into a satisfactory scenario. Shakespeare, we may surmise, saw the opportunities afforded by three details of the tale. After the murder, the Moor suffers from a deep melancholy because he 'had loved the lady more than his very eyes'. He had killed the thing he loved. Then there was the marriage of black and white with the possibilities involved of paradox, antithesis and symbol; and as the Devil was depicted as black, whereas the demi-devil of the play is white, this would suggest the diabolic imagery analysed by Leslie Bethell.[1] But perhaps the detail which most attracted Shakespeare was the contrast between the Ensign's fine appearance and his secretly depraved nature. This fitted in with one of Shakespeare's persistent obsessions – from Tarquin to Angelo and Claudius – of the difficulty of distinguishing seeming from being.[2] Perhaps this was a question of professional interest to an actor – as we can see from the stage references in *Richard III* and *Macbeth*. If an actor can take the part of angel or devil, male or female, how can one tell (when all the world's a stage) that any man is not acting a part? At the end of the third book of *Paradise Lost*, Satan, journeying to Eden to encompass the Fall of Man, encounters Uriel,

> The sharpest sighted spirit of all in Heav'n.

He does not recognise Satan, but directs him to Paradise. Milton comments:

> For neither Man nor Angel can discern
> Hypocrisie, the onely evil that walks
> Invisible, except to God alone,
> By his permissive will, through Heav'n and Earth:

> And oft though wisdom wake, suspicion sleeps
> At wisdoms Gate, and to simplicitie
> Resigns her charge, while goodness thinks no ill
> Where no ill seems.

Most hypocrites in literature succeed only in deceiving some people some of the time. Tartuffe and Pecksniff don't succeed with everyone. But Shakespeare seems to have shared Milton's view on the impenetrability of evil: and this is surely the answer to those who regard Othello as excessively stupid. Othello is deceived like everyone else in the play, and like the Archangel Uriel.

Despite numerous caveats on the danger of treating characters in a poetic play as characters in a novel or even as living human beings, there are still too many critics and some directors who continue the practice. We are told that Othello becomes jealous in only five minutes after the beginning of Iago's temptation, as though playing time could be equated with real time. It may be true, as Una Ellis-Fermor argued in her British Academy lecture,[3] that 'the genuine dramatic mode of thought, the fundamental quality which reveals the innate dramatic genius', and which 'distinguishes the essentially dramatic from all other kinds of genius' is the power of the dramatist to identify himself with each of his characters, each in turn and simultaneously. It is easy to see that Bernard Shaw can speak through Barbara and Cousins as well as through Undershaft; that Millamant, Mirabell, Lady Wishfort, Witwoud, Sir Wilfull and Marwood are magnificently realised; and that Eliot, who lacked this power, could create a Celia Copplestone but is less successful with the Chamberlaynes. Yet one cannot accept Professor Ellis-Fermor's formulation without certain qualifications. In

[1] 'The Diabolic Images in *Othello*', *Shakespeare Survey 5* (Cambridge, 1952), pp. 62–80.
[2] 'Seem' and its derivatives were used by Shakespeare nearly 500 times.
[3] *Shakespeare the Dramatist* (London, 1961), p. 18.

several of Marlowe's plays only one or two characters are fully realised, yet one would hesitate to say that he lacked innate dramatic genius; while, on the other hand, Browning who possessed a remarkable power of identifying himself with a wide variety of characters, wrote only unsuccessful plays. The power of self-identification is clearly not sufficient.

Then perhaps it should be stressed that the dramatist – the professional dramatist – relies on the actors to embody his characters, adding to them the physical presence of Burbage, Garrick, Mrs Siddons or Sir John Gielgud. A character on the page needs to be incarnated in a character on the stage. In *Measure for Measure* Barnadine is given only 7 speeches, Juliet 7 and Froth 8, with a total of only 232 words between the three characters. But Shakespeare knew that all three could be made into unforgettable figures.

The third qualification, or clarification, which needs to be made is that every good dramatist, especially the poetic dramatist, eschews the methods of naturalism. Ibsen said of *Emperor and Galilean* that he wanted to give the reader the impression that what he was reading was something that had really happened. But he was continually stressing that 'in the realm of art there is no place for pure reality, but only for illusion'.[1]

Yet there are still some critics who apply prosaic methods of analysis to Shakespeare's characters and arrive inevitably at absurd results. Part of the trouble is due to the fact that for the last 250 years the novel has been the dominant literary form; and during the last 100 years we have been urged to wring the neck of rhetoric. So we get the dramatic critic of the *Daily Telegraph* assuring us that Congreve was a bad dramatist; and the dramatic critic of the *Sunday Times* asserting on successive Sundays that a single line in Pinter's one-act play, *Landscape*, expresses love more successfully than anything in *Antony and Cleopatra*, instancing from the latter the lines:

Now boast thee, Death, in thy possession lies
A lass unparallel'd.

Dame Peggy Ashcroft spoke the Pinter line in question – 'Oh my true love I said' – in a way that enraptured Mr Hobson along with the rest of the audience. Here, he thought, was the true voice of feeling, as opposed to the rhetorical artifice of Shakespeare's lines. I admire Pinter 'on this side idolatry' as much as any, but it need hardly be said that he, too, indulges in rhetoric. He departs from the colloquial order of words to obtain poetic effects. The line admired by Mr Hobson is at the very end of the play; but, if it is read in its context, Pinter's rhetorical artifice will be apparent:

He lay above me and looked down at me.
He supported my shoulder...
So tender his touch on my neck.
So softly his kiss on my cheek...
My hand on his rib...
So sweetly the sand over me.
Tiny the sand on my skin...
So silent the sky in my eyes.
Gently the sound of the tide...
Oh my true love I said.[2]

Here are nice examples of anaphora and assonance; and the passage as a whole is as far removed from the colloquial speech of today as Shakespeare's lines were from the speech of Jacobean England.

This same fear of rhetoric has bedevilled a large number of recent productions of Shakespeare. David Warner is an excellent actor and he gave us an unforgettable portrait of Henry VI; but he tried to make the great Towton speech sound as colloquial as prose by inserting medial pauses and by pretending that the lines were not end-stopped. This was obviously wrong-headed, not merely because

[1] *Samlede Verher*, XVII (Oslo, 1946), 73; *ibid.*, XV (Oslo, 1930), 48.
[2] *'Landscape' and 'Silence'* (London, 1969), pp. 29–30.

the poetry was ruined, but because the following passage in which the son-killing father and father-killing son bewail the evils of civil war appeared to be absurd instead of emblematic. Another example of the same fear of rhetoric is the treatment of rhymed verse. We have heard in recent years a Beatrice who tried to conceal the fact that she was speaking a six-line stanza; a Romeo and Juliet who seem ashamed to be sharing a sonnet on their first meeting; and, worst of all, a Titania who guyed her instructions to the fairies about the entertainment of Bottom, by pronouncing *dewberries* as though it rhymed with *eyes* rather than *bees*:

> Hop in his walks and gambol in his eyes;
> Feed him with apricocks and dewberries,
> With purple grapes, green figs, and mulberries;
> The honey-bags steal from the humble-bees,
> And for night-tapers crop their waxen thighs.

This amused many of the audience, but it could not but make the judicious grieve.

Shakespeare's original audience has often been criticised, but at least they were willing to respond to poetry. I have touched on the fruitful interaction of Shakespeare with his fellow actors, who gave as well as demanded; but I have implied the collaboration of what must have been a magnificent audience. Whatever their defects, their favourite play was *Hamlet*: whatever the virtue of modern audiences, their favourite play is *The Mousetrap*.

It is often said that Shakespeare learnt more from the theatre itself and from the plays in which he performed than he did from books, and certainly the playwright's job can be learnt more effectively in the theatre than outside it. He quickly learnt to bombast out a blank verse as the best of his predecessors. But perhaps some recent critics have over-emphasised this aspect of his apprenticeship. It did not take him long to pick up everything that Marlowe, Lyly and Kyd could teach him. From his predecessors Shakespeare learnt a lesson every bit as valuable: he learnt what to avoid. But from treading the boards and experiencing the response of an audience he acquired a knowledge, which soon became a sixth sense, of how to play on them as on a pipe, how to surprise their laughter or their tears, or as Louis MacNeice put it, how to try their heart-strings in the name of mirth; how to point an epigram or make an effective exit; when to use music or the lyrical poetry which requires no accompaniment; the variation of pace, the use of gesture, of silence; the contrast of voices; even the use of slapstick.

But acting, it may be suggested, does not merely teach a playwright the tricks of the trade: it is also a stepping-stone to that more fundamental quality of a dramatist of making his characters live by living in them. Coleridge explained this ability 'to paint truly and according to the colouring of nature, a vast number of personages' by suggesting that Shakespeare 'had only to imitate certain parts of his own character, or to exaggerate such as existed in possibility'. Coleridge, again, said in a letter to Sotheby that Shakespeare alone reveals the ability 'to send ourselves out of ourselves, to *think* ourselves into the thoughts and feelings of beings in circumstances wholly and strangely different from our own'.[1] This, no doubt, is true as far as it goes; but it is an ability likely to be developed by acting.

We are all familiar with those passages in Keats's letters in which he describes the poetic character, which is more the character of the dramatic poet than of the poet *per se*:

When I am in a room with People, if I ever am free from speculating on creations of my own brain, then not myself goes home to myself; but the identity of every one in the room begins to press upon me that I am in a very little time annihilated.[2]

[1] S. T. Coleridge, *Shakespearean Criticism*, ed. T. M. Raysor (London, 1960), II, 85; *Letters*, ed. E. H. Coleridge (London, 1895), I, 372.
[2] *Letters*, ed. M. B. Forman (Oxford, 1935), p. 228.

So Hazlitt described Shakespeare's ability to identify himself with his characters:

The striking peculiarity of Shakespere's mind was its generic quality, its power of communication with all other minds – so that it contained a universe of thought and feeling within itself, and had no one peculiar bias, or exclusive excellence more than another. He was just like any other man, but that he was like all other men. He was the least of an egotist that it was possible to be. He was nothing in himself; but he was all that others were, or that they could become. He not only had in himself the germs of every faculty and feeling, but he could follow them by anticipation, intuitively, into all their conceivable ramifications, through every change of fortune or conflict of passion or turn of thought...There was no respect of persons with him. His genius shone equally on the evil and on the good, on the wise and foolish, the monarch and the beggar...He had only to think of anything in order to become that thing, with all the circumstances belonging to it...That which, perhaps, more than anything else, distinguishes the dramatic productions of Shakespeare from all others, is this wonderful truth and individuality of conception. Each of his characters is as much itself, and as absolutely independent of the rest, as well as of the author, as if they were living persons, not fictions of the mind. The poet may be said, for the time, to identify himself with the character he wishes to represent, and to pass from one to another, like the same soul successively animating different bodies. By an art like of the ventriloquist, he throws his imagination out of himself, and makes every word appear to proceed from the mouth of the person in whose name it is given...One might suppose that he had stood by at the time, and overheard what passed.[1]

This power, which Keats and Hazlitt agreed that Shakespeare possessed to a supreme degree, is one which is encouraged by acting. One has only to talk with any competent actor, even with amateurs, to recognise that to play any role successfully one has to identify oneself with the character. You cannot play Goneril or Regan successfully if you do not, for the time being, look at the situation from their point of view. But, of course, it is the business of the director to see that the proper balance of the play is maintained. We don't want another production in which the villains are excused. I suppose everyone who has taken part in a production of a play, either as an actor or as a director, would agree that one emerges from rehearsals with an increased understanding not merely of the play but of human beings; and if an actor has as much delight in playing Iago as Imogen, a poet will take as much delight in conceiving one as the other. The same power is present to some degree in the greater novelists, most noticeably in Dickens, who was an actor of genius and whose public readings enabled him to portray a wide range of characters.

Shakespeare, then, extended his powers of empathy by the practice of his profession as actor, and also by his profession as playwright. So that if we read the plays written between 1590 and 1608 we find an ever-increasing subtlety of characterisation. Richard III and Macbeth commit much the same crimes; but despite the fact that Shakespeare uses his knowledge of acting in depicting Richard, he remains outside the character. Macbeth, on the other hand, is depicted from within. By the time he came to write the great tragedies, Shakespeare could imagine himself as Hamlet and Claudius, Othello and Iago, Antony and Cleopatra. This imaginative identification went far beyond asking himself such a question as: 'If I were in Hamlet's position what would I do?' – though this is a salutary question for critics to ask themselves – it was more like a case of possession. One could almost say that though Shakespeare created Hamlet, Hamlet returned the compliment.

Although I have been stressing Shakespeare's professionalism, it would be a mistake to imagine that when we have analysed the skills of Shakespeare the Craftsman (as Professor

[1] *Lectures on the English Poets* (London, 1922), pp. 47–50.

Bradbrook calls him in her excellent Clark lectures)[1] we have plucked out the heart of his mystery. If he is distinguished from most other poetic dramatists by being fully professional, he is likewise distinguished from most professionals by the way he proved axioms – the great commonplaces – on his pulses; by the fact (as he admitted) that he had made old offences of affections new; and by the sense he gives us that each individual work illuminates all the rest, though each work

> Is a new beginning, a raid on the inarticulate.[2]

With *The Winter's Tale* and *The Tempest* in mind one cannot continue the Eliot quotation:

> With shabby equipment always deteriorating
> In the general mess of imprecision of feeling.

Nor, after *The Tempest*, if the Circus Animals deserted him, can we imagine Shakespeare like Yeats, lying down

> where all the ladders start
> In the foul rag-and-bone shop of [his] heart.[3]

I began by excusing Hardy and Bridges for their failure to appreciate that Shakespeare's plays were satisfactorily constructed for the Elizabethan theatre, because of the adaptations then in vogue. The wheel is come full circle. Adaptations are once again the fashion; and if one were to give advice to a young director, who had not yet made a name for himself, one might suggest that the quickest way to acquire a reputation would be to play Shakespeare straight, without cuts and without gimmicks. I presume the one thing that unites the readers of *Shakespeare Survey* is a suspicion that Shakespeare knew better than his adaptors.

More than sixty years have elapsed since Hardy said there was no future for Shakespeare in the theatre. It is surely strange that we are still without a theatre which approximates to the Globe or the Blackfriars, where we could see whether his stage-craft – on which so many critics have written eloquently – is successful in practice. I am not, of course, suggesting that all productions of Shakespeare should be on a replica of the Globe. They would seem very dull to those international audiences which have only a smattering of English; and in the theatre standardisation is death. I am not even opposed to some adaptations: for, however much we may admire the Granville-Barker style of production, we have to admit that change is desirable lest one good custom should corrupt the world of the theatre. I am merely suggesting that among the experiments Shakespeare's own method is worth trying.

I began by quoting Boswell, and it will be appropriate to end with a well-known passage in the *Life of Johnson*:

> *Boswell.* I remember many years ago, when my imagination was warm, and I happened to be in a melancholy mood, it distressed me to think of going into a state of being in which Shakespeare's poetry did not exist. A lady whom I then much admired, a very amiable woman, humoured my fancy, and relieved me by saying, 'The first thing you will meet in the other world will be an elegant copy of Shakespeare's works presented to you.' Dr. Johnson smiled benignantly at this, and did not appear to disapprove of the notion.[4]

It is to be hoped that besides being elegant the celestial edition would be purged of those errors in the text committed by careless compositors and over-confident editors. But one wonders whether even so this would be a fitting reward for a lover of Shakespeare. One would like, besides the elegant edition, a Playhouse in Paradise where his works would be performed by angelic actors, who would be able to resist Satanic temptations to cut, bowdlerise or improve the original scripts.

[1] *Shakespeare the Craftsman* (London, 1969).
[2] T. S. Eliot, *Four Quartets* (London, 1949), p. 22.
[3] W. B. Yeats, *Collected Poems* (New York, 1950), p. 391.
[4] III, 312.

© KENNETH MUIR 1971

SHAKESPEARE'S TALKING ANIMALS

TERENCE HAWKES

There is a tense moment at the end of certain modern dramatic productions (it is a feature which has recently shown itself at Stratford) when the actors suddenly turn on the audience and, in the name of communication, begin menacingly to advance on them with ferocious and implacable *bonhomie*. But let me put you out of fear. As this conference draws to an end, it is not my intention to come smilingly amongst you in any physical sense. I know my place. Nor does the title of my paper make mocking reference to any here present in their professional capacities. Dog does not eat dog.

But my subject does involve our communication with each other in a different, more general, but no less 'contemporary' way. For when Ben Jonson nominated language as 'the only benefit man hath to expresse his excellencie of mind above other creatures' (*Timber, or Discoveries*), he was articulating an idea that has had modernity thrust upon it. In fact the concept of man as the Talking Animal, with language his distinctive feature, marking him off from the other animals, is one of those currently fashionable notions redeemed, we might now profitably allow, by its antiquity. For the classification of man as *ʒoon logon echon* (a living creature possessing speech) enjoyed currency before Aristotle, and Cicero offers a formula no less positive than Ben Jonson's when he claims that 'it is in this alone, or in this especially, that we are superior to the animals; that we can converse amongst our-selves, and express our thoughts in speech' (*De Oratore*, I. 8. 32).

Such ideas obviously have particular force and relevance in societies where the act of talking, face to face, constitutes the fundamental mode of life and where speech seems not only to embody humanity, but to bring into being and reinforce all the communal social structures of 'civilisation'. In such societies, speech and man, language and culture, talking and 'way of life' must be very closely connected.

Elizabethan society was certainly not wholly oral in character. But equally certainly it was not wholly literate in any sense that would be meaningful to us. English then, as M. C. Bradbrook puts it, was still 'a tongue rather than a written language'[1] and the most recent estimates suggest that only between thirty percent and fifty percent of males in Shakespeare's London were minimally literate (this using the dubious standard of their ability to write their own names).[2] In any case, as W. J. Ong argues, oral habits and traditions still played dominant roles in spheres that were only potentially those of writing, and the writing of the period exhibits a formidable and formative

[1] M. C. Bradbrook, 'St. George for Spelling Reform!', *Shakespeare Quarterly*, xv (1964), 129–41.
[2] See Lawrence Stone, 'The Educational Revolution in England 1560–1640', *Past and Present*, xxviii (July 1964), 41–80; and 'Literacy and Education in England 1640–1900', *Past and Present*, xlii (February 1969), 69–139. Also, Carlo M. Cipolla, *Literacy and Development in the West* (Harmondsworth, 1969), pp. 38–61.

47

'oral residue' that he characterises as 'heavy in the extreme'.[1] So it is not surprising to find the notion of speech as man's distinctive and 'civilising' characteristic common amongst those who wrote of language at the time. 'It is', Ben Jonson continues, 'the Instrument of Society. Therefore Mercury, who is the President of Language is called *Deorum hominumque interpres*' (*Timber*). And the characteristically oral sense of identity between culture and language, man and speech, lies behind the commonplace notion that he expounds so memorably; '*Language* most shewes a man; speake that I may see thee' (*ibid.*).

It is difficult for us, who habitually read and write, to share Jonson's sense of speech's revealing inward qualities. And it is no less difficult for us fully to accept the implications of the fact that Shakespeare's plays were written for an audience most of whom would have shared it.

I am not concerned with the plays' own use of language in this context, and the characteristically oral qualities of their style: the rhapsodic, formulaic, incremental and serial structures that occasionally baffled the highly literate Dr Johnson. But I am interested in the ideas *about* language and its social role which they must in consequence implicitly manifest, and which constitute a neglected part of their world view, perhaps because we are anaesthetised to them by our own literacy. And these involve, primarily, a deep and almost certainly defensive commitment to language in its oral dimension: to the ideal as well as the idea of man as the animal that talks.

The history plays for example seem to embody and reinforce a fundamentally oral outlook, which of course differs markedly from our own. Frances Yates has recently brilliantly reminded us that the faculty of memory plays a crucial role in an oral setting, acting as the repository of the cultural tradition, and proving highly developed in response to that important function.[2] But memory's opposite, forgetting, is also important in the same process. Memory, it could be argued, acts as a selective filter, storing experience of continuing relevance to the society. Non-relevant experience is then systematically forgotten, in what has been termed a process of structural amnesia. As a result, the present permanently imposes its own shape on the past, so that in an oral society the world seems always to have been as it is now. Its 'past' looks exactly like its 'present'. Myth takes the place of 'history', and the overwhelming bias towards consistency between past and present makes such societies normally deeply conservative. Such changes as occur tend to be redressive and reconciling, reinforcing rather than innovatory, and at their most extreme take the form of rebellion rather than revolution.[3]

A context such as this seems to have generated the history plays' view of the world. In them, myth and 'history' merge, and the shape of the present determines that of the past. The upheavals chronicled have a redressive, reconciling, re-inforcing mode, and take the form of rebellion rather than revolution. The king is rejected, but not kingship.

In fact, the essence of what has been misleadingly termed the Tudor 'revolution' had been the establishment of the king as the vital and unifying communicative link between man and deity and man and man. Through him, men could symbolically 'speak' to one another, to God, and in English. And just as the Christian God is always characterised as a *communicator*, one who talks directly and personally

[1] W. J. Ong, 'Oral Residue in Tudor Prose Style', *PMLA*, LXXX (1965), 144–55.
[2] Frances A. Yates, *The Art of Memory* (London, 1966).
[3] I am here drawing heavily on the essay by Jack Goody and Ian Watt, 'The Consequences of Literacy', in *Literacy in Traditional Societies*, ed. Jack Goody (Cambridge, 1968), pp. 27–68.

to man,[1] so as God's vicegerent, the Christian king ought ideally to manifest the same 'civilising' quality.

Richard II, of course, notably does not, and his shortcomings in this connection seem to supply Shakespeare in the second tetralogy with a crucial purchase on the past. Under Richard's rule, civilised talking between people deteriorates beyond repair, bringing about its opposite, civil war.[2]

Nor does his successor fare any better in this respect. It is Bolingbroke's son Hal who, as Prince and 'the mirror of all Christian Kings', demonstrates a saving capacity for simple straightforward unifying oral communication with all speakers of the language from high to low, be they knave or knight, English, Welsh, Irish or Scot. His breezy inabilities outside his native tongue (exhibited in the courting of the French princess) serve to emphasise his capabilities within it.

In the course of their exhaustive probing after the nature of human reality, Shakespeare's tragic plays seem to take as their starting point the notion that man is fundamentally a communicator; that talking (and listening) make man human. In them, the tragedy seems to involve a denial, by villainy or circumstance, of man's communicative functions; a prohibition of the essential 'talking and listening' aspects of his nature. Only when these are restored is society able to function again in harmony with, and as a collective expression of, that nature.

To take the single example of *Hamlet*, it's clear that the attitudes towards language of the 'mighty opposites', Hamlet on the one hand and Claudius on the other, constitute a major dimension of the conflict that sparks the play. Under Claudius, talking at Elsinore deteriorates progressively, bringing with it a breakdown in exactly those personal relationships which underpin human society. From the early blandishments of Claudius, their polish concealing the truth of murder, usurpation and incest, through the 'indirections' of Polonius, Ophelia's ravings, the obstructive technicalities of the Gravediggers, and the gibberings of Osric, the process is an accelerating one of descent to a level of uncommunicative brutishness, where spying replaces talking and listening, and men become hunting and hunted animals. As Laertes discovers on his return to Elsinore, linguistic chaos is come again. It is as if

> the world were now but to begin,
> Antiquity forgot, custom not known,
> The ratifiers and props of every word...
>
> (IV, v, 103–5)

The way of life Hamlet opposes to Elsinore is one in which talking and listening, voice and ear, hold their rightful cherished place as civilising instruments. There, the Prince finds solace in Horatio as

> e'en as just a man
> As e'er my conversation coped withal.
>
> (III, ii, 55–6)

There, Claudius's poisoning of the King's ear is seen, in symbolic proportion, to violate 'the whole ear of Denmark' (I, v, 36).

There, too, the play's great metaphor of the theatre lays a good deal of emphasis on the oral faculties; on the notion that a professional actor's speech makes serious demands on his audience's ears. Hamlet's rueful acknowledgement of the Player's ability to communicate immediately and powerfully by means of his art, to 'cleave the general ear with horrid speech' (II, ii, 573), to 'speak out', to

> amaze indeed
> The very faculties of eyes and ears
>
> (II, ii, 575–6)

[1] See W. J. Ong, *The Presence of the Word* (New Haven and London, 1967), pp. 12 ff. and 73.

[2] See my article 'The Word Against the Word: the Role of Language in *Richard II*', *Language and Style*, II (1969), 296–322.

is as striking as the claims made for the play's own capabilities in forcing oral communication on the guilty, making them 'proclaim' their malefactions so that 'murder, though it have no tongue, will speak/With most miraculous organ' (II, ii, 605–6). Not surprisingly, the sum of Hamlet's advice to the Players is that they speak distinctly, paying due respect to man's talking–listening nature, so that they do not 'split the ears of the groundlings' (III, ii, 10).

For Hamlet, the essence of genuine humanity ultimately lies in the basic 'playing' situation itself, in the 'talking–listening' interaction of actors and audience across a stage: a process that, to an oral community, might not inappropriately seem the ultimate symbolic representation of itself. In the theatre, as outside it, people talk, others listen, as evidence of their humanity, and the player's oral art does indeed show 'the very age and body of the time his form and pressure'. Moreover, in a society whose investment in memory must, as has been said, be very great, the theatre will have the added function almost of a 'memory-bank'; a place where memory literally resides, is stored, and in performance is brilliantly displayed by the actors. Hamlet's promise to the Ghost to

> remember thee!
> Aye, thou poor Ghost, whiles memory holds a seat
> In this distracted Globe   (I, v, 95–7)

has, not merely by means of the oral device of the pun, this enlarging aspect. And it hints at such a theatre's immense but informal educative function in an oral culture as an institution serving to *remind* its members of accepted common values, and to confront them with a dramatic affirmation and confirmation of these, almost as a unifying and preservative act of *anamnesis*, of 'bringing to mind'.[1]

Given this, it is an odd delusion of the literate that the non-literate are dispossessed. The reverse might even be the case. William the Conqueror was illiterate. Moreover, it takes a considerable effort of detachment for us to realise that the prospect of literacy can appear somewhat alarming to an oral culture. On the positive side, it offers the possibility of a new and effective medium of communication which, by providing a visible and lasting counterpart of speech, enables it, apparently, to transcend ephemerality and to conquer space and time. Writing seems to make speech permanent and portable.

But a basically non-literate community might well take a more negative view, seeing in writing a potential subversion of its way of life. Far from reproducing speech, writing could be said to 'reduce' it. The full resonance of oral utterance, imbued with the personality, gestures, tone of voice and physical presence of its speaker, from whom it is never separated, vanishes in the abstracted impersonality and sheer silence of marks on paper. The solvent of written 'clarity' disperses the richness of oral 'ambiguity'.

When we turn to Shakespeare's earliest comedies, exactly these tensions confront us, and *Love's Labour's Lost* in particular seems largely to re-state a much older case in this connection.

In the *Phaedrus*, Plato presents a famous argument against writing. Re-telling the myth of its invention, he recounts the words of the Egyptian King to Theuth, who has invented letters:

If men learn this, it will implant forgetfulness in their souls: they will cease to exercise memory because they rely on that which is written, calling things to remembrance no longer from within themselves, but by means of external marks. What you have discovered is a recipe not for memory, but for reminder. And it is no true wisdom that you offer your disciples but only its semblance; for by telling them of many things without teaching them, you will make them seem to know much, while for the most part they

[1] For an account of a similar process in respect of poetry and drama in Hellenic culture, see E. A. Havelock, *Preface to Plato* (Oxford, 1963), pp. 41–3 and 48.

know nothing; and as men filled, not with wisdom but with the conceit of wisdom, they will be a burden to their fellows.[1]

In essence, that seems to be a reasonable account of what happens in *Love's Labour's Lost*, for in this 'the most linguistically oriented of all Shakespeare's plays'[2] the oral world of speech is comically opposed to the silent world of books. At its simplest, the action concerns a group of men who opt out of active oral society in pursuit of immortality, and in the name of what turns out to be the 'conceit of wisdom'. It tells the story of their realisation that true wisdom, true 'civilisation', true immortality, reside precisely in the oral community and its social and sexual processes which they have rejected. As 'bookmen' (as the play calls them) the members of Navarre's 'silent court' realise they have betrayed their true nature of 'talking animals'.

It is a commonplace that the main comic characters parody Navarre's courtiers in their various attitudes to language. The characteristically oral sense that speech is the man prevails. Armado and Holofernes have 'been at a great feast of languages and stolen the scraps', and if to speak is to be human, Armado hardly achieves that status. He does not speak, so much as utter writing, expending most of his interest literally on the 'external marks' of letters. His response to the inward animal disturbances of love is appropriately reductive:

I am sure I shall turn sonnet. Devise wit; write pen; for I am for whole volumes in folio.

(I, ii, 173 ff.)

For Holofernes, as for Nathaniel, it is *writing* not speech which distinguishes man from the animals, and both concur in dismissing the wretched Dull as one unredeemed by literacy's Eucharist;

he hath never fed of the dainties that are bred in a book. He hath not eat paper, as it were; he hath not drunk ink. His intellect is not replenished, he is only an animal.

(IV, ii, 23–5)

Holofernes's contribution to the debate about orthography consists, predictably, of the assertion that the rules of writing ought to dominate speech. He 'abhors' he tells us

such rackers of orthography, as to speak dout, fine, when he should say doubt; det, when he should pronounce debt, d,e,b,t, not d,e,t

(V, i, 18 ff.)

Berowne's rejection of 'speeches penned', the 'taffeta phrases, silken terms precise' of 'orthography', and his resolve to embrace their oral opposite, 'russet yeas and honest kersey noes' constitutes an important statement of the play's main theme. Access to reality, he discovers, lies not in books, but in involvement with other people: not in the domain of the eye, reading and writing, but in that of the voice and the ear, talking and listening. His sonnet to Rosaline is thus a reprise of his earlier 'reasons against reading':

If knowledge be the mark, to know thee shall suffice;
Well learned is that tongue that well can thee
                    commend...
                 (IV, ii, 109–10)

Women, in short, are the curriculum of *life's* academy. In Berowne's metaphor,

They are the ground, the books, the academes,
From whence doth spring the true Promethean fire.
                 (IV, iii, 299–301)

Knowledge, this seems to say, lies in life itself, in our interaction with others in the community, that talking–listening involvement which, the play makes clear, precedes and prefigures its necessary sexual counterpart. And like love, knowledge is no abstract entity that books can 'contain', or reading give access to. In Berowne's words

[1] Plato, *Phaedrus*, 275 a 2-b 2, trans. R. Hackforth (Cambridge, 1952), p. 157.
[2] Bradbrook, 'St. George for Spelling Reform!'

Learning is but an adjunct to ourself
And where we are our learning likewise is.

(IV, iii, 309–12)

Our way of life, that is to say, constitutes our knowledge. And in an oral society, as way of life and language are intimately related, so the language embodies, and indeed *is* knowledge for the community. There is no other source.

Berowne's punishment confirms this, for the burden placed on him is emphatically a linguistic one. His early love, on his own admission 'Formed by the eye, and therefore like the eye' (v, ii, 752) has proved shallow and vain. Now he must engage with the speech community, not deny it; recognise its 'theatrical' dimension, become a 'player' or an 'entertainer'. He must

this twelve month term from day to day
Visit the speechless sick, and still converse
With groaning wretches... (v, ii, 840–2)

The former '...merry madcap lord/Not a word with him but a jest' (II, i, 216–17) must become aware of the *reciprocal* 'dramatic' nature of speech. He must learn, as Rosaline rebukes him, that an audience's listening necessarily complements the actor's oral art, that

A jest's prosperity lies in the ear
Of him that hears it, never in the tongue
Of him that makes it...

(v, ii, 851–3)

In the *Phaedrus*, Plato also makes Socrates say 'anyone who leaves behind him a written manual, and likewise anyone who takes it over from him, on the supposition that such writing will provide something reliable and permanent, must be exceedingly simple-minded...'[1] At the end of the 1598 Quarto, the earliest surviving 'written manual' of *Love's Labour's Lost*, this phrase occurs: 'The words of Mercury are harsh after the songs of Apollo.' It is attributed to no particular character, and is set in a type larger than that used for the printing of the main body of the play. In the

Folio text the line remains, but is assigned to the 'Braggart' (i.e. Armado) who adds 'You that way: we this way' as an exit line for the characters assembled on the stage. The various editors of *Love's Labour's Lost* have responded in different ways to this choice of endings. Dover Wilson and Quiller-Couch in the New Cambridge edition, and Richard David in the New Arden edition are the exception amongst recent editors in preferring that of the First Quarto. Most others tend to assign the line to Armado, thus reducing its prominence, and the peculiar quality given it by the larger type. Possibly they share with E. K. Chambers the feeling that 'Mercury has nothing to do with what precedes'.[2]

Yet Mercury, it will be remembered, was associated by Ben Jonson with language, being styled its president. In his role as messenger of the Gods, Mercury (or Hermes) was also firmly associated with writing, often as its inventor, a connection he shared with his Egyptian and Scandinavian counterparts. As the various avatars of Mercury merge into a single figure in the Renaissance, this association becomes more and more established so that, for example, Nashe's *Summer's Last Will and Testament* (1592–3), in the process of a satirical account of the history of writing, can tell how Hermes/Mercury

Weary with graving in blind characters,
And figures of familiar beasts and plants,
Invented letters to write lies withall...

(1262 ff.)

Apollo, of course, symbolised no less a number of disparate ideas during the same period, but in respect of the contrast with Mercury here postulated will obviously be primarily con-

---

[1] *Phaedrus*, 275 c 5-d 2, p. 158.
[2] E. K. Chambers, *William Shakespeare, a study of Facts and Problems* (Oxford, 1930), I, 338. I am greatly indebted in connection with the point that follows to the hitherto unpublished work of my research student, Malcolm Evans.

nected with language in its oral form and its tonal aspects; a relationship appropriate to his role as god of music and harmony. Robert Stephanus's *Thesaurus Linguae Latinae* (1573) assigns to Apollo the specific role, amongst others, of protector of the vocal chords. In short, both Mercury and Apollo could be said to have a good deal to do with 'what precedes'.

The line 'The words of Mercury are harsh after the songs of Apollo' perhaps constitutes not so much a comment on the *subject* of *Love's Labour's Lost*, in which Mercury as Mercade the messenger brings his harsh words into the Apollonian atmosphere of the play, as a comment on the *form* of this play, on the nature of drama which it embodies and, hopefully, on the subject of the present paper. The 'words of Mercury' are surely *Love's Labour's Lost* seen in written form; in its printed Quarto version. It is itself part of the world of books which the play has urged us to reject. The 'songs of Apollo' are those oral words heard in the actual performance of the play, of which the book is a 'harsh' shadow. The book cannot 'contain' the play, as Dover Wilson discovered for himself when he was 'converted' by Tyrone Guthrie's production in 1936,[1] and the words are printed in a larger type, separate from the words of the play, for this reason. They constitute a comment on the *book* the reader of *Love's Labour's Lost* holds in his hand. Momentarily he is like the 'bookmen' of the play, engrossed in a 'reduced' world of writing, not in the 'real' world of oral interchange, of which the play in performance is a compelling version. The play's epigraph, which these words are, is perhaps intended to jolt him out of that state; to force him to raise his eyes from the 'speeches penned' and to encounter the world with voice and ear, in the oral spirit intended by Berowne. The words thus use the functions of Mercury to achieve the purpose of Apollo, uniting these opposites in characteristically Shakespearian

fashion. It is perhaps this aspect of his work that Ben Jonson celebrates in the lines he wrote for the great 'book of the plays' the First Folio, which refer explicitly to 'What He Hath Left Us';

> He was not of an age, but for all time!
> And all the muses still were in their prime,
> When like Apollo he came forth to warm
> Our ears, or like a Mercury to charm!

Nor is *Love's Labour's Lost* the only item of evidence he hath left us: there are the plays at large, the condition in which they have come down to us, and the point of view this condition perhaps embodies. G. E. Bentley has pointed out in some detail that Shakespeare manifests very little interest in his plays as works to be themselves read.[2] We may, as T. J. B. Spencer puts it, 'consider it incredible that he should not have expected his plays to be read as well as performed'.[3] I agree that it is incredible. Yet the very degree of our incredulity testifies perhaps to the effectiveness of the anaesthetic of literacy that has us 'bookmen' in its grip.

For to suggest an opposite view is to do nothing more startling than affirm the theme of this Conference, and to characterise Shakespeare as an artist supremely committed to the oral art of drama. 'He was naturally learned', Dryden said of him in his *Essay of Dramatick Poesie* (1668), 'he needed not the spectacles of books to read nature'. He is the Theatre Poet, that is to say, not the Book Poet, and the sense of that distinction and its related commitment in these plays is perhaps one of their most underestimated ingredients.

Because to be a Theatre Poet is, after all,

[1] J. Dover Wilson, *Shakespeare's Happy Comedies* (London, 1962), pp. 64 ff.

[2] G. E. Bentley, *Shakespeare and his Theatre* (Lincoln, Nebraska, 1964), pp. 1–26.

[3] T. J. B. Spencer, 'The Elizabethan Theatre-Poet', in *The Elizabethan Theatre*, ed. David Galloway (Toronto and London, 1969), p. 6.

and despite Anne Barton's eloquent and persuasive arguments to the contrary, to manifest a personal faith in language's oral dimension. It is to believe, perhaps, that true immortality ultimately resides more in the apparent ephemerality of speech, less in the apparent permanence of writing. As Heywood, Shakespeare's contemporary, put it in his *Apology for Actors* (1612), the drama's vested interest in speech as its raw material actually expands and improves the language:

Our English tongue, which hath been the most harsh and broken language in the world...is now, by this secondary means of playing, continually refined... so that in process from the most rude and unpolisht tongue it has grown to a most perfect and composed language.

In a sense, it is *that* truth which we manifest at this moment: you by your tolerant listening presence, I by my intolerable talking one. What links us with Shakespeare is exactly this reciprocal process, the oral process of the language that, 400 years since he used it, is still second – even first – nature to most of us.

I conclude with what must appear blatant special pleading, for my vowels have by now betrayed me. I was born and grew up in Shakespeare's county, just twenty-one miles from where we now find ourselves. Although this makes me what the New Cambridge editors call a mere 'pavement critic' it also makes it appropriate that it is I who voice a redressive doubt, however small, concerning the advice given in the First Folio to 'the Great Variety of Readers'. In the matter of Shakespeare's aptest memorial we risk an over-emphasis on the need to 'reade him, therefore; and againe, and againe'. On the contrary, I propose, as one Talking Animal to others; *si monumentum requiris, audi.*

© TERENCE HAWKES 1971

THE MORALITY OF
'LOVE'S LABOUR'S LOST'

J. J. ANDERSON

Edward Dowden noted that the death of the Princess's father at the end of *Love's Labour's Lost* gives the comedy a sour twist:

It is a strange end for a comedy, and we can hardly doubt that Shakespeare's meaning is this – a true education is not to be attained by removing from the world into a region of fantastical culture, but by submitting to the complete discipline of both joy and sorrow. He does not preach a doctrine; but his view of life is embodied in his art.[1]

In this connection the ending of the play is indeed significant. As Berowne complains:

> Our wooing doth not end like an old play;
> Jack hath not Jill: these ladies' courtesy
> Might well have made our sport a comedy.
>
> (v, ii, 864–6)[2]

The ending is not truly comic, with difficulties resolved and sins forgiven, but moralistic – punishments are meted out, nor is it clear that the eventual outcome will be a happy one.[3] Shakespeare may not have the dramatic morality tradition of the Middle Ages directly in mind, but there is much in *Love's Labour's Lost* which is reminiscent of the morality plays. Thus the subject matter is shaped, often to the point of stylisation, round the development of a moral theme. The set scenes which make up much of the play are related to each other more by the theme than by the extremely tenuous plot. The characters may not be personified abstractions, but Shakespeare does give thematic considerations a large say in their creation. The King, Berowne, Longaville, and Dumain

have similar characteristics and they are defined as a group with a particular function in the development of the morality; the same may be said for the four ladies, and for the 'common' characters.[4] The whole play depends on the moral theme for its coherence.

The morality is a very Shakespearian one, suggesting not that men should aim for spiritual perfection, but merely that they should be responsibly human. At the beginning of the play, the four noblemen are planning to do without women and the world for three years so that they can form a 'little academe' devoted to study. The bombastic rhetoric of the King's opening speech, fine as it is, raises doubts at once:

> Let fame, that all hunt after in their lives,
> Live register'd upon our brazen tombs,
> And then grace us in the disgrace of death.
>
> (i, i, 1–3)

[1] *The Comedies of Shakespeare*, ed. W. J. Craig, with introductory studies of the several plays by Edward Dowden (Oxford, 1911), p. 439.

[2] References are to the Arden edition, ed. Richard David (London, 1951).

[3] See E. M. W. Tillyard, *Shakespeare's Early Comedies* (London, 1965), pp. 176–8.

[4] Cf. Ralph Berry, 'The Words of Mercury', *Shakespeare Survey 22* (Cambridge, 1969), p. 69, who sees four main groups (Navarre and his followers, the Princess and her retinue, the clowns, and Armado, Holofernes, and Sir Nathaniel), characterised by their attitudes towards words. I am generally indebted to Berry's essay, although his focus differs from mine, and his conclusion, that '*Love's Labour's Lost* is a sustained inquiry into the nature and status of words' (p. 75), seems to me too limited.

It is too glib, too much of a cliché, a set piece on the old idea of the triumph of learning over death. There is no sign that the King has thought out his proposal, and it soon emerges that his friends are as drunk with words and ideas as he is. Longaville and Dumain reply in equally flamboyant language, and although Longaville shows that he does not take the King's scheme very seriously when he admits to the idea of keeping women away from the court by threatening them with loss of their tongues (I, i, 119–26), he clearly enjoys the game. Berowne goes further, pointing out that it is unreasonable 'Not to see ladies, study, fast, not sleep' (I, i, 48), threatening to set himself to study how to evade the King's conditions, noting that study can be profitless, that study for them is out of season, and so on. Berowne it is who points out that the embassy of the Princess of France is going to make the men break their oaths straightaway (I, i, 132–9). And yet, having listed so many weaknesses in the King's scheme, Berowne cheerfully subscribes his own name to it:

> But I believe, although I seem so loath,
> I am the last that last will keep his oath.
>
> (I, i, 158–9)

There is no question of a change of heart, as Berowne makes clear later in the scene:

> I'll lay my head to any good man's hat,
> These oaths and laws will prove an idle scorn.
>
> (I, i, 291–2)

Berowne's criticisms are soon shown to be justified. First Costard has to be solemnly sentenced to a week's fasting with bran and water for being with a woman (I, i, 284–5), and next the King has to meet the Princess of France out in the fields, calling down a lecture upon his head in so doing:

> I hear your grace hath sworn out house-keeping:
> 'Tis deadly sin to keep that oath, my lord,
> And sin to break it.   (II, i, 104–6)

Finally, the men all fall in love. But for all his awareness Berowne evidently takes his criticisms no more seriously than he does the scheme he is criticising. His language provides the clue, for if the others talk flamboyantly, Berowne is brilliant to the point where he can be completely carried away by his own ingenuity:

> Light seeking light doth light of light beguile:
> So, ere you find where light in darkness lies,
> Your light grows dark by losing of your eyes.
>
> (I, i, 77–9)

Berowne is more concerned to make rhetorical capital out of his perceptions than to persuade others to abide by them, or to abide by them himself. Perceptive as he is, he cannot resist the lure of the intellect. Fine words are the men's delight and downfall, Berowne's most of all.

The irresponsibility which goes with the wit is fully revealed when the men fall in love. The King's edict will do for such as Costard, but it does not take the men long to abandon it when they find it standing in the way of their own desires. The eavesdropping scene (IV, iii) shows them at their gayest and most irresponsible. The King, unaware of Berowne hiding in a tree and thinking he is quite alone, confesses his love for the Princess in a poem which he reads out. He then hides when Longaville appears to read another love poem, and Longaville in his turn hides from Dumain. The men then emerge from hiding in reverse order, each making accusations of perjury and hypocrisy, only to be exposed by the next to emerge. When it is obvious that they are all equally guilty they indulge in some childishly competitive denigration of each other's mistresses, and then call on Berowne to provide a justification for the perjury they have committed in breaking their oaths. They are 'plunging from one crude male immaturity to another',[1] and

[1] Tillyard, *Shakespeare's Early Comedies*, p. 145.

once more Berowne is the extreme case. After his boast that he would be 'the last that last would keep his oath', he appears to be first to fall in love. He is more self-righteous than any of the others, more tellingly exposed, and then after his exposure he is least concerned: 'we deserve to die', he says (IV, iii, 206), with blatant insincerity, before quickly going on to 'Young blood doth not obey an old decree' (IV, iii, 214). He now obliges his friends with a long peroration on the power of love, the most famous speech in the play, with splendid ringing verses which generate a sense of high excitement. But it is not difficult to see that the excitement comes not from conviction but from overblown rhetoric and an argument which becomes progressively more specious until it culminates in an outrageous sophistry:

> It is religion to be thus forsworn;
> For charity itself fulfils the law;
> And who can sever love from charity?
>
> (IV, iii, 360–2)

'It is all lovely and vigorous and persuasive and overdone.'[1] And of course Berowne's own experience of love has been not sublime but comic. The girl he falls for is not at all romantic towards him, preferring to cap his witticisms rather than be impressed by them. Shakespeare puts Berowne's love on a par with Armado's love for Jaquenetta – the lovers' conversations are similar (Jaquenetta turns every one of Armado's remarks against him in I, ii, 124–35), Berowne's soliloquy at the end of act III (on being conquered by love) has its counterpart in Armado's at the end of act I, and the two wooings come together in Costard when both lovers entrust their love letters to him. When Costard gets the letters mixed up, they suffer similar fates – Armado's has to submit to the Princess's scorn ('What plume of feathers is he that indited this letter?', IV, i, 93), and Berowne's has to suffer the indignity of Holofernes's criticism:

> Here are only numbers ratified; but, for the elegancy, facility, and golden cadence of poesy, caret.
>
> (IV, ii, 119–21)

No one would wish to dispute Holofernes's judgement, and there is little else in Berowne's behaviour to allow one to take him seriously as a lover. His soliloquy at the end of act III expresses not feeling for his mistress but amazement at himself and amused resignation:

> Well, I will love, write, sigh, pray, sue, and groan:
> Some men must love my lady, and some Joan.
>
> (III, i, 201–2)

Berowne is too detached, too much the connoisseur of experience. In a soliloquy at the beginning of the eavesdropping scene Berowne says that love has taught him to be melancholy, and the soliloquy is indeed anguished in movement:

> By the Lord, this love is as mad as Ajax: it kills sheep, it kills me, I a sheep: well proved again o' my side! I will not love; if I do, hang me; i' faith, I will not.
>
> (IV, iii, 6–9)

But the Berownian brilliancies are undiminished, and as in the first scene of the play they cast doubt on his *bona fides*, a doubt confirmed when the anguish vanishes once the eavesdropping game gets under way. Berowne is anguished only so long as he finds it interesting. Thus to take the 'affection's men-at-arms' speech as in any way sincere, as it is often taken,[2] is to ignore not only the nature of the rhetoric and argument, but also the character of Berowne as it has been developed up to this point. From beginning to end the speech is another performance, a 'salve for perjury' and an encouragement suited to the needs of the moment, and as such it is received:

> *King.* Saint Cupid, then! and, soldiers, to the field!
>
> (IV, iii, 363)

[1] Peter G. Phialas, *Shakespeare's Romantic Comedies* (Chapel Hill, 1966), p. 93.
[2] E.g. by Bobbyann Roesen, '*Love's Labour's Lost*', *Shakespeare Quarterly*, IV (1953), 419.

Longaville. Now to plain-dealing; lay these glozes by:
Shall we resolve to woo these girls of France?

(IV, iii, 367–8)

Berowne himself gives the game away at the very end of the scene. In a short speech reminiscent of his comment after he had subscribed his name to the original scheme ('These oaths and laws will prove an idle scorn'), Berowne shows that he doubts the course of action he has done so much to encourage and to which the men are now committed:

Allons! allons! Sow'd cockle reap'd no corn;
And justice always whirls in equal measure:
Light wenches may prove plagues to men forsworn;
If so, our copper buys no better treasure.

(IV, iii, 380–3)

The Arden editor's comment, that 'Berowne's note of warning here comes in rather inharmoniously after his magnificent address of loyalty to Love',[1] misses the point. We have seen before that Berowne's behaviour can be at odds with his perceptions, and his long speech is another instance of his inability to resist an opportunity to be brilliant, even when he knows better. All of the men are irresponsible in that they sacrifice rationality, conscience, and feeling to wit, but Berowne's irresponsibility is the most spectacular precisely because he is the most aware of what he is doing. Far from being 'a Chorus character throughout',[2] Berowne is the prime object lesson. He more than any of the others deserves Maria's censure:

Folly in fools bears not so strong a note
As foolery in the wise, when wit doth dote;
Since all the power thereof it doth apply
To prove, by wit, worth in simplicity.

(V, ii, 75–8)

Now the consequences of the men's attitudes begin to catch up with them. The show of the Muscovites, including the horseplay of the preparations, is a logical expression of their attitudes to love – it is a jolly good lark, and they hope to rush the ladies off their feet with it. But they fail, for the ladies, forewarned, play them at their own game, throwing their clevernesses back in their faces, as indeed they have always done. With characteristic perception, Berowne sees what is wrong – that their games lead only to counter-games because they are taken to be incompatible with serious feeling. But, equally characteristically, Berowne is unable to carry out his resolve to abandon affectation and to woo only with 'russet yeas and honest kersey noes' (V, ii, 413), for affectation has become so much a part of him; the very speech in which he confesses he is sick (V, ii, 417–23) exemplifies his sickness. The men may have failed, and they may know why, but they do not mend their ways. Instead they make another effort to impress by their wit, seizing the opportunity offered by the commoners' show of the Nine Worthies. There is an air almost of desperation about them now:

Dumain. Though my mocks come home by me, I will now be merry.
(V, ii, 625–6)

The commoners have always been easy game for the noblemen, for their failings are so obvious. Armado's language is ludicrously conceited, Nathaniel and Holofernes converse in an extraordinary mixture of Latin and English, and Costard's witty sallies are too often spoilt by his lack of command of the language:

I suffer for the truth, sir: for true it is I was taken with Jaquenetta, and Jaquenetta is a true girl; and therefore welcome the sour cup of prosperity!   (I, i, 294–6)

Their affectations blind them more obviously than do those of the noblemen. They are quite uncritical of themselves, Armado seeing himself as a fine gentleman, Costard gloating over the success of his sallies, and Holofernes unable to hide his pride in his 'foolish extravagant spirit':

[1] P. 116.
[2] Roesen, '*Love's Labour's Lost*', p. 412.

But the gift is good in those in whom it is acute, and I am thankful for it. (IV, ii, 71–2)

Even Dull's dullness has an air of smugness about it. But what they ignore in themselves they are all too ready to criticise in their fellows. Costard chooses to denigrate the intellectual capacities of Boyet, Armado, and Moth (IV, i, 138–47), Holofernes, the pedant, attacks Armado for being 'too picked, too spruce, too affected, too odd, as it were, too peregrinate, as I may call it' (V, i, 13–15), and Armado in his turn protests to the King that Holofernes is 'exceeding fantastical; too, too vain' (V, ii, 524–5). The commoners are always turning on each other; in particular, Costard and Armado are in conflict throughout the play, and Moth is critical of almost everybody, including his master Armado. The noblemen treat them as a joke, but there is irony in this, for the commoners' imperfections are, in essence, cruder versions of their own characteristics. The noblemen's wit is the commoners' misuse of language, the noblemen's competitiveness is the commoners' constant criticism of each other, the noblemen's pretension is the commoners' gross overreaching, and so on. The world of the commoners shows us that of the noblemen stripped of its veneer of sophistication. Moreover, this very lack of sophistication gives the commoners a moral strength which the noblemen do not have – they are simpler, more direct, more human, whatever their faults. When Berowne, after his love for Rosaline has been exposed, dismisses Costard and Jaquenetta with a sarcastic 'Will these turtles be gone?' (IV, iii, 208), Costard counters with:

Walk aside the true folk, and let the traitors stay.
(IV, iii, 210)

The justice of this is manifest, for Costard has at least always been true to himself, while the noblemen with their elaborate intellectualisations are traitors not only to their oaths but to any reasonable view of love or of human behaviour generally.

Matters come to a head in the Nine Worthies scene. The commoners have shown more than their usual self-conceit in tackling a subject far beyond their capabilities (at the suggestion of Holofernes: 'I say, none so fit as to present the Nine Worthies', V, i, 118–19). In the event they are more than usually ridiculous, and the noblemen respond with a torrent of cruel, if witty, abuse. Armado in particular is stripped of all his outward show and is forced to accept humiliating revelations. But the noblemen do themselves more real damage than they do their victims. After all, the commoners are doing their best to please, and however exasperated the noblemen may be with the outcome of their own show, there is no warrant for the ferocity of their attack. They now show that their wit can be not merely irresponsible but positively hurtful, and they reveal more clearly than before the selfishness and arrogance at the centre of their outlook. Holofernes has our entire sympathy with his reproach:

This is not generous, not gentle, not humble.
(V, ii, 621)

And Armado's appeal also wins us:

The sweet war-man is dead and rotten; sweet chucks, beat not the bones of the buried; when he breathed, he was a man. (V, ii, 651–3)

In spite of the idiosyncrasies of expression, such comments reveal more dignity than the noblemen are capable of, and the remark of Armado's points to a traditional symbolic significance of the Nine Worthies which I do not think has been noticed before in connection with *Love's Labour's Lost*, and which gives the performers' dignity a further dimension. It is true that in Elizabethan literature the Nine Worthies are often made into figures of fun, as indeed they are, on one level, in *Love's Labour's Lost*. But the original medieval tradition saw the Worthies as supreme examples of heroic lives, and the branch of this tradition which was dominant in the later Middle Ages linked them with the ancient *ubi sunt* theme as examples of famous men struck down by death, as in the alliterative poems *Morte Arthure* and *The Parlement of the Thre Ages*, in John Gower's *In Praise of Peace*, and in Lydgate's *Assembly of Gods*. In Bishop Barclay's *Ship of Fools* (1570), translated from the German, several of the Worthies are mentioned along with other heroes in the chapter headed 'Of the ende of worldly honour and power'. So the Nine Worthies came to be a *topos* of mortality, an aspect which gives bite to the scene in *Love's Labour's Lost* in that the show of the Worthies becomes more than a mere entertainment, bringing out not only the inhumanity but also the blindness and folly of the noblemen's behaviour. If they could only see it, the very performance they are mocking contains a warning that their arrogance is ultimately futile, that gaiety and wit are not enough, that human needs cannot be overridden for ever. Life is a fundamentally serious matter because all must die; death is one reality that cannot be ignored or disposed of in rhetoric, as the King disposes of it at the beginning of the play.

The climax of the scene, and of the play, comes when Marcade arrives with news of the death of the Princess's father:

Marcade. God save you, madam!
Princess. Welcome, Marcade,
  But that thou interrupt'st our merriment.
Marcade. I am sorry, madam; for the news I bring
  Is heavy in my tongue. The king your father –
Princess. Dead, for my life!
Marcade. Even so: my tale is told.

(v, ii, 705–11)

These few simple words, with their weight of meaning and restrained emotion, cut through the witticisms. Marcade's entrance is a splendid *coup de théâtre*, as has often been noted,[1] but it is also integral to the symbolic meaning; only on the literal level is it a bolt from the blue.

Marcade is the performers' vindication, a messenger of mortality who cannot be laughed at. His sudden arrival, brief announcement, and immediate fading from view again suggest something of the medieval personified Death itself, coming like a thief in the night.[2]

Armado emerges from the catastrophe with conscience intact and ready to profit from the damage he has suffered:

For mine own part, I breathe free breath. I have seen the day of wrong through the little hole of discretion, and I will right myself like a soldier.

(v, ii, 713–15)

His remark perhaps implies that he sees himself as better off than his persecutors, and certainly the noblemen have few resources left. Once more their show of wit, desperate this time, has failed in its object, as Marcade's news now demands all the attention of the ladies. Nor are the noblemen any better able than before to adjust to a new situation. Death and sorrow have finally shattered their world, demonstrating once and for all its moral inadequacy, but all they can do is urge their suits in the same old sophistic way. Their affectation has been discredited, as they recognise, but they still require to be purged, and the ladies take upon themselves the task of dispensing corrective punishments, understandably refusing to accept that the men are capable of genuine love without evidence that there is more to

[1] See e.g. the discussion of Phialas, *Shakespeare's Romantic Comedies*, p. 85, who however criticises the episode as 'sudden, unexpected, external'.

[2] Cf. Philip Edwards, *Shakespeare and the Confines of Art* (London, 1968), pp. 43–4: 'The entry of "Death" was wonderfully staged by Peter Brook in his production at Stratford-upon-Avon in 1947. There *was* no perceptible entry: the lights began to grow dim on the laughter at Armado's discomfiture. And as the light on the general scene went low, it slowly grew stronger on the black figure of Marcade, until he was seen and recognized. The laughter died away, and he spoke: "God save you, madam!" For all the audience could see, he had been standing there for a long time.'

them than wit and high spirits. The King is packed off to a hermitage for a year, and Rosaline requires Berowne to spend a year endeavouring to cheer sick people with his jests. When Berowne objects that 'Mirth cannot move a soul in agony' (v, ii, 847), Rosaline replies 'Why, that's the way to choke a gibing spirit' (v, ii, 848). Rosaline's attitude to Berowne has hardened in the course of the play as she has become more aware of the hurtful potential of his laughter. To begin with she thinks him merry 'Within the limit of becoming mirth' (II, i, 67), but now he is

> a man replete with mocks;
> Full of comparisons and wounding flouts
> (v, ii, 834–5)

The ladies have always stood apart from the men's attitudes, never becoming part of the world of the King's park. They too are devoted to wit – they enjoy their verbal battles with the men and with each other – but they differ from the men in that they make a distinction between what is proper to jest and what is not. They can see that life has its more serious side. They are scornful of the men's academy, and of their wooing games, for they see in these affectation being taken too far. For the men, affectation is a way of life, and they cannot help themselves, but for the ladies, consistently high-spirited as they undoubtedly are, it is more a means of passing the time agreeably, a matter of choice – they talk of *using* their wit (II, i, 226), and of 'a set of wit well play'd' (v, ii, 29). Much of what the ladies say and do is a comment, explicit or implicit, on the men's attitudes; the Princess's criticism of the King's scheme, when he receives her in the fields, has already been noticed, and Maria's censure of clever fools, quoted above, is part of a general condemnation of the noblemen which the ladies indulge in after Katharine has reminded them that love is not to be taken lightly, and that her sister died of love (v, i, 15).

The very first words that the Princess utters (II, i, 13–19) are a solemn rebuke to Boyet for the 'painted flourish' of his fulsome praise of her; honey-tongued Boyet is good for amusement, but the ladies keep him very much in his place throughout the play, and of course Boyet is very like the King and his friends, becoming virtually one of the King's party when he enters wholeheartedly into the jesting against the Worthies. At the beginning of the hunting scene (IV, i), the Princess deliberately misunderstands a remark made by the forester, insisting that he means to say she is not beautiful, and she gives him money 'for telling true' (IV, i, 18). She goes on to see desire for praise as dangerous when it leads to suppression of one's humanity, in words of obvious relevance to the noblemen's way of life:

> Glory grows guilty of detested crimes,
> When, for fame's sake, for praise, an outward part,
> We bend to that the working of the heart
> (IV, i, 31–3)[1]

In the Nine Worthies scene, the men's cruelty is underlined by the humanity of the Princess's occasional remarks:

> *Princess.* Speak, brave Hector; we are much delighted.
> *Armado.* I do adore thy sweet grace's slipper.
> (v, ii, 656–7)

The women expose faults and correct them. They are presented not as perfect, but as embodying norms of human conduct against which the aberrations of the noblemen are to be measured.

Thus love's labour is lost, because the lovers' affectations have made them unfit for love and life, and the play concludes with an oblique recapitulation of the morality in the

[1] Cf. the discussion of this episode in Berry, 'The Words of Mercury', p. 72. Berry notes that the Princess's speech on the deer (IV, i, 21–35) is 'the thematic counter to the King's opening speech in praise of "fame"', and that the Princess is 'beyond question the internal arbiter of the values of *Love's Labour's Lost*.'

two songs. Spring is a gay season, appropriate to the mocking voice of the cuckoo, but spring is inevitably followed by winter, a hard season, although it has its own soberer pleasures. The noblemen have behaved as though spring is the only season: all of them, like Berowne in his hospital, have to come to terms with the darker side of experience. 'The words of Mercury are harsh after the songs of Apollo.'

But, important as the morality theme is, it is wrong to take Shakespeare too seriously as a moralist. Richard Cody writes: 'The playwright who expected his audience to take much ethical satisfaction in such a play would be a simpler-minded stick than Shakespeare anywhere shows himself to be.'[1] The morality is lightweight – neither the sins nor the punishments do much hurt – and it is enveloped in fantasy. One must agree with Dowden that there is no preaching; there is no need to doubt that Shakespeare is concerned to make his point, but only so far as is consistent with artistic grace and neatness, as the two concluding songs well show. If, as is very likely, the exchange between Berowne and Rosaline in v, ii, 827–62 is a later version of v, ii, 807–12 (the unrevised version being inadvertently retained in the copy), then the revision, which directs the terms of Berowne's punishment more exactly to his fault, perhaps shows more concern for thematic appropriateness than for didactic effectiveness, fantastic as the penalty now becomes. At any rate there is no urgency about the play, nothing of the earnestness of the medieval playwrights, nor of the mordancy of a Ben Jonson. The dramatist's attitude is urbane throughout. Moreover, the morality, although it is central, is far from being the whole play. The characters and what they do, the jokes, songs, and shows have for the most part a simple entertainment value quite apart from their function in the scheme of the morality, and there is also the topical aspect, which has absorbed the attention of so many critics. *Love's Labour's Lost* is a many-sided play, and the morality does not swallow up the comedy.

[1] *The Landscape of the Mind* (Oxford, 1969), p. 118.

© J. J. ANDERSON 1971

SHAKESPEARE'S 'EARTH-TREADING STARS': THE IMAGE OF THE MASQUE IN 'ROMEO AND JULIET'

KATHLEEN E. McLUSKIE

Many of the commentators on *Romeo and Juliet* have suggested that the tragic outcome of the plot hinges merely on a series of coincidences in the time structure of the plot. Capulet hastens Juliet's marriage to Paris, Friar John arrives too late in Mantua and Juliet awakens just too late to prevent Romeo from suicide. Yet the play has far more force than simply a sad story of young lovers. The play is about 'the fearful passage of their death-marked love' and it arouses a feeling of tragic inevitability which runs throughout the plot and creates a suspense for which the tragic outcome is the only possible resolution. This feeling has to be aroused from the very beginning of the action and Shakespeare succeeds in this by presenting the meeting of the lovers in a masque. The masque solves perfectly the plot problem of how to get Romeo into the Capulet household but it also makes it into a theatrically significant event by the spectacular nature of the scene and the atmosphere which it creates. Romeo must enter the Capulet banquet as the herald of love and the masque evokes this atmosphere of youth and revelling. We see the associations of the masque for the characters involved when Capulet remembers

> the day
> That I have worn a visor and could tell
> A whispering tale in a fair lady's ear,
> Such as would please   (I, v, 23–6)

He regards it as a game of love for youth and we remember that the great novelty and attraction of the masque was that it allowed masqued strangers to mingle with the guests. We find in Hall an account of how Henry VIII met Anne Boleyn at a banquet given by Cardinal Wolsey where the king came masqued as a shepherd[1] and in all such accounts the masque is seen as high-spirited entertainment.

Romeo and Juliet are both going to the masque as lovers even before they have met. In the scene where the masque is first mentioned Benvolio persuades Romeo to go to the feast so that he may compare Rosaline with 'all the admired beauties of Verona'. He agrees to go 'to rejoice in splendour of mine own' and the magic of the masque enables him to find one even more splendid who will become his own in a way that Rosaline could never have been. In the following scene there is another reminder that the masque is a celebration of love for when Lady Capulet is talking to Juliet of her proposed marriage to Paris she says

> Can you love the gentleman?
> This night you shall behold him at our feast...
>   (I, iii, 80–1)

The masque, however, has other more sinister connotations since it allows hostile strangers entrance to another house with possibly dangerous consequences. In Holinshed we find how 'Thomas Walsingham and divers others...write that conspirators meant upon the sudden to have set upon the king in the

---

[1] Hall, *Chronicle* (London, 1809), pp. 239–40.

castle of Windsor under colour of a masque or mummery and so to have dispatched him.'[1] It is important that in the context of the Montague and Capulet feud Romeo is a potentially hostile stranger and in the midst of the revelling the reminder of the feud comes home to the audience in Tybalt's furious

> What, dares the slave
> Come hither, covered with an antic face,
> To fleer and scorn at our solemnity.
>
> (I, v, 53–5)

To Tybalt a masque can only be a temporary cover for the activities of the real world where names and families, the outward aspects of a man, are the reality for which he is prepared to violate all ceremony, and the ceremony of the masque insisted on by Capulet when he refuses to allow Tybalt to challenge Romeo is meaningless. To offset Tybalt's attitude we have the other various statements made about masking in the play. Romeo's first reference to masks talks of

> These happy masks that kiss fair ladies' brows,
> Being black, puts us in mind they hide the fair.
>
> (I, i, 228–9)

The mask is hiding something more beautiful than itself.

For Mercutio the mask is permanent and the visor which he puts on before the Capulet ball is simply an alternative to the mask of every day. He says

> Give me a case to put my visage in.
> A visor for a visor! What care I
> What curious eye doth quote deformities?
> Here are the beetle brows shall blush for me.
>
> (I, iv, 29–32)

In the context of the play a masque provides a suitable protective anonymity and creates a world where Romeo and Juliet can meet simply as a young man and a girl. This is made explicit in the scene after the banquet when Juliet, realising that Romeo has overheard her expression of love, says

> Thou knowest the mask of night is on my face,
> Else would a maiden blush bepaint my cheek...
>
> (II, ii, 85–6)

From behind their masks the lovers can create a delightful world of holy palmers expressed in the perfect symmetry of the sonnet which is formed by their first greeting. Nevertheless the insecurity of this world is shown by placing immediately before the sonnet Tybalt's threatening reminder of the outside world

> I will withdraw; but this intrusion shall,
> Now seeming sweet, convert to bitt'rest gall.
>
> (I, v, 89–90)

Thus within the one scene of the masque we have all the elements of the story and its tragic outcome. The arrival of Romeo with masquers brings in the love affair which is the centre of the plot but it also enrages Tybalt against him, causing their later duel with all its tragic consequences of banishment and death. The image of the masque, moreover, is echoed in other situations throughout the play, referring back to the scene of the lovers' meeting and contrasting with the later tragic events.

The first scene where the events of the tragedy begin to crowd in on the lovers is the death of Tybalt, and here again there is the echo of the masque in the challenging exchange:

Tybalt. Mercutio, thou consortest with Romeo.
Mercutio. Consort! What, dost thou make us minstrels? An thou make minstrels of us, look to hear nothing but discords. Here's my fiddlestick; here's that shall make you dance. Zounds, consort!

(III, i, 43–7)

Mercutio is here being quarrelsome and simply playing with Tybalt's words but it is significant that his word-play should develop into the

[1] Holinshed, *Chronicles* (1586 ed.), II, 515. Quoted in *A Book of Masques in Honour of Allardyce Nicoll*, ed. T. J. B. Spencer (Cambridge, 1967), p. 438.

imagery of music and dancing associated with the masque. Tybalt is coming to settle the score for Romeo's intrusion into the Capulet feast and Mercutio's words are a reminder of how Tybalt did not take part in the dancing on that occasion. In the Zeffirelli production of the play the fighting as well as the dancing was seen as just another activity of the lively youth of Verona. But just as Romeo and Juliet took the game of love in the masque seriously enough to get married, in this scene we see the game of duelling being played for high stakes and Romeo is plunged into the real world where he has to avenge a friend and then take the consequences of his action. Duelling can only be a game if all the participants are following the same rules, but just as Tybalt refused to play by the rules of the masque, the rules of hospitality and the convention of not recognising the masquers, here he breaks the convention of the duel and fatally wounds Mercutio under Romeo's arm.

With the death of Tybalt the action moves on to a more mature level. The lovers have to be seen to be adults for the play to evoke tragedy rather than pathos. Romeo has become a man in first refusing to join in the spurious game of honour. He will not fight with Tybalt since he is now committed to the higher level of his love for Juliet. His later challenge to Tybalt is based on the reality of Mercutio's death and he then has to cope with the real consequences of a manly action.

Similarly in the scene where the nurse brings Juliet news of her cousin's death we see her movement to maturity in love which is based, not on the excitement of a masque and a moonlit encounter in an orchard, but on the commitment of her new role. Her immediate reaction to the news of Tybalt's death takes us back again to the masque for she feels, as Tybalt did on that occasion, that Romeo's was a 'serpent heart, hid with a flowering face'. Through the course of this scene, however,

she comes to realise the narrowness of this division into serpents and flowers, Montague and Capulets. She realises that she must now stand with her husband in a world where the comfort is partial –

My husband lives that Tybalt would have slain
And Tybalt's dead that would have slain my husband.

(III, ii, 104–5)

In this world created by the death of Mercutio the masque is no sanctuary and the next time we hear the image of the masque it heralds not a joyful meeting but a sorrowful parting. When the lovers part at daybreak after their wedding night Juliet, seeing the dawn, insists

Yond light is not daylight; I know it, I:
It is some meteor that the sun exhales
To be to thee this night a torch-bearer,
And light thee on thy way to Mantua...

(III, v, 12–15)

We have seen how the masque, throughout the plot, becomes a kind of double image containing the seeds of joy as well as tragedy and this feeling is reinforced by the ideas behind the images which are used to talk about the masque and the physical presence of the masquers. When Capulet first mentions the banquet to Paris he says

At my poor house look to behold this night
Earth-treading stars that make dark heaven light.
Such comfort as do lusty young men feel
When well-apparell'd April on the heel
Of limping winter treads, even such delight
Among fresh female buds shall you this night
Inherit at this house.

(I, ii, 24–30)

The masque is being associated with youth and the spring of the year, but this has been fitted into a more general discussion of time with reference to Juliet's being too young for marriage. 'Well-apparell'd April' may come upon the heel of limping winter but all this is only part of a cyclical progression and after

April comes the summer which Capulet had said 'will wither in their pride'. We are reminded of all the images of time and the wheel which turns joy to sorrow.

The earth-treading stars are an echo of the 'solemne feast' in *Hero and Leander* where

> resorted many a wandering guest
> To meet their loves; such as had none at all
> Came lovers home from this great festival
> For every street like to a firmament
> Glistered with breathing stars (I, 94–8)

This again associates the feast with the birth of love but it also foreshadows the physical arrival of the masquers who, with their torches, are the embodiment of light brought to the banquet. They *are* the earth-treading stars and especially Romeo who is not in fact a masquer but a torch-bearer. He insisted to Benvolio

> Give me a torch; I am not for this ambling;
> Being but heavy, I will bear the light.
> Let wantons, light of heart,
> Tickle the senseless rushes with their heels . . .
> I'll be a candle-holder and look on
> (I, iv, 11–12, 35–6, 38)

The choice of this image is important since it suggests the image of a feast reflecting the harmony of the stars as well as their light. The masquers will be earth-treading stars since dancing was meant to reflect the harmonious movement of the heavens. Elyot's *The Boke named the Governour* has a chapter on dancing where he says that

> The interpreters of Plato do think that the wonderful and incomprehensible order of the celestial bodies, I mean stars and planets and their motions harmonical, gave to them that intensively and by deep search of reason behold their courses in the sundry diversities of number and time, a form of imitation of a semblable motion which they call dancing.
> (book I, chapter xx)[1]

Dancing at its highest figures the harmony of the spheres and we see in the masquing scene Capulet's vain attempt to maintain this

harmony at his feast when he forbids Tybalt to challenge Romeo. Nevertheless, we know then that the heavenly harmony of the lovers cannot survive in Verona since it is dealing with a 'Bewtie too rich for use, for earth too dear'.

The next time that the star image appears Juliet is talking of death, although happily, within the context of her love for Romeo:

> Come, gentle night, come, loving black-brow'd night,
> Give me my Romeo; and, when he shall die,
> Take him and cut him out in little stars,
> And he will make the face of heaven so fine
> That all the world will be in love with night,
> And pay no worship to the garish sun.
> (III, ii, 20–5)

The lovers could be harmonious stars through their love but this could also be achieved through a death which would not deny their love.

The association of love and death was a marked feature of Renaissance imagery as Wind has pointed out in his chapter on 'Amor as a God of Death' in *Pagan Mysteries in the Renaissance*.[2] There is the story of the exchange of arrows between love and death which is found in emblem books from Alciati onwards,[3] where the young who should have been lovers die and the old fall in love, and this is what happens in this play. Death could also be a higher kind of love and love demanded a certain death to the outside world. Wind shows how

> the loves of the gods appeared on sarcophagi with remarkable frequency. The love of Bacchus for Ariadne, of Mars for Rhea, of Zeus for Ganymede, of Diana for Endymion – all these were variations of the

---

[1] Elyot, *The Boke named the Governour*, ed. A. T. Eliot (London, 1834), p. 63.
[2] Edgar Wind, *Pagan Mysteries in the Renaissance* (London, 1967), chapter x *passim*.
[3] Alciati, *Emblematum Liber* (Antwerp, 1581), emblems 154, 155. Also Geoffrey Whitney, *A Choice of Emblems* (Leyden, 1586), and Francis Thynne, *Emblems and Epigrammes* (London, 1600).

same theme; the love of a god for a mortal. To die was to be loved by a god and partake through him of eternal bliss.[1]

This kind of correlation between love and death has specific relations with revelling and feasts, for Wind notes 'that in Philostratus, *Imagines*, I, 2, the figure of Revelry standing at the gate of a nuptial feast is described in the posture of a funerary Eros, slumbering though he stands, holding his torch downward and crossing his legs'.[2]

Similarly Romeo goes to the masque as a figure of revelry not unlike the funerary Eros for he is carrying a torch and has deliberately rejected the role of Cupid. Mercutio had said to him

> borrow Cupid's wings
> And soar with them above a common bound
>
> (I, iv, 17–18)

but Romeo replies that he is

> too sore enpierced with his shaft
> To soar with his light feathers... (19–20)

He is not here specifically a figure of death since we cannot assume that Shakespeare is making a direct comparison with Philostratus and at this stage Romeo is still carrying the torch high. Nevertheless it is important to see how in contemporary thought there is the shadow of death over ideas of revelry as well as in the plot of Romeo and Juliet.

In the later part of the play Romeo and death are specifically related. The next feast that takes place is the preparation for Juliet's wedding and here death in the midst of feasting seems actually to be true. Capulet tells Paris

> the night before thy wedding day
> Hath Death lain with thy wife. There she lies,
> Flower as she was, deflowered by him.
> Death is my son-in-law, Death is my heir;
> My daughter he hath wedded. (IV, v, 35–9)

The Death who had lain with Juliet was Romeo but since we know that she is in fact alive we see that he has only brought her death in the world of the Capulets. There is thus hope that the final death is also death of true love to the world outside and the road to immortality on a higher sphere. Warren Smith has pointed out that the rosemary which bestrews Juliet's corpse was used at weddings as well as funerals, for it is a symbol of rebirth and immortality.[3] The funeral procession will take Juliet to her final wedding with Death who, as Capulet has said, is Romeo. Paris's lament over Juliet

> O love! O life! – not life, but love in death!
>
> (IV, v, 57)

suggests the final fate of the lovers who die in love and through their love in order to attain the harmony of the stars which is impossible in the world of Verona.

The feeling of triumph is very strong in the graveyard scene and this is achieved by bringing in the theme and imagery of the first banquet. When Romeo goes to bury Paris in the Capulet vault he exclaims

> A grave? O no! A lantern, slaught'red youth;
> For here lies Juliet, and her beauty makes
> This vault a feasting presence full of light
>
> (V, iii, 85–7)

'A feasting presence full of light' is surely a reference to the simply theatrical effect of the arrival of torch-bearers at a banquet and the image of light reminds us of Juliet as she was at that banquet. The first time he sees her Romeo says

> O, she doth teach the torches to burn bright!
> It seems she hangs upon the cheek of night
> As a rich jewel in an Ethiop's ear...
>
> (I, v, 43–5)

The echo of the banquet is a tragic recollection of their early love but where there is feasting there is the love of 'earth-treading

---

[1] *Pagan Mysteries*, p. 154.
[2] *Ibid.*, p. 158, n. 19.
[3] Warren D. Smith, 'Romeo's Final Dream', *MLR*, LXII (1967), 579–83.

stars' and in the grave Romeo believes that 'unsubstantial death is amorous'. He has come as Death to a different kind of banquet and he brings a different kind of death whereby

> Thou art not conquer'd; beauty's ensign yet
> Is crimson in thy lips and in thy cheeks,
> And death's pale flag is not advanced there.
>
> (v, iii, 94–5)

But the triumph of the lovers in their death cannot hinge on the feeling of this scene alone, however important this is in the theatre. The feeling is created and backed up by the image of Romeo's dreams which goes through the play and is also associated with the masque. Later writers of masques at the court of James I, like Daniel in *The Vision of the Twelve Goddesses* and Jonson in *The Vision of Delight*, actually placed their masques in the context of premonitory dreams showing that they created a special kind of world of vision and truth. Similarly the masque in *Romeo and Juliet* is placed in a context of premonitory dreams by the discussion of Romeo's dream when the masquers are preparing.

Romeo is worried about going to the masque because of his dream which has foreshadowed

> Some consequence, yet hanging in the stars,
> Shall bitterly begin his fearful date
> With this night's revels, and expire the term
> Of a despised life clos'd in my breast,
> By some vile forfeit of untimely death.
>
> (i, iv, 107–11)

Mercutio rejects the possibility of significant dreams, for as far as he is concerned dreams are merely the result of direct sense impressions and an idle romanticising of the everyday world. The dream of love is caused by Queen Mab galloping through lovers' brains and dreams of kissing are only due to the feel of Queen Mab on ladies' lips. We would like to be able to agree with Mercutio when he is denying Romeo's fears, but we see how his attitude also makes it impossible to accept the dream of

love, as we see when he jeers at Romeo after the masque and his scorn takes on the explicitly sexual note of

> If love be blind, love cannot hit the mark.
> Now will he sit under a medlar tree,
> And wish his mistress were that kind of fruit
> As maids call medlars when they laugh alone.
>
> (ii, i, 33–6)

Mercutio rejects both the love and the tragedy but we see in the play that in the world of Verona it is impossible to have one without the other.

The masque is indeed an unreal dream world in that it releases the lovers from the limitations of everyday life. The fact of its being a dream, however, does not make it any less true, for as Thomas Hill explains in his *Most Pleasaunte Arte of the Interpretacion of Dreames*: 'those dreames which are caused before the sonne rysing do signifye matters to come, and those at the rysing of the sonne do signifye matters present and at the instant'.[1]

When Romeo leaves Juliet, just at sunrise, he is 'afeard/Being in the night all this is but a dream' and here the waking dream of the masque and the scene in the orchard does 'signifie matters present and at the instant'. The truth of the earlier dream although related to the masque will only become apparent during the course of the action whereas the truth of the later dream is seen immediately in the continuing love of Romeo and Juliet. Nevertheless, just as the masque combines the joy of meeting with the danger of Tybalt's anger, the two dreams react together and we have to believe the whole truth of Romeo's statements. The dream of the meeting in the orchard has come true but it is still 'too flattering sweet to be substantiall' and its truth must be modified by the truth of the earlier dream. The premonition in the dream of impending death

---

[1] Thomas Hill, *Most Pleasaunte Arte of the Interpretacion of Dreames* (London, 1576), sig. c 1ᵛ.

gives an ironic undercurrent to the scene of the masque which is made explicit in Tybalt's reminder of the real world. The fact that the masque itself is seen as a dream again emphasises the precariousness of the lovers' happiness.

The image of the dream occupies the same kind of paradoxical position in the play as that of the masque. Romeo and Juliet's love is a dream and so it cannot exist in the world of sense and action occupied by Mercutio and the Nurse for whom one man is much the same as another. Yet if Romeo's premonitory dream is true, the dream of love is also true on a level beyond that of the world of Verona. The acceptance of both fulfilled love and tragedy allows the lovers to achieve a glory denied to the exponents of the world of sense.

The final scene, with its images of light and feasting, is also given a note of triumph by the final dream. Before Romeo hears of Juliet's death he has another dream:

I dreamt my lady came and found me dead –
Strange dream, that gives a dead man leave to think! –
And breath'd such life with kisses in my lips
That I reviv'd and was an emperor.   (v, i, 6–9)

On one level this dream is poignantly ironic since it is Romeo who comes and finds Juliet dead and her last kisses are an attempt to kill herself with the poison from his lips. Nevertheless the premonition is not simply a reversal of what happens but foretells the events after Juliet has kissed Romeo. The dream of love does give a dead man leave to think, for their love makes their death part of the progress beyond the world of sense. The world of action can only provide the kind of death which comes to Mercutio who dies cursing, and in any case it is based on the much more false dreams of spurious honour and sexual prowess.

The masque in *Romeo and Juliet* provides an image of the brief moment of harmony in which it was possible for Romeo and Juliet to fall in love. It is presented theatrically in the stage picture of the 'feasting presence full of light' and poetically in the image of the earth-treading stars. This moment of harmony becomes a central point of reference for the whole play, and its controlling images of revelry within danger, sudden light in darkness, and a dream which transcends reality, are the opposites, contrasting and yet reconcilable, which make for the vitality of the play.

© KATHLEEN E. McLUSKIE 1971

'HAMLET' AND THE
'SPARING DISCOVERIE'

DAVID KAULA

In writing *Hamlet* Shakespeare, with his usual versatility, seems to have used several sources of various kinds. Not only did he draw on a previous version of the story but he also found material for his purposes in such works as Lyly's *Euphues*, Bright's *Treatise of Melancholie*, and Nashe's *Pierce Pennilesse*.[1] Another work which offers considerable evidence that it may belong to this list is a little-known pamphlet published in London in 1601, one of the several polemics which emanated from the current disputes within the English Catholic priesthood known as the Archpriest Controversy. Admittedly this is not the kind of work which Shakespeare, so far as we know, was in the habit of utilizing. Among his recognized sources the only one that even remotely resembles it, indeed the only example of a religious polemic, is Samuel Harsnet's violently anti-Catholic *A Declaration of Egregious Popish Impostures*. Yet the pamphlet shows so many verbal and other resemblances to *Hamlet* that it raises the question whether it might have a connection with the play.

The two parties involved in the Archpriest Controversy, usually referred to as the 'Jesuits' and 'seculars', were divided over the question of how the underground Catholic movement in England should be organized and what its objective should be.[2] To the Jesuits and their followers the only acceptable goal was the eventual restoration of England to the Church. Certain members of the secular clergy, on the other hand, felt that this policy could only have the negative result of antagonizing the government and increasing the penalties English Catholics had to endure. They hoped to convince the government that the great majority of Catholics, rather than supporting the Jesuits and their subversive schemes, were loyal to the Queen and accepted the Protestant regime, and that all they wished was the limited freedom to practise their religion in safety. To publicize these views the seculars between 1601–2 produced more than a dozen pamphlets, nearly all of which were published in London with the covert approval of the authorities.[3] The main target of their attacks and the most active spokesman for the other side was Robert Persons, the prominent Jesuit who was then serving as rector of the English seminary in Rome.

The pamphlet in question, one of those produced by the seculars, shows the following matter on its title-page:

[1] See Kenneth Muir, *Shakespeare's Sources* (London, 1961), pp. 110–22.

[2] The fullest summaries of the controversy appear in T. G. Law, *A Historical Sketch of the Conflicts between Jesuits and Seculars in the Reign of Queen Elizabeth* (London, 1889) and J. H. Pollen, *The Institution of the Archpriest Blackwell* (London, 1916). There are shorter accounts in E. I. Watkin, *Roman Catholicism in England from the Reformation to 1950* (London, 1957), pp. 51–9, and Patrick McGrath, *Papists and Puritans under Elizabeth I* (London, 1967), pp. 284–99.

[3] See Gladys Jenkins, 'The Archpriest Controversy and the Printers, 1601–1603', *The Library*, 5th series, II (1948), 182–3.

A SPARING DISCOVERIE OF OVR ENGLISH IESVITS, and of Fa. *Parsons* proceedings vnder pretence of promoting the Catholike faith in *England*:

For a caueat to all true Catholiks our very louing brethren and friends, how they embrace *such very vncatholike, though Iesuiticall deseignments.*

Eccles. 4. *Vidi calumnias quae sub sole geruntur, & lachrymas innocentium, & neminem consolatorem.*

Newly Imprinted. 1601.

A well-printed quarto volume of eighty-two pages, the *Sparing Discoverie* offers evidence that it was published in London rather than abroad. Indeed, according to the most recent and reliable bibliographical authority on recusant literature it came from the press of James Roberts, the printer who entered *Hamlet* in the Stationers' Register in July the following year and produced the Second Quarto edition of 1604.[1] The pamphlet includes a preface signed 'W.W.', the initials of William Watson, the most aggressive and prolific of the anti-Jesuit writers. Near the end of the preface Watson intimates, however, that the body of the tract is the work of another author, and since it is written in a style decidedly more lucid and coherent than his own there is no reason to doubt him. One indication of this writer's identity appears in a letter the Jesuit Anthony Rivers wrote to Persons in July 1602, where in discussing some of the seculars' pamphlets Rivers mentions that Christopher Bagshaw is thought to be the author of the *Sparing Discoverie.*[2] Since in both content and wording the *Sparing Discoverie* coincides at several points with another pamphlet almost certainly by Bagshaw, *A True Relation of the Faction Begun at Wisbich* (1601), it seems likely that he was the author.[3]

In *Hamlet* there are no longer passages of a half-dozen lines or more which closely duplicate single passages in the *Sparing Discoverie*. Most of the verbal similarities between the two works are rather of the smaller, scattered variety, such as those which can be seen, say, between *King Lear* and Harsnet's

Declaration. Among the elements they share are nearly two dozen words which Shakespeare never used before in his plays, and these will be listed later. An example of parallel phasing may be seen in the following sentence from the preface of the pamphlet, in which Watson makes the typically unsupported claim that the Jesuits were responsible for the papal bull of excommunication issued against Queen Elizabeth in 1570:

For this cause it is that they (the Spanish faction I meane) haue labored these *30.* yeers space and vpward (for so long it is since the Bull of *Pius Quintus* came out by the Iesuiticall humorists procurement) for depriuing her Maiestie of her life, Kingdome, Crowne, and all at once... (sig. a2ᵛ)

In *Hamlet* the final portion of the sentence is paralleled in two places, in the Ghost's line:

> by a brother's hand
> Of life, of crown, of queen at once dispatched...
> (I, v, 74-5)

and, more fully, in Claudius's proposal to Laertes:
> we will our kingdom give,
> Our crown, our life, and all that we call ours...
> (IV, v, 205-6)

A detail worth noting here is the way the phrase 'and all at once' at the end of the

[1] A. F. Allison and D. M. Rogers, 'A Catalogue of Catholic Books in English Printed Abroad or Secretly in England, 1558–1640', *Biographical Studies*, III, iii–iv (1956), no. 64. Contrary to Allison and Rogers, Gladys Jenkins assigns the printing of the *Sparing Discoverie* to Felix Kingston ('The Archpriest Controversy', p. 184), as does the *STC*, no. 25126.

[2] Henry Foley, *Records of the English Province of the Society of Jesus* (London, 1877–83), I, 42.

[3] One of the leaders of the anti-Jesuit faction in the Archpriest Controversy, Bagshaw earlier took part in the notorious quarrels among the priests imprisoned at Wisbech Castle, the so-called Wisbech Stirs of 1595–7. His *True Relation* shows a large number of similarities to *King Lear*, and a study of this work as a possible new source for the play is forthcoming in the *Shakespeare Quarterly*.

quotation is divided between the two lines in the play. In condemning the Jesuits for trying to instigate rebellions against the Queen, Bagshaw writes:

Hereunto may be added...how many they haue intituled to the Crowne of this Kingdome: as the Duke of *Parma*, the Earle of *Darby*, and others, exciting some of them by force of armes to assayle her Maiestie, and buzzing into their eares how easily the Scepter might be wrung out of her hands, and they obteyne it. (p. 8)

The phrase 'buzzing into their eares' resembles a line on Laertes's rebellion:

And wants not buzzers to infect his ear...
(IV, v, 90)

and 'by force of armes to assayle her Maiestie' a line on Fortinbras:

To give th' assay of arms against your majesty.
(II, ii, 71)

Here the similarity is strengthened by the fact that 'assay' in one of its now-obsolete meanings was synonymous with, and indeed apparently influenced by, 'assail'.[1]

Again on the subject of rebellion, Bagshaw blames the Jesuits for advocating 'that the people may depose their Princes, and choose others at their pleasures...' He then asks: 'what Prince will indure such persons in his Kingdome, as vnder pretence of Religion, shall infect his subiects with such hatefull conceits, so dangerous to his estate?' Further on he presents a sequence of three images:

This only we will say, that our pretended Fathers build Castles in the ayre, and feede themselues with their owne follyes: as though where the people do once get a head, it be not as hard a matter to suppresse them, as to stop the breach of the sea, when in fury it hath once mastered the banks.
(pp. 14–15)

Certain elements here are paralleled in Claudius's and the Messenger's accounts of Laertes's rebellion just before he enters with his rabble. First, the notion that the people may depose one prince and 'choose' another:

They cry, 'Choose we! Laertes shall be king!'
(IV, v, 106)

A few lines before this Bagshaw's comparison of a popular uprising which has gained a 'head' to a sea which has mastered its banks is matched in the Messenger's lines:

The ocean, overpeering of his list,
Eats not the flats with more impiteous haste
Than young Laertes, in a riotous head,
O'erbears your officers. (IV, v, 99–102)

Before this occurs a line which suggests Bagshaw's other two images, 'build Castles in the ayre, and feede themselues with their owne follyes' – if, that is, 'clouds' is taken as equivalent to 'Castles in the ayre':

Feeds on his wonder, keeps himself in clouds...
(IV, v, 89)[2]

Yet another resemblance may be seen between the phrases, 'what Prince will indure such persons in his Kingdome...so dangerous to his estate', and Claudius's earlier remark on the homicidal Hamlet:

The terms of our estate may not endure
Hazard so near's... (III, iii, 5–6)

A numerical correspondence appears in this sentence in the *Sparing Discoverie*: 'Whereupon Doctor *Barret* in the behalfe of the Colledge fel in debt 3000. crownes: the Iesuits all the while keeping him from the annuall pension' (p. 64). Both '3000. crownes' and the notion of an 'annuall pension' occur in the line on Fortinbras:

[1] *OED*, 'assay', v., II, 14.
[2] The conventional connection between clouds and castles in the air is indicated by a passage in Fairfax's translation of Tasso, *Godfrey of Bulloigne* (1600), p. 294: 'oft the clouds frame shapes of castles great/ Amid the aire, that little time do last...'

Gives him three thousand crowns in annual fee...

(II, ii, 73)[1]

Although Fortinbras's situation is hardly comparable to that of Dr Barret, the rector of the seminary at Douai, the correspondence seems more significant when we notice that this is the only place in *Hamlet* where crowns are mentioned, the standard currency elsewhere being the ducat.[2] In another reference to the Jesuits' mishandling of money Bagshaw writes: 'You haue heard how the Iesuites became our Collectors, or rather not ours, but their owne: to whome for their accompts the false Steward in the Gospell we suppose may giue place' (p. 19). In the next sentence Bagshaw alleges that a Jesuit 'stole 27. pound of the common money' belonging to the priests imprisoned at Wisbech Castle. The combination of 'false Steward' and 'stole' appears in Ophelia's line:

It is the false steward, that stole his master's daughter.

(IV, v, 171)

Some other short phrases in the *Sparing Discoverie* which also occur in *Hamlet* are the following: 'continuall practise' (p. 1, V, ii, 200), 'most holy and religious' (p. 1, III, iii, 8), 'particular thoughts' (p. 24, I, i, 67), 'take Armes against' (p. 65, III, i, 59), 'out of ioynt' (p. 67, I, v, 188), and '*filius terrae*', which corresponds to Rosencrantz's 'children of the earth' (p. 56, II, ii, 224).

'*Filius terrae*' is one of Bagshaw's several uncomplimentary epithets for Persons, an allusion to his plebeian background. Although he pretends he is reluctant to do so, Bagshaw repeats another, more serious slander the seculars often directed at Persons, that he

is by his birth a bastard, begotten vpon the bodie of a very base woman by the Parson of the parish where hee was borne...Which defect, because it did not proceede from any fault in him, we could haue wished had bin omitted by our very reuerend brethren in their late declaration to his holinesse...   (pp. 41–2)[3]

In his curious meditation on the 'vicious mole of nature' Hamlet expresses the same notion, that a person will be slandered for his 'birth' even though 'it did not proceede from any fault in him':

So oft it chances in particular men
That for some vicious mole of nature in them,
As in their birth, wherein they are not guilty...

(I, iv, 23–5)

As Bagshaw speaks of a 'defect' and 'fault', so Hamlet in his ensuing lines also uses these terms in the phrases 'stamp of one defect' and 'particular fault' (I, iv, 31, 36).

In addition to these similarities in verbal detail the *Sparing Discoverie* shows various broader resemblances to *Hamlet*, some of which involve traits of character. One of the more prominent features of the pamphlet is its portrayal of the Jesuits as busy politicians obsessed with plots and stratagems and forever meddling in affairs irrelevant to their calling. Bagshaw declares: 'Let these men brag as much as they list of their pollicies, their foresights, and their pragmaticall wisedome, they shall neuer whilest we liue, haue in these courses our approbation' (p. 10). Bragging of policies and foresights is a habit also displayed by a certain character in the play, one who likes to think of himself as among those 'of

[1] This is the line as it appears in both the First Quarto and Folio. In the Second Quarto it reads: 'Giues him threescore thousand crownes in annuall fee'. Since the addition of '-score' here makes the line hypermetrical it could be plausibly assumed that Shakespeare originally wrote 'three' rather than 'threescore'.

[2] As in 'a hundred ducats apiece for his picture in little' (II, ii, 357), 'five ducats, five' (IV, iv, 20), 'twenty thousand ducats' (IV, iv, 25).

[3] The 'late declaration to his holinesse' is one of the first pamphlets published by the seculars, the *Declaratio Motuum* (London, 1601), which began their attack on Persons's character and career. Persons answers the completely groundless charge that he was illegitimate in *A Briefe Apologie or Defence of the Catholike Ecclesiastical Hierarchie* (Antwerp, 1601), ff. 197–197[v].

wisdom and of reach' (II, i, 64). In describing the Jesuits' schemes and stratagems Watson and Bagshaw often make use of such terms as 'drifts, practises, and deuices', 'plotting and compassing', 'cunning fishing', 'hunting', 'ginnes', and 'traps' (sig. A3ᵛ, pp. 8, 23, 27, 32). Polonius shows his predilection for this sort of language in 'encompassment and drift of question' (II, i, 10), 'here's my drift' (II, i, 37), 'Your bait of falsehood takes this carp of truth' (II, i, 63), and 'Hunts...this trail of policy' (II, ii, 47). Watson claims that he could

deduct a triple alphabet intire of Machiuilian practises vsed by the Iesuites...how, when, amongst whom, and by whom, this & that stratageme is to be practised: what maximes, axiomaes, or rules are generall or common to all: and which are speciall...How this politician or state-father is to be imployed in Princes Courts as a lieger for aduice...how to insinuate himselfe in proper person or by his agents into his Soueraignes fauour, or some neerest about the seate of Maiesty, to know all the secrets of the land...

(sig. a2)

Polonius likewise has his collections of stratagems and maxims, takes pride in being an 'assistant for a state' high in his sovereign's favor, and devotes his energies to ferreting out secrets. In addition, there is a more precise resemblance between one of Watson's phrases – 'how, when, amongst whom, and by whom, this & that stratageme is to be practised' – and a verbal idiosyncrasy Polonius displays as he is contriving stratagems for Reynaldo:

Enquire me first what Danskers are in Paris,
And how, and who, what means, and where they keep,
What company, at what expense...   (II, i, 7–9)

The *Sparing Discoverie* offers an analogy to one of Polonius's particular activities in Bagshaw's detailed account of a device he claims the Jesuits invented 'to enrich and increase their order':

It is tearmed by them an holy exercise, and is put in practise when they finde any, that are meet to serue

their turnes, either for their extraordinary pregnancy of wit and learning, or for their parentage and friends, or for their wealth and possessions, and cannot otherwise allure them to their society.   (p. 21)

After explaining how the Jesuit conducting the exercise first subtly works on the candidate's emotions so as to place him in a receptive frame of mind, all the while treating him 'with all kinde of sweete behauiour and curtesy', Bagshaw describes how the exercise itself proceeds:

The partie at the time appointed, comming to the holy Father who must deale with him, is recluded from the speech of any body but the sayd Father for a certaine time. Vpon his first reclusion the Father commeth vnto him, and giueth him a meditation to study vpon for some foure or fiue houres: willing him in the meane while carefullie to remember all the cogitations that do come into his minde. The sayd foure or fiue houres expired, in commeth this good Father: and then the partie must be confessed, and is to reueale all his particular thoughts of what matter soeuer good or bad that came into his head, all the time of his aforesayd meditation.   (p. 24)

The most suggestive phrase here is, 'the Father...giueth him a meditation to study vpon for some foure or fiue houres'. Although Polonius does not do precisely this with Hamlet, as he is contriving his meeting with Ophelia he mentions the same time period:

You know sometimes he walks four hours together
Here in the lobby   (II, ii, 160–1)

and a few moments later Hamlet comes in '*reading on a book*' (II, ii, 167, s.d.). At this point, by asking Claudius and Gertrude to leave, Polonius in effect 'recludes' Hamlet 'from the speech of any body' but himself. Then in the course of their following dialogue he enacts what could be taken as a parody of the inquisition described in the excerpt, as he questions Hamlet about the 'matter' of his cogitations:

Polonius. What do you read, my lord?
Hamlet. Words, words, words.
Polonius. What is the matter, my lord?

(II, ii, 191–3)

Shortly after this episode Hamlet makes a remark to Rosencrantz and Guildenstern which resembles the phrase, 'thoughts of what matter soeuer good or bad':

for there is nothing either good or bad but thinking makes it so.   (II, ii, 247)

The word 'exercise' in the specifically religious sense, which Shakespeare used only once before in his plays (in *Richard III*), occurs in Polonius's lines to Ophelia as he is about to expose her to Hamlet. Like Bagshaw's Jesuit, he both gives her a 'meditation to study vpon' and prepares here for 'reclusion':

Read on this book,
That show of such an exercise may colour
Your loneliness.   (III, i, 44–6)

By forcing Ophelia to perform this kind of 'show' or 'pious action', Polonius illustrates yet another one of the many vices Watson and Bagshaw attribute to the Jesuits, a 'catholick shew of so true religion' or 'externall shew of pietie' (sigs. A3ᵛ, a1).

The *Sparing Discoverie* reveals several other resemblances to *Hamlet* of the more general variety, but these would need a good deal of space to illustrate and would largely repeat the kind of evidence which has been presented. It remains to list those words which appear in both works but in none of the twenty-two plays Shakespeare wrote before *Hamlet*. Most of these words are not unusual, but since the list is fairly extensive it does provide one means of assessing a possible influence, in that Shakespeare conceivably could have been prompted to use them by his reading of the pamphlet.[1] Those words which occur in no other Shakespeare play before or after *Hamlet* are indicated with an asterisk:

anticipation (p. 20, II, ii, 290)
appurtenance (p. 57, II, ii, 362*)
associates (as a noun – sig. a1, p. 59, IV, iii. 44*)
calumny (sig. a2, III, i, 137)
comply (sig. A4ᵛ, II, ii, 363)
disioynt (sig. A4ᵛ, I, ii, 20)
document (p. 1, IV, v, 177*)[2]
equiuocation (pp. 6, 11, V, i, 129)
gules (sig. A3, II, ii, 445)
incest (sig. a2, I, v, 83)
inuentor (p. 7, V, ii, 374)
marshal (as a verb – p. 55, III, iv, 206)
occurents (sig. a2, p. 7, V, ii, 346*)
ouercrow (sig. a1, V, ii, 342*)
ouertop (sig. a1, V, i, 240)
pourport (sig. A3, II, i, 82*)
Prouinciall (sig. a3ᵛ, p. 18, III, ii, 266)
schoolfellowe (p. 43, III, iv, 203*)
sheepes skin (p. 40, V, i, 106*)
statist (p. 43, V, ii, 33)
towring (sig. a1ᵛ, V, ii, 80)
traduced (pp. 9, 34, I, iv, 18)

A word of special significance here is 'equivocation', which in the play occurs in Hamlet's comment to Horatio on the quibbling of the Gravedigger. It is the clearest indication in the play that Shakespeare was aware of the current disputes between the Jesuits and seculars. Equivocation was one of the subtle practices for which the Jesuits were repeatedly condemned by their opponents, and indeed in the *Sparing Discoverie* Bagshaw devotes more than a page to describing what he calls 'their equiuocating, which you may tearme in plaine english, lying and cogging' (pp. 10–12). There may be other, less explicit allusions to equivocation in *Hamlet* (one for instance in Claudius's opening speech

[1] An example of this kind of influence appears in the many words in *King Lear* which Shakespeare seems to have picked up from his reading of Florio's *Montaigne*. For a list of these see *King Lear*, New Arden edition by Kenneth Muir (London, 1959), p. 250.

[2] In both works this word is used in the less usual sense of 'lesson'. In the play it occurs in Laertes's comment on Ophelia's flower speech: 'A document in madness'.

from the throne[1]), as well as several possible references to other matters related to the Archpriest Controversy, some occurring in passages which so far have not been adequately explained. These would require extensive investigation, however, and so must be considered in another place.

In general, the various similarities between *Hamlet* and the *Sparing Discoverie* seem unusually plentiful, even when we allow for the fact that two such works written at nearly the same time are bound to show some common features in their language. If individually the similarities do not always seem remarkable, as they accumulate they tend to appear less and less accidental. Although not too well-known today, the Archpriest Controversy was a widely-publicized affair in London at the time, and there would be nothing peculiar about Shakespeare's taking an interest in such matters. A few years later he was to pay close attention to another work in which Persons and his colleagues are attacked when he used Harsnet's *Declaration* as a source for *King Lear*. One objection which could be raised to the assumption that Shakespeare used the *Sparing Discoverie* is its date. According to Pollen, the pamphlet was published in October, 1601.[2] It has been argued that Shakespeare must have written *Hamlet* before February of that year, the evidence for this being the marginal note in Gabriel Harvey's copy of Chaucer, which refers to Essex in the present tense before

mentioning 'Shakespeares...tragedie of Hamlet, Prince of Denmarke'.[3] It has been questioned, however, whether the note was necessarily written before Essex's execution in February,[4] and in any case a casually jotted note cannot be considered too formidable a piece of evidence, especially in the absence of any supporting evidence. A more definite terminal date for *Hamlet* is established by Roberts's entry in the Stationers' Register of July 26, 1602. Between the preceding October and that date Shakespeare would have had time enough to read and make use of the *Sparing Discoverie*.

[1] One of Claudius's lines, 'In equal scale weighing delight and dole' (I, ii, 13), anticipates the use of the same image of equal weighing in the Porter's remark in *Macbeth*: 'Faith, here's an equivocator, that could swear in both scales against either scale' (II, iii, 7–9); and it is also paralleled in Brabantio's lines: 'These sentences, to sugar, or to gall,/Being strong on both sides, are equivocal' (*Oth.*, I, iii, 216–17). The implication is that the new regime in Denmark is based on an equivocal mixture of truth and falsity, and Hamlet's comment on the Gravedigger's quibbling, like the Porter's on the equivocator, would have a significance which extends well beyond the immediate episode.

[2] *Institution of the Archpriest*, p. 102.

[3] See E. A. J. Honigmann, 'The Date of *Hamlet*', *Shakespeare Survey 9* (Cambridge, 1956), pp. 24–6.

[4] Leo Kirschbaum, 'The Date of Shakespeare's *Hamlet*', *Studies in Philology*, XXXIV (1937), 168–75.

© DAVID KAULA 1971

'HAMLET' IN FRANCE 200 YEARS AGO

J. D. GOLDER

Only as recently as 200 years ago, on Saturday, 30 September 1769, to be precise, was a French theatre audience treated for the first time to a stage version of a Shakespeare play. The play was *Hamlet* and its adaptor Jean-François Ducis. This was by no means the first the French had heard of Shakespeare or indeed of the Prince. Voltaire had frequently labelled the play an unbridled monstrosity and its author an ignorant barbarian. True, he had been unable to avoid recognising that Shakespeare had an undeniable natural genius, but what Voltaire could not forgive was the Englishman's ignorance of the rules of the drama and his abhorrent lack of good taste. Voltaire's criticisms were repeated, though in less virulent terms, by other eighteenth-century French critics such as L'Abbé Prévost and L'Abbé Le Blanc. The La Place translation of the play, which appeared in 1746, was a miserably emasculated effort which failed to fulfil the promise of its author's very perceptive preliminary 'Discours' and succeeded only in proving once more that the neo-classical concept of tragedy was still very much alive. If at heart Voltaire was a devout Racinian and believed unquestioningly in the validity of Aristotle's rules, in the unities, in propriety, in dignity of language and in, to use Racine's own formula, 'une action simple, chargée de peu de matière', he was none the less aware of the need for tragedy to speak a little less to the ears and a little more to the eyes and advocated a slightly less stringent application of the

basic doctrine. Would not a few slight shifts of scene be permissible? A little blood on stage? A little more action?

Ducis, who never sought to hide his admiration for Voltaire, agreed wholeheartedly with these proposals. What is more, Ducis was an ardent worshipper of Shakespeare, even going as far as celebrating la fête de Saint-Guillaume each year by crowning with a laurel wreath a bust of the Bard. But unfortunately, to a very large degree, Ducis was defeated before he started by his ignorance of the English language and his need, therefore, to rely on La Place's truncated version as his source. Even with the stimulation of the contemporary tide of Anglomania which was sweeping France, this was a barrier which no amount of good will, adulation or reforming zeal could overcome satisfactorily. Whether he liked it or not, Ducis was a prisoner of convention, a mouthpiece of the attitudes of his day, and what his audience at the Comédie-Française saw in 1769, far from being an epoch-making innovation and providing a perspicacious insight and fuller understanding of the Shakespearian concept of tragedy, served merely to underline the essential incompatibility of two diametrically opposed cultures.

Ducis's dramatis personae lists only eight speaking roles: Hamlet, Gertrude, Claudius, Ophélie, Polonius, Norceste (Horatio), Elvire (an invention of Ducis) and Voltimand ('*capitaine des gardes*'). Fortinbras, Laertes, Cornelius, Rosencrantz and Guildenstern, the

Ghost, the Gravediggers, the Strolling Players, Osric, Bernardo, Marcellus and Francisco are dispensed with. The scene is set exclusively inside the '*Palais des rois de Danemarck*' and there are no visits up on to the battlements, into Polonius's apartments, into Gertrude's closet, to any adjacent cemeteries or distant sea-side plains. And whilst the action of Shakespeare's plot demands a matter of months in which to be acted out, Ducis confines his to no more than the actual performance time.

No prior acquaintance with either Shakespeare's *Hamlet* or any of the conventional classical French tragedies is required for one to be able to deduce from these physical statistics that there is a fundamental difference in the nature of these two plays and that in them two very different dramatic techniques are at work. Shakespeare's sprawling, baroque canvas of people and incidents is reduced by Ducis to a claustrophobic palace intrigue from which all but the aristocratic and their attendants are excluded.

Within such a framework Ducis fashions a much modified version of Shakespeare's original plot.[1] Hamlet's father is murdered by Claudius and Gertrude who poison him in his bed. When the play opens, Claudius, an ambitious first prince of the blood, is not yet married to Gertrude. He is intent upon the throne and, with the aid of Polonius and a band of conspirators, is plotting to dispose of Hamlet before the prince's coronation. The ghost of his father has twice appeared to Hamlet in dreams, revealed all and demanded summary vengeance and the deaths of both criminals. Ophélie, Claudius's daughter, now appears to tell Gertrude how, in defiance of the old king's decree, she has fallen in love with Hamlet. Gertrude, eager to atone for her crime and devote the rest of her life to her son, approves of the match. Ophélie hastens to inform Hamlet of the good news but he is all weakness and tears and can only offer the

enigmatical reply that happiness is sometimes further off than one thinks. By presenting his mother with the funeral urn in which her husband's ashes have been placed, Hamlet extracts a confession from Gertrude. Unable, however, to obey the ghost's order to kill his mother, Hamlet rushes out to deal with Claudius instead. The usurper has attacked the palace with his revolutionaries whom he has duped into believing that Hamlet has killed his own father but Hamlet, with the help of some support hastily mustered by Norceste and the volatile mob to whom Gertrude finally reveals the truth, quells the insurrection. Claudius stabs himself and, in a dying gesture, gives Hamlet the dagger to take to Gertrude. She, utterly overcome with remorse, also commits suicide, leaving Hamlet to reign with Ophélie.

The divergencies from the original are self-evident. Professor F. C. Green, contrasting the 'a priori or hypothetical approach to natural truths' of the classical French dramatists with Shakespeare's 'experimental approach',[2] provides a useful clue for the understanding of the reasons which prevented Ducis from reproducing Shakespeare. The tragedy of Shakespeare's Hamlet does and can only emerge after a review of a complicated series of events and circumstances treated in chronological order. When the curtain rises on Ducis's tragedy, however, Hamlet is already faced with his dilemma. The moment of truth is at hand and the action is already largely played out.[3] In so far as the

[1] For the original manuscript version of Ducis's *Hamlet*, as performed in September 1769, see Mary Vanderhoof, 'Hamlet, A Tragedy adapted from Shakespeare (1770) by Jean-François Ducis: A Critical Edition', *Proceedings of the American Philosophical Society*, xcvii (1953), i, 88–142. It is upon this manuscript version that my article is based.

[2] F. C. Green, *Minuet, A Critical Survey of English and French Literary Ideas in the Eighteenth Century* (Cambridge, 1935), p. 36.

[3] Indeed the very first word of the play, '*Oui*', indicates in itself that we join Claudius and Polonius

event which sparks off the tragedy, the murder of the king, has already taken place, as of course in the English play too, Shakespeare for once momentarily walks on common ground with the classical French dramatists. But in Ducis far more than this one event has taken place before the play opens. Gertrude has already felt remorse and decided to break with Claudius. Claudius has already taken action to get rid of Hamlet. The ghost has already appeared to Hamlet and demanded vengeance. All that Ducis leaves himself is a situation, a moment of crisis, ready to be analysed, not a story waiting to be told. As he explained to Garrick in a letter some months before *Hamlet* opened, his intention was 'to create an interesting role of a parricidal queen and especially to portray in Hamlet's pure and melancholy soul a model of filial love'.[1]

Indeed, if Gertrude is not the heroine of Ducis's play, her role is at least as important as Hamlet's.[2] In sharp contrast to Claudius, she is a glowing paragon of repentance and even if Ducis does go further than Shakespeare and involves her unequivocally in her husband's murder, he never dwells on her guilt. It is a belief in man's inherent goodness, or at least in the rehabilitation of repentant sinners, together with an adherence to the tradition of French tragedy and the Aristotelean precept that in spite of their sins all characters must maintain a dignified nobility befitting their rank, which obliges Ducis to make radical changes in the character of Shakespeare's Gertrude. In some respects she becomes more like a Racinian or Voltairian heroine. Torn between her son, and the would-be usurper, she could be Voltaire's Mérope. Haunted by terrible dreams of her crime, she is Racine's Athalie and unburdening her sins to the attentive Elvire, she becomes Phèdre confessing her guilty passion to Oenone. Moreover, whereas Shakespeare stresses the evil side of human nature, Ducis always strives to depict

virtue and good and is forever at pains to render the queen a less revolting specimen of humanity. And of course the proprieties dictated a high standard of relative respectability. Although it was she who placed the poisoned chalice by her husband's bedside, she instantly repented. Unfortunately, before she could retrieve it, the king had drunk down its contents. Her motive for murder was not base ambition, but love. And again this was no torrid, physical love, but a sophisticated passion quite unsullied by incest since Claudius is not her husband's brother. All in all, Gertrude is made to look quite innocent. Before her very first appearance she has determined to defy Claudius, forget all ideas of marriage to him and to atone for her sins by spending the rest of the play in persistent manifestations of maternal love. She never tires of reminding us of her intentions:

C'est de voir couronner un prince, un fils que j'aime...
De nourir dans mon sein le remords que j'endure
De mériter encore de sentir la nature.[3]

or of crystallising her emotions into a nicely turned platitude:

Seul bien des criminels, le repentir nous reste.[4]

She, and not Claudius as in Shakespeare, will ask Norceste to ascertain the cause of Hamlet's inordinate sorrow. And she, overruling her late husband's edict, will allow and encourage Ophélie to marry Hamlet. At the end of the play she makes public confession of her misdeeds and, with a dagger dripping with Claudius's blood commits suicide, a brief

in mid-conversation, that things have already begun to happen. Compare the opening line of Racine's *Andromaque*, *Iphigénie* or *Athalie*.

[1] Ducis's letter to Garrick is dated 14 April 1769. See P. Albert, *Lettres de Ducis* (Paris, 1879), p. 7.

[2] It is not until Talma takes over in 1803 that the prince's role becomes the heaviest in terms of lines. In the original version, Ducis gives Gertrude some 420 lines to speak and Hamlet some 370.

[3] 1769 ms., act I, scene ii.

[4] *Ibid.*

homily on the folly of infidelity on her lips. If this was traditional practice in neo-classical tragedies, in the present situation, after continual demonstrations of remorse, Gertrude's ultimate expiation seems an unnecessarily drastic measure. The expedient, however, could not have failed to warm the hearts of an audience for whom the theatre was very much a school for morality and tragedy itself looked to as the champion of virtue.

To Ducis's French mind, Shakespeare's *Hamlet* is not really a tragedy at all. The predicament of the English prince could by no means have been relied upon to interest a neo-classically minded eighteenth-century audience. They would have had little truck with an ineffectual specimen prevented from acting by his own ratiocinations and basic concern with the problems of living. To them, once the ghost has spoken, Hamlet has simply to go ahead and obey. His filial duty demands that he kill Claudius and forgive his mother. The time is out of joint and the universal order is unbalanced. He has received a supernatural directive and there is nothing to prevent him setting the world right and redressing the natural balance. Ducis evidently feels the need for a psychological conflict. He therefore provides his Hamlet with a tragic dilemma such as Corneille might have contrived. This he achieves by simply transferring the ancestry of his Ophelia from Polonius to Claudius. Now once he has heard the ghost's story, Hamlet finds himself confronted with the most celebrated of all Corneillian conflicts, that of love and filial duty, passion and the voice of nature. Avenging his father now means for Hamlet, just as it did for Le Cid, killing the father of the woman he loves. Inability to resolve this dilemma is a perfectly rational and acceptable explanation of the prince's inertia. But Ducis makes his Hamlet's problem doubly difficult by having the ghost demand the death of Gertrude as well as that of Claudius. The

very thought of killing his mother is too unnatural a crime to even bear consideration. Thus the French prince is afforded a second quite understandable reason for delay. Putting antic dispositions on becomes totally superfluous, since he is well aware of the reasons for his melancholy. He lacks will and freely admits as much.

As such, this weak and sensitive Hamlet, a melancholy soul and the plaything of his own emotions, is a reflection of Ducis himself and very much a product of the cult of *sensibilité* which overcame the second half of the eighteenth century. For Ducis, sentiment was the first truth. 'Je demanderai,' he once said, 'si au théâtre le jugement des pleurs ne l'emporte pas sur celui de la raison.' Tears are the outward manifestation of the heart at work. And the heart and natural feelings are a less fallible guide to upright moral conduct than reason. This Hamlet is an '*âme sensible*' and much given to tears,

J'enhardis, en tremblant, mon âme encore flottante
La pitie m'attendrit, le meurtre m'épouvante.[1]

But, although he will briefly contemplate suicide as an alternative to obeying the ghost, so strongly is he attached to the seventeenth-century attitudes towards parental rights that ultimately he is prepared to sacrifice love to filial respect.

Not until brought face to face with Ophélie, made to look his dilemma between the eyes as it were, can Hamlet solve his problem and stir himself to a Corneillian course of action. It is perhaps appropriate therefore that this Ophelia, far from reflecting her Shakespearian counterpart, should betray a distinctly classical upbringing. In some scenes she is almost a pure-bred Corneillian heroine. Quick to put her principles of duty before her love, she acts and speaks in the manner of Chimène:

[1] 1769 ms., act II, scene iii.

Ophélie. Tu vas souiller ta gloire.
Hamlet. Ma gloire est d'être fils.
Ophélie. Et la mienne à mon tour
  Est au devoir du sang d'immoler mon amour...
  Mon devoir désormais m'est dicté par le tien.
  Tu cours venger ton père et moi sauver le mien.[1]

She embodies the masculine, self-willed aggressiveness of an Emilie as she asserts her independence and fearless attitude towards dying in the service of her honour and the fulfilment of her personal *gloire*. Her love for Hamlet is illegal and defiantly asserts itself once the old king is dead. One cannot help but see in her plight a suggestion of that of Aricie in Racine's *Phèdre*. She, too, is loved by the son of the man who has decreed that she should never marry. Though from their clash of wills Hamlet will emerge set on revenge, Ophélie will not go mad and drown herself. It is not in the nature of the Corneillian heroine to capitulate. Her virtue and dutiful conduct will reap the same just rewards as those of Hamlet and they will finally marry.

Thanks to Ophélie, Hamlet is free to face the cardboard figure of Claudius, the conventional usurper. He is a monstrous villain, cruel and motivated by ambition. But, as is the case with all of Ducis's villains, he is quite naive and uncomplicated. And even here Ducis is eager to alleviate in some mild way the man's callousness by almost presenting him with a valid excuse for murder. The old king's decree forbidding Ophélie to marry amounts to an injustice towards his family and even Gertrude does not deny that her husband acted harshly towards Claudius in failing to give due recognition to the latter's services to the state.[2] And when his time comes, Claudius has the decency to commit suicide and so spare Hamlet the trouble of soiling his hands with his blood.[3]

Of Norceste, Polonius and Elvire little need be said. Classical tragedy traditionally required *confidents* to fill the basically technical role of wheedling out of their superiors their states of mind, or acting as chorus or messenger, bringing to the attention of the audience knowledge of events which either time, place or decency prevented from being shown on stage. Norceste is such a man. Replacing Horatio, Rosencrantz and Guildenstern, he prompts Hamlet to explain the visitations of the ghost and obligingly goes and fetches the urn for the prince. Polonius, relieved of the parentage of Ophélie, becomes the usurper's right-hand man, a kind of Narcisse to Claudius's Néron, and is required simply to act as silent interlocutor whilst Claudius gives a ninety-one-line exposé of the initial political situation. After the first scene of the play, he is given nothing more to say.[4] Elvire is asked to do nothing except listen patiently to Gertrude's confession and report dutifully to her mistress the details of the final offstage battle. All three are simply instrumental in a dastardly classical plot to substitute for action words, words, words.

The lengthy *récit* is an inevitable consequence of the observance of the unity of place and, as we have seen, Ducis religiously respects the unities of place, time and action.

The theorists saw unity of tone as a necessary corollary to unity of action and consequently ruled out any mixing of genres. To this was inseparably bound a respect of the proprieties. Since tragedy concerned kings and princes, the general action of the play had constantly to

[1] 1769 ms., act IV, scene ii.
[2] 1769 ms., act I, scene ii.
[3] Ducis appears to have been dissatisfied with Claudius's fate, however, for in the first publication of the play, in 1770, he has the usurper steep himself deeper in crime by stabbing Gertrude and then jesting wickedly about it in the fashion of a Richard III. This time an offstage suicide would have been altogether too noble an end for Claudius. Hamlet, accordingly, runs him through in full view of the audience.
[4] Polonius does reappear very fleetingly just once at the end of the play (v, iv), at the head of the rebels. And we hear from Elvire that he ultimately receives just punishment for his misdeeds.

reflect the genteel and dignified elegance of a social elite. The characters were made to speak in highly polished alexandrine verse, so falsely noble and unreal that often an elaborate periphrasis was needed to avoid calling a spade a spade. Ducis bows politely to this set of harsh principles.[1] The Gravediggers, whose vulgar and humorous remarks would lower the tone of the proceedings, are excluded. The wandering wit of Polonius's senile mind is similarly inadmissible. And Ophélie's new-found father provides her with the noble blood she will need if she is to aspire to the regal hand of a Hamlet who has never heard of Wittemburg University. Gone, too, is the comic effeminacy of Osric, whose services are not required in any case since there is no fencing match. Indeed Ducis is careful to avoid any suspicion of unseemly violence and clash of swords on stage in his *dénoûment*. Hamlet deals with the insurrection in the wings and the audience is left to reconstruct the battle from Elvire's inoffensive narrative.

A major offence to unity of tone for Ducis is Shakespeare's play within a play. However, he lights upon an ingenious – if not entirely original[2] – substitute which not only acts as a 'Mouse-trap' but also replaces in part the closet scene. The urn's the thing in which Ducis will catch the criminal conscience. Having publicly carried around and exhibited the urn containing the dead king's ashes, partially to inspire himself to vengeance and partially to force the criminals to betray their guilt, Hamlet encounters his mother and, thrusting it at her heart,[3] forces her to swear her innocence over the said urn. She cannot do so and faints.

It is perhaps hardly necessary to explain that, for reasons of propriety, this interview between mother and son takes place in an unspecified main chamber of the palace and not in Gertrude's private closet. But that Ducis was taking a bold step in including such an interview at all is undeniable. However, here as elsewhere, he tempers his rashness by toning down Shakespeare's realism. Though the prince accuses his mother and even raises his arm to her in momentary defiance of the natural instincts of filial tenderness, his actual language to her is no more licentious than it has been to Ophélie. Here good taste and breeding forbid any reference to 'reechy kisses' just as earlier they had forbidden any talk of 'country matters'. Hamlet is very polite and even when Gertrude faints Ducis sees to it that there is no untidiness. An armchair is conveniently at hand to catch the unconscious queen.[4]

Despite, or perhaps because of, the two abortive attempts by Voltaire to introduce a ghost on to the stage,[5] Ducis is embarrassed by the supernatural element and, albeit reluctantly, sacrifices the ghost as a visible stage presence, leaving him in Hamlet's mind's eye.[6]

---

[1] In the 1770 edition, in an obvious attempt to render the murder of the old king a little less improbable, Ducis has Gertrude tell us that her late husband

Empruntait le secours de ces puissants breuvages
Dont un art bienfaisant montra les avantages...

In other words, the old man was on medicines!

[2] Charles Collé (*Journal et mémoires, 1748–1772* (Paris, 1868), p. 238) was quick to point out that a similar urn device had been successfully employed by Sophocles in his *Electra* and badly imitated by Voltaire in his *Oreste*.

[3] The 1769 ms. stage direction reads, '*il lui apuye l'urne sur la poitrine*'.

[4] In later versions of this scene, Ducis also provides a strategically-placed table upon which Hamlet can quietly replace the urn.

[5] In *Eryphile* (1732) and *Semiramis* (1748). It should be remembered that it was the presence of spectators seated on stage which had robbed Voltaire's spectral entrances of their effect and turned them into ludicrous farces. By 1769, however, this particular inconvenience was a thing of the past.

[6] Even though Ducis himself makes it quite clear in his letter to Garrick (quoted above) that he must regretfully dispense with Shakespeare's Ghost, confusion still exists as to whether, for at least one performance, Ducis did not change his mind. In a variant scene added to the 1770 edition, the ghost is heard to

But if dreams and the hero's imagination can accommodate with classical unobtrusiveness the ghost's physical presence, the contemporary taste for the funereal is a different matter. Again the fateful urn is shaped to this purpose and with its ashes actually groaning as Hamlet carries it about with him –

Hamlet (*montrant l'urne*). Mais de mon père, o ciel !
je sens frémir la cendre
Mes transports jusqu'à lui se sont-ils fait entendre?
O poudre des tombeaux, qui vient vous agiter?
Est-ce pour m'affermir ou pour m'épouvanter?
Cendre plaintive et chère, oui, j'entends ton
murmure:
Oui, ce poignard sanglant va laver ton injure;[1]

it becomes a fitting source of morbid pleasure for an audience taught by Baculard d'Arnaud how to appreciate the grim insignia of death and the strange power they had to titillate the emotions.

It is all too easy to discard this first French adaptation of Shakespeare for the stage as a gross travesty without fully recognising the fact that Ducis did extend Shakespeare's foothold on the continent.[2] He gave to the Bard a viewing audience in France where formerly he had only had a reading public. And this audience applauded loudly even though at the outset the play was something of a *succès de scandale*. First-night critics were by no means unanimous in their praise. Diderot suggested that it was only a frenzied display of histrionics by Molé in the title role that saved the play from being hissed.[3] Indeed the audience had jeered Hamlet at one point, for daring to threaten his mother with a dagger in the closet scene. The critics were divided in their opinion of the urn device. Some, though surprisingly regretting the suppression of the play scene, found the urn to be a happy invention. Others, like Collé, for whom the play as a whole was nothing short of '*une plate abomination*', flatly denied it any validity.[4] Diderot, who liked the urn, thought that Shakespeare's Ghost, if a

ghost was necessary in the first place, was infinitely preferable to Ducis's. At least he did not command Hamlet to kill his mother. Of the play as a whole, Diderot said that he was more readily able to suffer Shakespeare's monster than Ducis's scarecrow and suggested that Ducis would be better advised to leave playwriting well alone.

But Ducis chose to ignore Diderot's advice. Indeed, carried forward on a wave of public acclamation, he proceeded to adapt five more of Shakespeare's plays before the end of the century.[5] His *Hamlet*, however, was to remain a problem for him. Within two weeks of its opening night, after only five performances, Ducis began to rework his first draft. When Talma took over the role of the prince in 1803, bringing with him a sound knowledge of English as well as enormous acting talent, revision work was intensified. But if the influence of Talma on subsequent versions of *Hamlet* was great, still greater had been that of the Revolution and fast-evolving literary taste. There was also the considerable role played

order Hamlet '*Frappe*' as the prince prepares to strike his mother. There is one interesting report, however, quoted by Mme Sylvie Chevalley in her article, 'Ducis, Shakespeare, et les comédiens français, 1', *Revue d'histoire du théâtre*, IV (1964), 332, n. 14, which reads: 'L'ombre d'un roi assassiné paraissait dans le quatrième acte et prononçait d'une voix lugubre, l'arrêt de mort de ses meurtriers…M. Ducis fut obligé d'affaiblir sa pièce pour la rendre plus raisonnable' (*Journal de Paris*, 17 April 1803).

[1] 1769 ms., act IV, scene iii.

[2] Ducis's *Hamlet* was translated into Italian, Spanish and Dutch, his *Roméo et Juliette* into Swedish and his *Roi Léar* and *Othello* into Russian (Ph. van Tieghem, *Le Préromantisme* (1947), III, 246–8). Ducis's *Hamlet* was still being played in the Netherlands as late as 1878 (see Brian Downs, Anglo-Dutch Relations, 1869–1900', *MLR*, XXXI (1963), 335).

[3] Diderot, *Œuvres complètes* (Paris, 1875–7), VIII, 471–6.

[4] Collé, *Journal*.

[5] *Romeo and Juliet* (1772); *King Lear* (1783); *Macbeth* (1784); *King John* (1791); and *Othello* (1792).

by Pierre Letourneur, who from 1776 to 1782 gave the French a relatively faithful translation to read. The effect of all this was to make Ducis bolder and his *Hamlet* received some small benefit. In 1809 a recognisable equivalent of the 'To be or not to be' soliloquy was inserted. Whilst the urn was still used to extract a confession from Gertrude, a device much more akin to the play within a play was introduced to catch the conscience of the criminals: Norceste relates how an anonymous English monarch has recently been poisoned by his consort. The fifth act was entirely revised, in one version Claudius actually being killed by Hamlet on stage. But despite these modifications, the play in which Talma starred for twenty-six years and which did not finally leave the repertory of the Comédie-Française until 1851, after 203 performances, was fundamentally the same as that first seen in 1769. The scarecrow finally died aged eighty-two.

© J. D. GOLDER 1971

THE HAMLET IN HENRY ADAMS

CHARLES VANDERSEE

The world is a fit theatre to-day in which any part may be acted. There is this moment proposed to me every kind of life that men lead anywhere, or that imagination can paint. By another spring I may be a mail-carrier in Peru, or a South African planter, or a Siberian exile, or a Greenland whaler, or a settler on the Columbia River, or a Canton merchant, or a soldier in Florida, or a mackerel fisher off Cape Sable, or a Robinson Crusoe in the Pacific, or a silent navigator of any sea. So wide is the choice of parts, what a pity if the part of Hamlet be left out!

> HENRY DAVID THOREAU, diary entry for 21 March 1840; first published in the *Atlantic Monthly*, January 1905.

The aim of the artist is psychologic, not historic truth.

> JAMES RUSSELL LOWELL, 'Shakespeare Once More' (1868).

I

As Thoreau recognized in 1840, America was not a land likely to produce Hamlets. The mood of the country was expansionist and brash, the summons of the West being responded to with fervor and the needed technology for a bustling nation rapidly developing. 'Puritan fanatics like Goodyear brought to the vulcanization of rubber the same intense passion that Thoreau brought to Nature', Lewis Mumford has observed (*The Golden Day*), and it hardly needs adding that the national passion which was to gain the ascendancy was decisively that for rubber. It was not that Americans were incapable of serious reflection and patient philosophizing. But one undertook such concerns at his peril,

and in direct opposition to the frenetic spirit prevailing in his compatriots. As soon as America spied a thinker, it grew apprehensive. Thus Emerson, though issuing a bold manifesto in his famous 'American Scholar' address of 1837, felt himself called upon to operate from a defensive position also. With ill-concealed sarcasm he noted his countrymen's excessive alarm.

Our age is bewailed as the age of Introversion. Must that needs be evil? We, it seems, are critical; we are embarrassed with second thoughts; we cannot enjoy any thing for hankering to know whereof the pleasure consists; we are lined with eyes; we see with our feet; the time is infected with Hamlet's unhappiness,
  'Sicklied o'er with the pale cast of thought.'

Paradoxically, *Hamlet* was popular in America at this time (as throughout the century), perhaps because of Hamlet's very contrast to the admired national types.[1] The young, literate, and introspective Prince would have been an odd bird indeed to American audiences, and his play a glimpse of the pathos and tragedy that seemed, from a New World point of view, to be receding happily into the very distant past. To be sure, there were some cultivated men on the Eastern seaboard for whom the play was filled with power rather than merely curiosity. One such

---

[1] See Esther Dunn, *Shakespeare in America* (New York, 1939), pp. 209, 211, and elsewhere; Robert Falk, 'Shakespeare in America: A Survey to 1900', *Shakespeare Survey 18* (Cambridge, 1965), pp. 102–19.

was the former President of the United States, John Quincy Adams. Turned out of office by the Tennessee democrat, Andrew Jackson, Adams was reduced to the office of Massachusetts Congressman in 1839 when the Shakespearian actor James H. Hackett wrote to ask his opinion of Hamlet. Widely known as a Shakespeare buff, his idolatry beginning in childhood, Adams was eager to reply. His habit was to rise at 4 a.m. in order to take care of his private correspondence before going off to the Capitol, and the letter he wrote runs to seven printed pages. To him, Hamlet was 'the personification of a *man*, in the prime of life, with a mind cultivated by the learning acquirable at a university, combining *intelligence* and *sensibility* in their highest degrees, within a step of the highest distinction attainable on earth, crushed to extinction by the pressure of calamities inflicted, not by nature, but against nature – not by physical but by moral evil'.[1]

Just at the time Adams declared his enthusiasm for Hamlet, and Thoreau feared his absence in America, there was born in Boston the thinker and writer who was to become the American Hamlet. This was, oddly enough, John Quincy Adams's grandson, Henry Brooks Adams, born in 1838. *The Education of Henry Adams*, immodestly but accurately called by its publishers 'quite simply the greatest autobiography of American letters', has also and accurately been termed 'the autobiography of an American Hamlet'.[2] It was the climax to a literary career that had included two novels (*Democracy* and *Esther*), two biographies, the masterly nine-volume *History* of Jefferson and Madison, and *Mont-Saint-Michel and Chartres*. By a fitting coincidence Adams was in the process of writing his *Education* in the very year, 1905, that Thoreau's diary reference to Hamlet appeared in print for the first time. Whether Adams saw this plea is not known, but what is perfectly clear is that Adams intended to portray himself as a Hamlet figure, that un-

likeliest of characters in nineteenth-century America. Four allusions in the *Education* help make this clear, two of them occurring as Adams neared Hamlet's own age of thirty. Both passages allude to lines from Hamlet's famous soliloquy on indecision:

> Thus conscience does make cowards of us all;
> And thus the native hue of resolution
> Is sicklied o'er with the pale cast of thought,
> And enterprises of great pitch and moment
> With this regard their currents turn awry,
> And lose the name of action.   (III, i, 83–8)

The first instance referred to the English anti-slavery 'eccentrics' of the 1860s, men such as Henry Reeve of the *Edinburgh Review*, whom Adams had known when he spent the Civil War years in London as secretary to his father, the American minister to the Court of St James's. As Adams recalled them forty years later, these men had the virtue of moral earnestness, but it was cancelled out by dogmatism and cautious reserve. Idealists they were, but rigidly so, and as a consequence they turned out to be 'mute and useless' in the political arena. 'As a class', wrote Adams, 'they were timid – with good reason – and timidity, which is high wisdom in philosophy, sicklies the whole cast of thought in action' (192). Such men were 'the followers of Tocqueville, and of John Stuart Mill', and Adams, as he wryly confessed elsewhere,[3] felt himself one of them. Later on

---

[1] To James H. Hackett, 19 February 1839. Hackett, *Notes and Comment upon Certain Plays and Actors of Shakespeare, with Criticisms and Correspondence* (New York, 1863), p. 193.

[2] Halford Luccock, *Contemporary American Literature and Religion* (Chicago, 1934), p. 137. *The Education of Henry Adams* was published privately in 1907 and by Houghton Mifflin (Boston) in 1918. Later printings, including the Modern Library edition, have the same pagination. Page references are in parentheses.

[3] Years later Adams wrote to Charles Milnes Gaskell, an English friend: 'Our epoch of John Stuart Mill and de Tocqueville and Henry Reeve and the Duke of Argyll, is as far away as that of Rousseau and of John the Precursor. What is to happen next does

in the *Education*, when he described how his own days of backstage politics and muck-raking journalism ended, and his 'nervous energy ran low' (316), the Adams of the *Education* came to look more and more like these English 'eccentrics'.

The second passage had to do not with politics but with evolutionary theory. Like other thinking young men of the 1860s, Adams had come under the spell of Darwinism – everybody's 'new hobby' (231) – and the idea of progress that it implied. To most intellectuals the Darwinian scheme was one more truth happily discovered in an increasingly comprehensible world. An interval of Hamlet-like introspection revealed to Adams, however, that he himself cared nothing about how true the hypothesis was, but only about how interesting it was. He concluded, uncomfortably, that 'he was a Darwinian for fun'.

Mr. [Charles Francis] Adams, the father, looked on [this attitude] as moral weakness; it annoyed him; but it did not annoy him nearly so much as it annoyed his son [i.e. Henry], who had no need to learn from Hamlet the fatal effect of the pale cast of thought on enterprises great or small. He had no notion of letting the currents of his action be turned awry by this form of conscience. To him, the current of his time was to be his current, lead where it might. (232)

The 'conscience' of which Adams spoke was a name for mental scrupulousness, or what he here described as a 'mania for handling all the sides of every question, looking into every window, and opening every door' (232). James Russell Lowell, in his 1868 essay, 'Shakespeare Once More', was to point out to American readers that Shakespeare's 'conscience' meant 'consciousness'.[1] The *Zeitgeist* would not, as Adams foresaw, tolerate excessive consciousness – a Hamletizing scrutiny of its fashionable dogmas or its frenetic enterprises. It was 'fatal' to one's 'practical usefulness in society' (232). Adams's vow, therefore, was to circumvent the temperamental Hamlet in himself and to

adopt, with proper seriousness, the dogmas and attitudes of his time. It is this temperamental Hamlet in Adams that we shall be exploring, in so far as Adams enforces the parallel on his readers in the *Education*, a highly stylized portrait of himself.

Adams's own awareness of the parallel is sufficient to evoke scrutiny, but the very circumstances of his life, as he chooses certain details and incidents for the *Education*, offer striking parallels to Hamlet's, and thus provide a most intriguing context within which to study the temperamental affinity. Both Hamlet and Henry Adams were royal personages, Hamlet literally and Adams as member of a three-generation dynasty that had supplied the United States with two presidents. ('You'll be thinkin' you'll be President too!' the Irish gardener had told young Henry [16].) Both men in young manhood found 'the times out of joint', Hamlet in the reign of his murderous uncle, and Adams nervously watching from London as the Civil War turned the nation into a battlefield. Both voiced despair in the middle of a glittering world, Hamlet amid the drunken revelry that gained the Danish court notoriety (I, iv, 8–22), and Henry Adams amid the boisterous Gilded Age of American plutocracy as well as *fin-de-siècle* Paris. Both were university scholars, one gracing Wittenberg as student and the other Harvard as both student and professor of medieval history. Both had loves who died tragically, the fair Ophelia driven to madness and the witty but suicidally disturbed Marian, whose presence in the *Education* is established only by enigmatic references to her tombstone in Rock Creek Cemetery (329). Both men had close friends

not necessarily concern us' (10 March 1902). *Letters of Henry Adams 1892–1918*, ed. Worthington Chauncey Ford (Boston and New York, 1938), p. 377.
[1] 'Shakespeare Once More', *Among My Books* (Boston, 1870), p. 213. Originally published in *North American Review*, 106 (April 1868), 629–70.

who functioned as important foils in their life stories: Hamlet's Horatio and Henry Adams's political confidant John Hay. Both believed themselves forced into situations requiring redress, and both undertook it with pathetically mixed results. Hamlet succeeded, circuitously, in revenging his father but died himself; Adams failed to reform a corrupt American government and thus to render viable his family's political ideals, but he survived to write his testament of failure. Both were victims of education, Hamlet suffering from information conveyed him by his father's ghost, Adams tormented by a harrowing vision of the future havoc that science seemed to be calling down upon the world. Finally, and most significant (since the aforementioned correspondences are more curious and informative than really meaningful), both men were tormented by the twin curses of the brilliant and sensitive mind: conscience and consciousness. The two men were, in these respects, near twins in temperament, as many of the most famous passages in the *Education* hint. Adams, for example, claimed to have spent much of his time as a Harvard undergraduate in 'desultory and useless reading' (60), and he later described himself as a typical Harvard student of that era: 'perhaps his worst weakness was his self-criticism and self-consciousness' (65). In the *Education* the theme of his life as professor, journalist, and 'stable-companion to statesmen' (317) turns out to be failure, and not only his famous failure to be educated for life in a modern multiverse. Involved also is his failure to profit from the advantages handed to him, and the failure of his country to persist in the ideals and moral standards of its founders.

II

In the *Education*, the memoirs and the moral fable of the Hamlet who survived, the conscience we encounter is active but ineffectual,

and the operation of consciousness is at best inconclusive. For more than one reason Adams divided his book into two chronological parts, omitting the years between 1872 and 1891. Part one, from birth in 1838 to the corrupt Washington of 1871, deals with Adams's formidable New England conscience and its contribution to Adams's extraordinary discomfort and failure of sorts. Part two, from 1892 until the death of John Hay in 1905, is concerned with consciousness and its role in alienation. As in *Hamlet*, these two leading themes artfully interweave in the *Education*. But the emphasis in the beginning is on conscience (accompanied by ignorance), whereas the last half of the book develops the idea of consciousness (or awareness) and leaves the reader to make his own inferences about the place of conscience.

The conscience of Henry Adams is the 'instinctive' morality that imbedded itself in his character from earliest infancy. This, at least, is what Adams insists that we understand:

Resistance to something was the law of New England nature; the boy looked out on the world with the instinct of resistance; for numberless generations his predecessors had viewed the world chiefly as a thing to be reformed, filled with evil forces to be abolished. (7)

The word 'instinct' is one of Adams's carefully chosen words; elsewhere he refers to his 'nervous system' (148), reinforcing the idea that moralism is something he was born with, an aspect of innate temperament. Insuperably and unchangeably moralistic, this 'nervous system' unfitted him for viewing politics as a mere game or as an impersonal power struggle. Politics could only be seen on the lofty plane of statesmanship: how to administer with justice and prudence the affairs of the people. ''Tis sweet and commendable *in your nature*, Hamlet,/To give these mourning duties to your father', remarks Claudius (I, ii, 87–8; italics mine). The acknowledgment of Hamlet's innate temperament is the same thing Adams seeks from his reader, and it is from this point that the tension in the *Education* begins to mount. For Adams's notion of being born into a Boston morality has a great deal to do with duties to the fathers, not alone the Adams line of statesmen but the 'moral tradition' of New England. Yvor Winters, with his customary thoroughness, has traced the genealogy of this tradition back six centuries to 'the paternity of Ockham',[1] but one need not be quite so precisely concerned with origins. Adams himself was inclined to delve much farther back than the Middle Ages when seeking certain of his moral principles, political ethics in particular. 'It was the old Ciceronian idea of government by *the best* that produced the long line of New England statesmen', remarked Adams in fixing on perhaps the central tenet of his political morality (32, italics Adams's). Speaking more generally, his moral principles went back even further: 'he inherited dogma and *a priori* thought from the beginning of time' (26). Adams's whimsical point here is to stress firmly the impact of traditional values upon himself. Whether one liked the idea of being bound by fixed standards of ethics or not, one *was* bound. 'Grant's administration outraged every rule of ordinary decency' (280), Adams bluntly asserted later in the book. 'The moral law had expired – like the Constitution.' This is virtually the same decisive tone of voice used by Hamlet in referring to his own land under a corrupt and sinning sovereign: ''Tis an unweeded garden,/That grows to seed' (I, ii, 135–6).

For our purposes the implications of such a conscience require attention in order to see why Adams is able to use Hamlet as a spiritual point of reference but at the same time is unwilling to draw a detailed parallel. Looked at in broad terms, the *Education* has a tension that most life studies do not, and certainly most Victorian-era biographies do not. The usual life has as its beginning focus of interest the

question, 'What *can* I do?' as opposed to Adams's implied question, 'What *must* I do?' The typical American questions go on something like this: What am I fitted for? Where do my talents lie? How can I get somebody to recognize my worth? Where can I get some leverage? How far can I finally get? The narrative is of a struggle to get a place, to rise in esteem and worldly goods, to place oneself in as prominent a place as possible within the endlessly expanding American economy. Obstacles can always be overcome (or else the route easily changed); opportunities are as frequent as the rising of the sun. Adams is noticeably different. The question compulsively raised in the whole first section, 'What *must* I do?' means, in Adams's own phrases, 'What do my "New England nature" and my peculiar "nervous system" *compel* me to do in life?' Far from becoming the American self-made man, which John G. Cawelti has recently well characterized,[2] Adams is in quite a different situation. He has *been* made and shaped already; he is not entrusted with making himself. The breath of life called 'education' simply needs to be breathed into his well-shaped Boston nostrils, and thus his pre-existing shape will be filled out.

If his attitude seems dutiful and deferential – even fatalistic – we should immediately recognize a second implicit question that Adams raised, one which will seem as arrogant as the first question is modest. If one has New England values imbedded, *a priori*, in one's 'system',

[1] 'Henry Adams, or the Creation of Confusion', *In Defense of Reason* (New York, 1947), p. 391. 'The history immediately relevant to an understanding of Adams's mind might be said to begin with the first great theological critics of Aquinas, especially with Ockham' (*ibid*. p. 374). See also Austin Warren, *The New England Conscience* (Ann Arbor, 1966), pp. 170–81, for discussion of Adams's moral heritage.
[2] *Apostles of the Self-Made Man* (Chicago, 1965). Cawelti rightly points out that Adams in his best known novel, *Democracy*, deals with self-made men in the realm of American electoral politics (p. 267).

and if one also finds these values subsequently confirmed empirically (e.g. the 'slave states', glimpsed at the age of twelve, represent 'the sum of all wickedness'), then other questions must perforce arise: Not only, 'What must *I* do?' but then 'What must *they* do?' – *they* being, at various times, the Confederate leaders, Grant and his cabinet, the general American public, and the various foreign powers (especially the English ministers), all of whom seemed to lack the Adams/Boston ethical nervous system. That question leads, as a necessary consequence, to two others, much more painful: 'Why aren't they doing it?' 'How can I get them to do it?' To sum up, the leading moral issues in the life of Adams as depicted in the *Education* disregard entirely the ultra-American question, 'Where am I going and how fast will I get there?' in favor of a more complex question filled with a great many more dramatic possibilities. 'Where do *we all have* to go, and how do *I* get us started?' This question accounts for the rich interplay of tensions in the first part of the book, and contributes as well to the surprising modernity of the book, which made it a sort of bible early in the 1920s to a series of lost Americans for whom the Horatio Alger values had paled.

Here in basic outline is Hamlet unmistakably, though Adams avoids a direct comparison. Personal career and wellbeing are secondary; the important thing is to be where one's moral influence can operate, where one can act out one's ethical imperatives. Hamlet abandons Wittenberg, ostensibly at the request of Claudius and his mother, but also in order to stay in Denmark and keep an eye on the suspicious couple. Adams in his early twenties follows his father to London as legation secretary for eight long years, doing secret and propagandistic journalism for part of that time, in order to keep an eye on Gladstone, Russell, and Palmerston. Neither young man worries about gaining a foothold on the ladder of life; his place is virtually guaranteed. Claudius acknowledges Hamlet as 'chiefest courtier', and Adams remarks apropos of his own auspicious family name: 'His social position would never be questioned... Never in his life would he have to explain who he was' (64). The role of *son*, the role of *a priori moralist*, the role of *keen observer* – these are the key similarities, to which must be added the gilt setting: for Hamlet the king's court; for Adams, access to the most crucial diplomatic post of the Civil War and later, briefly, admission to the confidence of high Washington officials during the Reconstruction era (243–82).

From here the pattern in Adams's *Education* diverges slightly from *Hamlet*. The revenge and subterfuge which are so important for Hamlet are played down in the *Education*, though they were fully present in Adams's life and quite often can be discerned between the lines of the *Education*. Adams devotes two striking pages, for example, to his extensive but anonymous journalism in 1860–1 (120–1). On some thirty occasions he had sent indiscreet dispatches from London, which editor Henry Raymond of the New York *Times* gladly and prominently published. For the American minister's son to be using pen and ink at the Legation for purposes of criticizing England in a home newspaper was dangerously indiscreet. Moreover, his advice to the North is rightly understood in retrospect as an attempt to stage a play that would catch the attention (if not necessarily the conscience) of the Queen's ministers. Adams stressed the need for military victories, for immediate emancipation of slaves, for anything that would make the North appear strong and thus keep Foreign Secretary Russell from supporting the Confederacy.[1] This Hamlet-like subterfuge Adams

[1] Ernest Samuels discusses this phase of Adams's life in *The Young Henry Adams* (Cambridge, Mass., 1948), pp. 97–112. Adams also wrote letters to the son of Secretary of State William H. Seward as a part

passed over quickly in the *Education*, and he omitted entirely his one great effort to revenge his fathers. This was the now-famous biography of John Randolph, which he published in 1883. The outspoken Randolph, a Virginian, had been a bitter enemy of John Adams and John Quincy Adams both, and family enmity (compounded by regional suspicion) had remained inflamed over the decades. Henry Adams's scorn is amply evident throughout the book, as he portrays to the point of caricature the madness and ill temper of Randolph. Adams's biographer refers to the book as his 'golden opportunity' for revenge against the man who had denied his grandfather re-election as President. The eccentric Virginian appears in *John Randolph* as an irresponsible Quixote and a jealous Iago; in private Adams called him a 'lunatic monkey' and complained about having been 'obliged to treat him as though he were respectable'.[1] Randolph's moral failure lay in traducing the Adamses' standards of statesmanship: he was 'violent, tyrannical, vicious, cruel, and licentious in language as in morals' – 'unintelligible and monstrous' to what Adams called 'a New England man'. To Adams's considerable satisfaction, the book sold well.

But again, within the pages of the *Education* both the filial revenge and the behind-the-scenes contriving are underplayed, lest the Hamlet analogy appear too blatant. The conscience-laden Hamlet that remains is the observer, the lamenter, and the would-be reformer. A. C. Bradley in 1904, the year before Adams wrote the *Education*, speculated of a younger Hamlet that 'Doubtless in happier days he was a close and constant observer of men and manners'.[2] The Adams of the *Education* uses the image of a card game to make the same point about himself: 'Probably no child, born in the year [1838], held better cards than he...As it happened, he never got to the point of playing the game at all; he lost himself in the study of it, watching the errors of the players' (4). The moral errors were those that were especially noticeable, and Adams throughout the book vivified them by making them visible to the eye as well as referring to them abstractly. Slavery, seen in Maryland in 1850, struck him in this manner:

The railway, about the size and character of a modern tram, rambled through unfenced fields and woods, or through village streets, among a haphazard variety of pigs, cows, and negro babies who might all have used the cabins for pens and styes, had the Southern pig required styes, but who never showed a sign of care. This was the boy's impression of what slavery caused... (44)[3]

The seasoning he underwent in London during the Civil War, being privy to his father's diplomacy, gave him a chance to observe the presumed duplicity of Earl Russell. This too had a visual embodiment: '*Punch*, before 1862, commonly drew Russell as a schoolboy telling lies, and afterwards as prematurely senile, at seventy' (164). The horrifying scandals under Grant's administration likewise were visible to the eye, in Adams's two vivid metaphors:

The worst scandals of the eighteenth century were relatively harmless by the side of this, which smirched executive, judiciary, banks, corporate systems, professions, and people, all the great active forces of society, in one dirty cesspool of vulgar corruption... already he [Adams] foresaw a life of wasted energy, sweeping the stables of American society clean of the endless corruption... (272–3)

of his quiet but determined activism. They are printed with an introduction in Charles Vandersee, 'Henry Adams Behind the Scenes: Civil War Letters to Frederick W. Seward', *Bulletin of the New York Public Library*, 71 (April 1967), 245–64.

[1] Ernest Samuels, *Henry Adams: The Middle Years* (Cambridge, Mass., 1958), pp. 186–7. Adams, *John Randolph* (1883; rpt New York, 1961), pp. 25, 184.

[2] *Shakespearean Tragedy*, 2nd ed. (London, 1905), p. 114.

[3] I am quoting a less familiar passage to make the point. Most readers of the *Education* will also recall his famous analogy between the badness of the road that leads to Mount Vernon and the evil of Southern slavery (47).

To function as 'close and constant observer' was thus literally to confront evil with the senses as well as with the mind. We recollect Hamlet vividly speaking of the 'salt of most unrighteous tears' and the 'incestuous sheets' of his mother, and the 'funeral bak'd-meats' that 'Did coldly furnish forth the marriage tables' (I, ii, 180–1).

The next step for a moralist beyond mere observation is protest – some verbal articulation of outrage. Adams's chapter 'Free Fight' (1869–70) begins with remarks about his 'splenetic temper' (269) in the face of the 'unnecessary evils' of nature – bad climates and the differentiation of sexes. Behind this banter (not too far removed from Hamlet's discerning of camels, whales, and weasels in the clouds), lay the serious moral outrage over existing political evils. Adams again used journalism as the outlet for his anger and devotes the chapter to two scandalous occurrences in particular. One was the notorious and brazen effort by financier Jay Gould to corner the US gold supply in 1869, which Adams wrote up for the *Edinburgh Review*. The other scandal was within the government itself, as executive, legislative and judicial branches all engaged in mutual destruction. The Senate chamber was a particular focus for this national chaos, being 'a scene of irritated egotism that passed ridicule. Senators...picked quarrels with each other, and no one objected, but they picked quarrels also with the Executive and threw every Department into confusion' (278–9). The newspapers, reported Adams, 'discussed little else than the alleged moral laxity of [President] Grant, [Congressman] Garfield, and [Speaker of the House] Blaine' (280). Adams himself summarized it all in a long and angry essay for the *North American Review* ('The Session').

His intent was destruction, annihilation of the evil itself and thorough reformation of the men. Both articles struck their mark, but with little consequence. Hamlet's dramatic simula-tion of his father's murder had at least the effect of interrupting the performance and driving his uncle from the audience. Adams's articles were instantly read widely and pirated by other periodicals, and the 'Session' piece dealing with Congress was even 'reprinted by the Democratic National Committee and circulated as a campaign document by the hundred thousand copies' (292). The moral effect, however, was nil. Readers he had, but the cry of conscience, the 'active enmity' to-ward corruption that the articles represented (281), failed to arouse the American public. 'Not one person, man or woman offer[ed] him so much as a congratulation, except to call him a begonia' (292). Begonia was the epithet applied to him by a Wisconsin senator, evidently in scornful measurement of the weak-ness of a moral stance in the America of 1870 – an 'unweeded garden' if ever there was one. Or, to use Adams's own specific allusion to *Hamlet*: 'On the whole, even for Senators, diplomats, and Cabinet officers, the period was wearisome and stale' (295).

The conflicts thus set up between the New England conscience and the succession of British and American politicians do not, as in *Hamlet*, lead into violent combat and a spec-tacular denouement. 'Barren and dangerous' the Washington politicos might be (297), but Adams does not emerge as a knight to combat them in the political arena directly or as a shrewd gamester to defeat them with clever strategy. His moralizing is verbal and direct, much as the Hamlet who cries to his mother, 'O shame! Where is thy blush?' But none of the soiled politicians find themselves con-victed – none cries that his heart is cleft in twain. A mere 'begonia', Adams is not even honored with an attempt to be bought off, much less exalted, like Hamlet, with a commission to have his head struck off. For all practical purposes, except for one transitory political campaign, he is ignored. The first half of

Adams's book ends with Adams quite resigned to failure. 'Henceforth, he went on, submissive' (313). This is the last line of the last chapter in the first section, appropriately titled 'Failure'. We recognize that the Hamlet analogy which up to now has seemed so plain is an analogy concerned specifically with temperament, which Adams wisely refuses to carry into plot or structure. Hamlet plunges on; Adams withdraws from the struggle.

III

What occurs in the second half of the *Education* is therefore not a heightening of the specific moral tensions and conflicts of the first part. Instead, it is an attempt to examine thoroughly the world in which they take place, the world in which 'moral law' seems to have expired. This examination shows us the other aspect of Hamlet's character residing in Adams, the quality of consciousness and awareness. We see Adams putting forth this trait for our consideration as we begin the chapter entitled 'Twenty Years After'. The year is now 1892, and Adams's days of journalistic activism and moral outrage have been left behind. The twenty years had been spent teaching medieval history at Harvard, editing the illustrious *North American Review*, writing nine volumes of American history, and quietly penning two novels. 'Henry Adams thought his own duties sufficiently performed and his account with society settled' (315–16). There is thus a distinct chronological separation that Adams insists upon: one's hereditary 'duties', moral and vocational, occupied the first half of life, and now to be undertaken is serious thought, the painful exertion of the intellect. The mind as active probing agent takes over to replace the mind as passive repository of *a priori* morality. As noted, this sharp dichotomy perhaps more than anything else prevents Adams from enforcing the Hamlet analogy step by step throughout the *Education*. In *Hamlet*, con-

science and consciousness exist inextricably; it is ludicrous to try to think of Hamlet relaxing his vigil or becoming 'submissive'. Adams, with a whole lifetime to portray, finds the dichotomy structurally important, in setting off his life into distinct phases. Yet in the long run the reader cannot help noticing that Adams wants things both ways. He wishes to emphasize consciousness in the last half of his life, yet he makes plain from the beginning that a predisposition toward that consciousness does exist from boyhood. 'Restless-minded, introspective, self-conscious' are the adjectives Adams applies to himself and his brothers from childhood on (28). As early as the fourth page of his narrative he stresses that in him were intensified certain New England traits, 'the habit of doubt; of distrusting his own judgment ...; the tendency to regard every question as open...' (6). In short, we are to understand that a predisposition to self-consciousness and mental awareness exists in Adams from boyhood, even if this seems to be operating only at half-capacity during the first three-and-a-half decades of life. The critical and questioning faculty, dormant and unaware of the right questions to ask, coexists in the boy and man with an unthinking *a priori* moralism. Contradictory as this sounds – a habit of distrust going along with unquestioning assent – Adams seems to insist upon it. His reason becomes clear only in the second part of the book. We need only contrast two passages, the first from chapter two:

Viewed from Mount Vernon Street [the Adams boyhood home], the problem of life was as simple as it was classic. Politics offered no difficulties, for there the moral law was a sure guide. Social perfection was also sure, because human nature worked for Good, and three instruments were all she asked – Suffrage, Common Schools, and Press. On these points doubt was forbidden. (33)

On these principles, and with faith in this Mount Vernon trinity Adams had operated, unconscious of their virtual obsolescence, until the decade of the 1870s. One might very well be born with a propensity for doubt, but doubt stopped at these three icons. The Adams of 1892, however, was beginning to wake into full consciousness, and with consciousness the secure icons of youth vanish in a mist of uncertainty. The second passage is from chapter 21:

The new world he faced in Paris and London seemed to him fantastic. Willing to admit it real in the sense of having some kind of existence outside his own mind, he could not admit it reasonable [i.e. by his old Mount Vernon standards]...As he saw the world, it was no longer simple and could not express itself simply. It should express what it was; and this was something that neither Adams nor [his friend John] La Farge understood. (317)

Two ideas are here for our attention. First, the consciousness which had always existed, but only in latent form, now arouses itself. Second, the stimulus for this arousing is the very newness of the modern world, which has become so striking as finally to make an impact on the mind. It is this acute awareness of the 'new world' – and the *sudden* awareness, Adams would have us believe – that defines the consciousness of Adams, his own peculiar 'pale cast of thought' that kept him for the remaining twenty-odd years of his life trying to find scientific and social patterns to deal with this newness.

The fruit of this contemplation finally turned out to be a theory of history that would account for the direction of history if not for its details. We recall that Hamlet, in the speech Adams has twice referred to, meditates on the likely consequences of consciousness: 'enterprises of great pitch and moment...lose the name of action'. Hamlet does not articulate in the speech the path he himself follows, a path which unites thought with action, which puts consciousness to active use so that effective action may follow. That is also the path that Adams follows in the

last half of the *Education*. It is the quest to find out what is going on in the world, so that one can deal with it. Hamlet follows the movements of the King, has clandestine conversation with the Queen, interrogates Rosencrantz and Guildenstern, and in general conducts himself as a sleepless and earnest one-man intelligence-gathering agency. And he is finally able to have his acquired knowledge consummated in action. Adams moves on a philosophical level. He tries to find out what is going on in terms of science and history. And the final result of his efforts culminates not in action for himself but in a gentle hope that others may benefit. If man wishes to lead a successful life, his only hope lies in this very consciousness or awareness, not in mere action alone, which is the flaw of most Americans (297), and not in mere reflex response to *a priori* morals. The famous lines of the preface express quite clearly the intended link between Adams's theorizing and a later generation's practice that might follow from it: the 'object, in this Volume, is to fit young men, in universities or elsewhere, to be men of the world, equipped for any emergency' (xxiv). Thus it is here again clear that the basic temperament of Adams is akin to that of Hamlet, and in a general sense their aims are similar. Only at the end is there a sharp divergence, for if Adams had pushed the analogy too far he would have had to make his book a tragedy. As we shall later spell out, this is by no means the logical outcome or the chosen intent.

The temperamental affinity of Adams with Hamlet, as an inquiring spirit determined to find out what is going on, begins to develop in the second chapter of the second section of the *Education* (chapter 22). Here Adams talks about 'a starting point for a new education' (337), about seeming 'to feel that something new and curious was about to happen in the world' (338), about discovering that 'life had taken on a new face' (339). The year is now 1893, notable to Adams for a panic in Wall

Street, a world's fair in Chicago, and the re-appearance in his life of his iconoclastic brother Brooks, 'a vigorous thinker who irritated too many Boston conventions ever to suit the [Boston] atmosphere' (338). These three novelties combined to suggest to Adams more things than he had dreamed of in his philosophy before. The panic seemed to demonstrate that even the shrewdest and wisest men of the world – those who manipulated money – were victims of 'some very powerful energy at work' which 'nobody understood' (338). The Columbian Exposition in Chicago, with its anachronistic architecture and fantastic Midway, was an 'in-conceivable scenic display', an utterly chaotic 'Babel of loose and ill-joined...vague and ill-defined and unrelated thoughts and half-thoughts and experimental outcries' (340). As for Brooks, he brought to Adams a new hypothesis, or 'law of history', that seemed to prove the real nature of things to be 'instability' tending toward 'anarchism' (339). In short, when the dormant mind woke up in 1893 it found that the world it looked upon was chaos. One seems for the moment, at this critical point in the *Education*, to be transposed out of *Hamlet*, where 'the time is out of joint', into *Lear*, where 'all's cheerless, dark, and deadly'. Is chaos the law, or is there order in the chaos? This was the question to occupy Adams until he wrote the *Education* in 1905–6 and then for some ten more years.

It must be noticed that Adams's pursuit of scientific and metaphysical truth is on a dif-ferent plane from Hamlet's pursuit of existential truth. To seek to discover how the world runs is a different problem from trying to find out what is on Claudius's calculating mind and what is making Gertrude act the way she does. Yet the alertness of the intellect is the same, and, more important, the self-conscious aspect of the pursuit looms large in both minds. Both Adams and Hamlet keep holding open house in their minds, as it were, pointing out to the

audience how well aware they are of what they are doing and what they hope to accomplish by it. We readily accept the device of soliloquy in *Hamlet* as one convention that places us in the self-revealing mind of the speaker, but we have in addition such self-conscious interior revelation as Hamlet's declaration of aware-ness to Guildenstern: 'You would play upon me...you would seem to know my stop, you would pluck out the heart of my mystery... you cannot play upon me' (III, ii, 380 ff.). Or, the self-conscious explanation of his destined role, spoken to Gertrude after having stabbed Polonius:

Heaven hath pleas'd it so,
To punish me with this [Polonius] and this with me,
That I must be their scourge and minister.

(III, iv, 173 ff.)

The maps of Adams's mind and charts of his mental voyaging during the late years are open for inspection on page after page of the *Education*, the author being, as he frankly admits, 'engaged in studying his own mind' (434). The closing chapters of the *Education* give us a sense of isolation, a feeling that Adams as an old man is gradually withdrawing into the dark recesses of his mind to commune with himself and with whatever wisdom is available between the pages of books. 'He got out his Descartes again; dipped into his Hume and Berkeley; wrestled anew with Kant; pon-dered solemnly over his Hegel and Schopen-hauer and Hartmann...' (431–2). The names of scientists further sprinkle his perplexed pages: Gibbs, Pearson, Stallo, Haeckel, Mach, Poincaré. The conflict which Adams is thus engaged in as he nears the climax of his book is one which involves the clash of competing theories, a combat of abstractions rather than a duel with rapier and dagger. Adams himself was uncomfortable with his ending; to try to tack an argumentative conclusion onto a book that has been predominantly narrative seemed an error of form.[1] But there is consistency of theme, as the consciousness latent in the 'eighteenth-century' Boston child from the beginning becomes an active and struggling force seeking mastery of twentieth-century chaos the world over. Fully aware that consciousness 'makes cowards', Adams and Hamlet both set up strong resistance to this tendency.

IV

Specific focus on these two traits of temperament, conscience and consciousness, is to suggest why it is that readers over the years have sensed an affinity between Adams and Shakespeare's Hamlet. The extended comparison does not exhaust the similarities, for in addition to the biographical parallels mentioned earlier one can without much difficulty construct a much longer list of temperamental and emotional affinities. Such a list is attempted by an affectionate reader of the Adams self-revealed in his published letters, as distinguished from the highly stylized view that Adams gives of his life in the *Education*. Louis Kronenberger declares:

If Henry Adams was Hamlet in that he lacked the resolution to help avenge the murder of his grandfather's and his great-grandfather's dreams; if he was Hamlet in that he, in the *Education*, like the Prince of Denmark in his soliloquies, had a fine gift for dramatizing himself, if he was Hamlet in possessing a reflective and humorous nature, veined with sensibility and streaked with cruelty and disgust, and masculine in its thinking and feminine in its emotions – if he was Hamlet in all these things, he was Hamlet in one thing more: in relishing his privileged place in life ... year after year Henry Adams crossed to Europe on luxury liners and for months on end moved about Europe at least as much prince as Hamlet – in a succession of splendid hotels and country houses, and in an atmosphere not always so conspicuous for seriousness of thought or loftiness of purpose ...

Kronenberger is wrong in his initial statement, regarding a lack of resolution to avenge his ancestors, as we have noted above. But the rest of his remarks, pertaining as they do mostly to Adams's life rather than to his book, suggest further lines that might be followed if one were to read between the lines for a more extensive parallel between the two men. Briefer analogies by other scholars are also suggestive. Ernest Samuels, whose three-volume biography is authoritative, observes Adams's 'Hamlet-like indecision which was the other side of his passion for dogmatic generalization'. This is in reference to Adams's skeptical ambivalence toward the scientists he was reading and from whom he was deriving his law of history. Grant C. Knight, apropos of the same scientific researches, intriguingly suggests that Adams was 'a "Hamlet" substituting the second law of thermodynamics for a father's ghost'. Richard Chase, in his dialogue, *The Democratic Vista*, has one character remark: 'Adams is the most famous example of the modern American Hamlet, whose character and thought are finally neutralized by contradictions, rather than being inspirited and enlivened by them.'[2]

[1] Mixing 'narrative and didactic purpose and style' is something that 'cannot be successfully done'. 'I found that a narrative style was so incompatible with a didactic or scientific style, that I had to write a long supplementary chapter to explain in scientific terms what I could not put into narration without ruining the narrative.' To Barrett Wendell, 12 March 1909, in *Henry Adams and His Friends: A Collection of Unpublished Letters*, ed. Harold Dean Cater (Boston, 1947), p. 645.

[2] L. Kronenberger, 'The Letters–and Life–of Henry Adams', *Atlantic*, 219 (April 1967), 83. Samuels, *Henry Adams: The Major Phase* (Cambridge, Mass., 1964), pp. 383, 25. G. C. Knight, *The Strenuous Age in American Literature* (Chapel Hill, 1954), p. 145. Luccock, *Contemporary American Literature and Religion*; R. Chase, *The Democratic Vista* (Garden City, 1958), p. 41. A list of similarities, both basic and trivial, could carry on endlessly. It is not surprising to find the authors of a recent study-guide to the *Education* asking as their first practice question why Henry Adams could 'be considered a Hamlet figure'. Their prefabricated answer is rather more

All of this is not to say that *The Education of Henry Adams* cannot be understood without reference to *Hamlet*. The point is rather that an understanding of how *Hamlet* lurks inside and underneath Adams's moody life story is to approach that subtle book with the alertness that it demands, and moreover to gain at least a small sense of what the great English playwright meant to this American whose whole life was lived within the drama that political history provides. 'Toward the real artists', Adams once wrote to the woman he loved, 'I take no attitude except that of staying quiet on my knees, as I do before Shakespeare and Rembrandt and George Washington and you.'[1]

Having made this far an excursion into the effect of Hamlet on Henry Adams, we have still not discussed the most significant reference to the play in Adams's *Education*. This is a particularly important one because it occurs in the last paragraph of the book, at the very point at which a reader is compelled to inquire 'What now?' What is the prospect for the future, now that Adams's consciousness has chastened us into awareness of our chaotic modern world? How does he get himself out of the book, having built up not to Alger-like success but merely to a sort of hesitant affirmation after talking almost endlessly of 'failure'? That *Hamlet* should have occurred to him as an exit device is for several reasons not at all surprising, as a bit of investigation into cultural and personal history will suggest.

In 1904, the year before Adams wrote his book, A. C. Bradley published in England his famous lectures on *Shakespearean Tragedy*, where he noted that *Hamlet* was the most popular of Shakespeare's plays on the English stage at the end of the nineteenth century.[2] This was true in America as well as England, and had been for some time. Boston alone, for example, had the chance to see eleven stagings of the play between 1870 and 1876, the years that Adams had taught at Harvard.[3] Adams's

teacher, James Russell Lowell, was one of the many American critics who studied the young Dane and the troubling play that recounted his irresolution. Lowell, in fact, apparently valued *Hamlet* highest among Shakespeare's plays, if we judge by the length and passion of the *Hamlet* section in his 1868 essay 'Shakespeare Once More'.[4] In America at large during Lincoln's time there was 'widespread knowledge' of the stock situations in Hamlet, says a historian who has studied the matter. McGuffey's famous Readers, as one contribution to this knowledge, presented for young readers Hamlet's speech concerning Yorick's skull, marked with the desired inflections and pauses.[5] Practical young Americans at the time of Adams's boyhood were thus doubly enriched – encountering principles of elocution along with their exposure to great dramatic literature. It was this haphazard familiarity with the great lines from *Hamlet*, parroted in the schools, that Mark Twain exploited in perhaps the most comic scene of *Huckleberry Finn* (published 1885, but set in the 1840s): the charlatan duke's rendition of 'Hamlet's soliloquy', which

intelligent than occur in most books of this kind, and it makes, among other obvious points, the observation that 'although the man Adams was known to be fond of scociety, the speaker that one finds in the *Education* is quiet, withdrawn, and meditative, much like Hamlet. Adams is also given to soliloquies, or long periods of vocal soul-searching – in a very real sense, the entire *Education* can be considered an extended soliloquy on Adams' view of society'. James and Colette Lindroth, *The Education of Henry Adams* (Monarch Notes and Study Guides, New York, 1966), p. 70.

[1] To Mrs J. Donald Cameron, 28 December 1891, in Adams Papers, Massachusetts Historical Society, Boston. Quoted by permission.

[2] *Shakespearean Tragedy*, p. 91.

[3] Eugene Tompkins, *The History of Boston Theatre, 1854–1901* (Boston–New York, 1908).

[4] See also Falk, 'Shakespeare in America: A Survey to 1900', p. 114.

[5] Dunn, *Shakespeare in America*, pp. 281–2, 233–5. See, for example, *McGuffey's New Fifth Eclectic Reader* (Cincinnati, 1866), p. 34.

turns out to be a preposterous pastiche (chapter 21).

Mid-century in America, the period of Adams's collegiate years, had seen the rise to fame of Edwin Booth, the illustrious son of Junius Brutus Booth and brother to John Wilkes. Edwin Booth's *Hamlet* was in the repertoire of his first visit to Boston in the spring of 1857, when he was twenty-three and Henry Adams in the audience was nineteen. Newspaper reviews of his performance were mixed. The Boston *Transcript* reviewer reported that Booth indeed looked the part of Hamlet, but that the production on the whole was barely an average job. A correspondent to the *Transcript*, however, asserted that Booth's Hamlet was 'beautiful' – not so much in energy expended but in intensity of portrayal.[1] When Booth returned to Boston with Hamlet in November of 1859, Mrs Julia Ward Howe poured out nineteen effusive stanzas on the performance, which Lowell published in the *Atlantic Monthly* under the title 'Hamlet at the Boston'. Two of her romantic quatrains give an idea of why Booth's powerful characterization lingered in the memory:

And, beautiful as dreams of maidenhood,
   That doubt defy,
Young Hamlet, with his forehead grief-subdued,
   And visioning eye.

    .   .   .   .   .

'Tis with no feigned power thou bind'st our sense,
   No shallow art;
Sure, lavish Nature gave thee heritage
   Of Hamlet's heart.[2]

A junior at Harvard in 1857, Henry Adams saw Booth's first Hamlet at the Boston Theatre and came away from it moved by the sheer theatricality of the young Edwin. Adams was to see *Hamlet* twice more very soon, once in 1858 in Berlin and once in 1860 in Düsseldorf. The Berlin performance, probably starring Louis Dessoir, reminded him of Booth's triumphant debut in Boston. In a letter to his family he drew a comparison between Booth's production and the one he had just seen at Berlin's *Schauspielhaus*: The German version

was well done; remarkably well done. Setting aside the scenery, which is always perfect here, it was an exceedingly well acted piece. But Dessoir was not equal in stage effects to Booth and I've seen Mrs. Barrow [of the Boston Theatre permanent repertory company] do Ophelia much better than the little Fräulein Fuhr, who didn't at all satisfy me.

There was also, he observed, a loss in the translation; 'the German spoils it to an Englishman. The speech "'Tis not alone my inky cloak, good mother" begins in the German "Gnädige Frau". The whole thing sounds flat to me in German.'[3]

Of his theater experiences during those two years in Europe, this was quite the longest response that Adams set down in writing. There is little doubt that the play itself had something to say to him – something he did not try to explain but only hinted at when he described Bogumil Dawison's performance in Düsseldorf, his third *Hamlet* in four years: 'It was a very remarkable rendering, something entirely new and very striking, but repulsive and painful. I don't want to see it again and yet it showed more genius than any I ever saw.'[4]

No wonder, then, with the early imprint of at least three *Hamlets* on his mind, Adams dropped fragments of the great Shakespearian lines into his letters and writings during the late 1850s and 1860s. Probably it was Booth's

[1] Eleanor Ruggles, *Edwin Booth: Prince of Players* (New York, 1953), pp. 85–9, 96.
[2] 'Hamlet at the Boston', *Atlantic Monthly*, 3 (February 1859), 172–3. Booth's Hamlet was to become 'a national institution, a legend'. See Charles H. Shattuck, 'Edwin Booth's *Hamlet*: A New Promptbook', *Harvard Library Bulletin*, 15 (January 1967), 20.
[3] To Charles Francis Adams, Jr, 17–18 December 1858, in *Letters (1858–1891)*, p. 8.
[4] To Charles Francis Adams, Jr, 25 November 1859, in *Letters (1858–1891)*, p. 55.

Hamlet, or perhaps an early reading of the play, that came to mind in January of 1858 when he delivered a college oration at festivities of the Hasty Pudding Club. In 'The Cap and Bells' he made reference to the scene at Yorick's grave and to the 'great revenge' contemplated by Hamlet in his 'half-real madness'.[1] A letter to his brother from Washington in 1861 made semi-comic use of Hamlet's speech to Horatio in I, v, 129–31: 'I for one am going upon the business or the pleasure that shall suit me, for every man hath business or desire such as it is, and for my own poor part – look you – I will go write an article for the *Atlantic Monthly*.' Ophelia's mad song from act IV comically launched a spirited letter to his brother in 1862:

> Good morrow, 'tis St. Valentine's day
> All in the morning betime.
> And I a maid at your window
> To be your Valentine.

The same 'undiscovered country' lines from Hamlet's soliloquy that would later give Howells the title for a novel provided Adams in 1866 with a humorous reflection upon his brother:

Charles and his wife are so happy in Italy that I could envy them if it were not for that 'something ere the end', that undiscovered country from whose bourne no bachelor returns makes me rather 'accept the ills I have, than' the rest – Hamlet's logic is good for more cases than suicide.

In 1867, looking at the wretched state of post-war politics, he complained to his brother, 'The world is out of joint, and Hamlet was a damned fool for trying to set it right instead of trying to make money on it.'[2] Oddly enough, it was during this very decade that Adams had an excellent chance to contemplate his grandfather's spirited affection for *Hamlet*. In 1862 James H. Hackett published in New York a little volume with a long title, *Notes and Comments upon Certain Plays and Actors of Shake-*speare, which included the long letter about *Hamlet* that John Quincy Adams had written him in 1839. 'I look upon the tragedy of *Hamlet* as the master-piece of the drama – the master-piece of Shakespeare – I had almost said, the master-piece of the human mind', enthusiastically declared the ex-President and then-Congressman (p. 192).

Saturated in *Hamlet* at an early age, it is no wonder that at the other end of his long life Adams should find the words and situations of Hamlet coming back upon him. His first visit to the real Denmark had been in 1862, two years after his Düsseldorf *Hamlet*. Nearly forty years elapsed before his second visit, in 1901, as the *Education* was possibly beginning to germinate in his mind. In the early autumn of that year he boarded a ship in Sweden and crossed the Baltic Sea 'to Helsingfors where Hamlet's father's ghost was sitting on his terrace waiting'. Early in 1904 the Ghost re-appeared, as Adams, now sixty-six, contributed to the memorial volume put out by the Century Club in New York in honor of the late Clarence King. The brilliant geologist King, who was to figure so prominently in the *Education*, had in 1894 gone with his friend Adams to visit pre-revolutionary Cuba (*Education*, 349) and had gregariously roamed about in the wilds becoming friendly with the brigands and conspirators of the island. The incongruous situation amused Adams, as he depicted himself and the ebullient King: 'There were two elderly men; bald-headed [Adams]; gray-haired, or at

---

[1] 'The Cap and Bells', *The Harvard Magazine*, 4 (April 1858), 125.

[2] To Charles Francis Adams, Jr, 13 February 1861, in *Letters (1858–1891)*, p. 88. To the same, 14 February 1862, in *A Cycle of Adams Letters 1861–1865* (Boston and New York, 1920), I, 112. To John Gorham Palfrey, 4 May 1866, in Cater (ed.), *Henry Adams and His Friends*, p. 29. To Charles Francis Adams, Jr, 16 February 1867, in Adams Papers, Microfilms (Massachusetts Historical Society, Boston, 1954–9), reel 581.

least sable-silvered, like Hamlet's father [King], literary and scientific gentlemen...'[1]

Twice, therefore, in four years the Ghost of Hamlet's father had made its appearance in the mind of the ageing Adams. Was he the Hamlet perceiving this ghost? We may guess that the implication was intended, and that to close friends and correspondents this role was not a new one for Adams to adopt. At least twice in the 1890s he had made the persona quite explicit. Writing in 1891 to his closest friend, Elizabeth Cameron, wife of a Pennsylvania senator, he had lamented their impossible relationship. 'Why send you what I have written in this letter? I know it cannot give you pleasure, and is likely to give you pain...I cannot with propriety lead a life fit for you to associate with. I must be a nuisance to you and myself – like Hamlet...' Here the Hamlet persona thus had a very personal implication, opening up a realm additional to the political and moral implications that we have already noticed in the *Education*. Traveling in France in 1899, Adams was still writing to Mrs Cameron, though he had managed to stabilize his romantic feelings. He could now jest about his passion for 'twelfth century churches and literature', and declare of himself to Mrs Cameron, nineteen years his junior: 'I am a sexagenarian Hamlet with architectural fancies.'[2]

Adams published his *Education* privately in 1907, in 100 copies for friends. Presumably most were keen enough to perceive both Hamlets, the romantic 'nuisance' and the political moralist, though the former is quite absent from the text. For the rest of us, the Hamlet of the *Education* is the man who tried heroically to consummate a difficult relationship between himself and the world, between conscience/consciousness and the recalcitrant circumstances of an amoral and chaotic world. Possibly aware that the psychological resemblances between himself and Hamlet in the *Education* were becoming too striking, Adams

at the end backed away. Throughout the book he had been adhering, in effect, to his mentor Lowell's dictum that 'the aim of the artist is psychologic, not historic truth',[3] but even so he could hardly so disregard history as to end the book on a fully tragic note. He had not, after all succumbed; his mind in its quest had invented a great formula, a 'Dynamic Theory of History' (473), and had in fact seemed to see a bit of light flickering at the end of the historical corridor. Perhaps the modern mind *could* deal with the remarkable new forces and energies that seemed to buffet from all sides: 'Thus far, since five or ten thousand years, the mind had successfully reacted, and nothing yet proved that it would fail to react – but it would need to jump' (498). Adams himself is thus left wearied by mental struggle but in fact quite alive and even hedgingly triumphant. The death that marks the end of the book is that of Adams's long-time friend, John Hay, and it is not a tragic death. No Hamlet, Hay in eight years as Secretary of State 'had solved nearly every old problem of American statesmanship, and had left little or nothing to annoy his successor' (503). Never introspective, Hay had had brilliant success in the active world as poet, editor, businessman, biographer, and statesman. Yet Adams, in what is perhaps one of the two or three artistic blunders of the *Education*, tried in the last sentences to shift the role of Hamlet from himself to Hay. Hay, the cheerful man of affairs and symbol in the book of cynical politician but also devoted public servant, prepares to die, and in doing so echoes Hamlet. To which Adams responds as Horatio:

[1] To Mrs J. Donald Cameron, 28 September 1901, in *Letters (1892–1918)*, p. 355; Adams, 'King', in *Clarence King Memoirs* (New York, 1904), p. 174.

[2] 10 November 1891 and 26 September 1899, in Adams Papers, Massachusetts Historical Society. Quoted by permission.

[3] 'Shakespeare Once More', *Among My Books*, p. 208.

when the treatment ended, three weeks later, and he [Hay] came on to Paris, he showed, at the first glance, that he had lost strength...He was conscious of it, and in his last talk before starting for London and Liverpool he took the end of his activity for granted. 'You must hold out for the peace negotiations' [of the Russo-Japanese War], was the remonstrance of Adams. 'I've not time!' he replied. 'You'll need little time!' was the rejoinder.   (504)

'Had I but time', was the way Hamlet put it, in Shakespeare's words. Fixing on Hay's remark as a fortuitous way to lead himself out of the *Education*, Adams somewhat incongruously moves into the final paragraph of the book with himself still in the role of Horatio, survivor:

There it ended! Shakespeare himself could use no more than the commonplace to express what is incapable of expression. 'The rest is silence!'...It was not even the suddenness of the shock, or the sense of void, that threw Adams into the depths of Hamlet's Shakespearean silence in the full flare of Paris frivolity in its favorite haunt where worldly vanity reached its most futile climax in human history; it was only the quiet summons to follow – the assent to dismissal.

(504–5)

Perhaps, indeed, it was not so severe a mistake suddenly to throw over Hamlet and close out the narrative as Horatio. For Adams no doubt had in mind the succeeding words of Horatio: 'Let me speak to the yet unknowing world/How these things came about'. Moreover, as the ambiguous reference to 'Hamlet's Shakespearean silence' suggests, Adams was possibly trying to play both roles at once.

In the final analysis, however, the importance of the Hamlet persona in the *Education* has to do neither with the facts of John Hay's life nor with Adams's apparent switch in roles at the end. The larger implications are suggested by Lowell and Thoreau, the authors providing epigraphs for this study. Writing in 1840 as an American fully cognizant of the new nation's great destiny, Thoreau registered a mild and

even humorous dissent, as was his custom. He pointed to the bustling, active world of whaling, homesteading, selling, fighting, fishing, sailing – and included in his Whitman-like catalog of possibilities the fantasy of carrying mail in Peru or falling victim to a Siberian exile. But he reserved the end of his list for the least likely possibility to entice a young American (Thoreau was twenty-three): 'what a pity if the part of Hamlet be left out!' One might read about Hamlet in school readers, but the very idea of an American boy growing up that way! Esther Dunn points to the manner in which McGuffey handled Shakespeare's biography in his Readers – stressing his good marriage, his joint-ownership of a theater, and the fact that he 'accumulated some property'. *There* was Shakespeare; there was nothing of the Hamlet in the man who wrote *Hamlet* – school children, please note. Apprehensive parents were alerted by James Russell Lowell, lover of Shakespeare and well acquainted with the reflective life in his capacity as Smith Professor of French and Spanish at Harvard, but at bottom a practical man. Toward the end of the 1868 essay already cited, 'Shakespeare Once More', Lowell made a remark which hits strikingly close to the Henry Adams temperament and is almost a verbal foreshadowing of Adams's self-deprecating description of himself as failing to play his hand in the card game of life. It was not of Adams, Lowell's student of ten years before, that he was speaking, however. Lowell was cautioning against a Hamlet tendency that seemed to be catching on in America generally in the Gilded Age, not just among thin-lipped Bostonians. A modern American reader cannot help respond with a feeling of irony and may well rub his eyes in disbelief, but here is what Lowell was writing: 'It is certainly curious how prophetically typical the character [of Hamlet] is of that introversion of mind which is so constant a phenomenon of these latter days, of that over-consciousness which wastes itself in analyzing the motives of action instead of acting' (*Among My Books*, p. 225). Thoreau thought the absence of this phenomenon a pity in America; to Lowell, even in the middle of a business-oriented era, it was nothing but waste.

To have examined one such figure out of the era under discussion (Adams was two years old as Henry Thoreau wrote in his journal), is to consider the reality of the tension in America between act and thought, even in Adams's lifetime (1838–1918), an era usually understood in terms of enterprise, aggrandizement, decisiveness, and 'get-up-and-go'. The Hamlet side of the American character, as we see it cropping out in such diverse literary characters as James's Lambert Strether, Howells's Silas Lapham, and the 'I' in Emily Dickinson's poems is – Lowell notwithstanding – the side of America that can increasingly be seen as more attractive and even necessary than the average citizen has learned to acknowledge. Society, that is, does not remain humane unless consciousness and conscience are sensitively functioning at all levels. Consciousness provides imaginative awareness not only of different possibilities for growth and change but of their respective implications and of the need for choice, while conscience keeps pace, ready to take stands based on considered principle and to pass moral judgment on public actions.

It might well be argued that there is thus a kind of ideal, Platonic Hamlet toward which men aspire, which neither Shakespeare's Hamlet nor the Henry Adams of the *Education* is able really to be. Neither man, admirable in many ways, will serve us adequately as a model. The Hamlet temperament is one that too easily debases itself into either gothic monomania or cynical passivity. Toward the latter Adams tended in real life, and of the former in America Faulkner gives us a picture in the haunting figure of Henry Sutpen, who murders his sister's suitor in Mississippi in 1865 (*Absalom, Absalom!*): 'that gaunt tragic dramatic self-hypnotized youthful face like the tragedian in a college play, an academic Hamlet waked from some trancement of the curtain's falling and blundering across the dusty stage from which the rest of the cast had departed . . .'

That, however, is another story. Meanwhile, the Henry Adams whose conscience cried out to save his morally floundering nation and whose consciousness incisively discerned what are still central problems of a technological society is perhaps the most poised and balanced – and therefore useful – reincarnation of Hamlet that America has yet produced.

'PERICLES'
AND THE DREAM OF IMMORTALITY

J. P. BROCKBANK

Criticism of Shakespeare's *Pericles* has most often concerned itself with those of the play's problems that might offer a solution to patient inquiry. If the results have been disappointing, they have been intelligibly so; and yet, were the evidence less fragmentary and indecisive, and we could reach confident conclusions about authorship, literary genesis, and the skills and frailties of compositors *A* and *B*, the essential mystery of the play might still elude us, for it has to do with the insights and devices by which art attempts to encompass human mortality. If we wonder why the plays of Shakespeare's time, flourishing as they do upon a medieval root, offer so little reassurance about personal survival in a life to come, we may reflect with Wittgenstein that, 'Death is not an event of life. Death is not lived through'. The plays are pre-eminently about what is lived through.

The last pages of the *Tractatus Logico-Philosophicus*[1] may remind us that doctrines of immortality cannot in any case do what they are meant to do:

Is a riddle solved by the fact that I survive for ever?
Is this eternal life not as enigmatic as our present one?
The solution of the riddle of life in time and space lies outside space and time...

The riddle does not exist...

The solution to the problem of life is seen in the vanishing of this problem.

(Is not this the reason why men to whom after long doubting the sense of life became clear, could not then say wherein this sense consisted?)

Shakespeare's last plays seem both to touch upon the riddle and to set it aside; to seek answers 'outside space and time' and yet to discount whatever is adumbrated:

Thou thy worldly task hast done,
Home art gone, and ta'en thy wages...
(*Cym.* IV, ii, 261–2)
We are such stuff
As dreams are made on...
(*Tempest*, IV, i, 156–7)
The fixture of her eye has motion in't,
As we are mock'd with art.
(*W. Tale*, V, iii, 67–8)

The false deaths, the strange evaporations and the miraculous resurrections of the last plays allow to our experience in the theatre some solace of immortality that cannot readily take dogmatic form. 'Whereof one cannot speak, thereof one must be silent'; but the poet is not under the philosopher's obligation to keep silence – he finds a language to express the inexpressible. What cannot be held by dogma or reached by systematic thought may be intimated to the experience of our affections through the 'fine frenzy' of metaphor and rhythm.

The intimations of *Pericles* may need no gloss – 'he that hath ears to hear, let him hear'; but it is nevertheless of some consequence to our larger perspective of literary understanding to notice that they have multiple sources. The sources in part are perennial and experiential –

[1] Quotations are from the 1962 impression of the 1922 edition.

in continuing human endeavours to foil suffering and loss with dream and vision; but they are also dramatic and literary, to be traced in Shakespeare's own art, in the elements of romantic tale and (as F. D. Hoeniger has well observed[1]) in the traditions of the miracle play.

For a rendering of the relevant human experience, it happens characteristically that we may look to Shakespeare's own art. When Clarence in *Richard III*, I, iv, tells Brackenbury of his ominous dream, death by drowning finds a significantly resonant place in the play's poetry. The chronicle gave but slender occasion for it. As a child Clarence had crossed the water to meet Philip of Burgundy, and in the dream he is crossing to Burgundy again, with Richard of Gloucester 'upon the giddy hatches'. The dream is an intimation of risk ('Methought that Gloucester stumbled') and of the coming-on of a Senecal doom ('that grim ferryman'), but returning to the scene after reading *Pericles* it enables us to measure the distance of the dreamer's sense of reality from the political and human exigencies of the mundane world. 'What was your dream?', asks Brackenbury, gaoler to a political prisoner, 'I long to hear you tell it'. And Clarence tells of 'reflecting gems' that 'in scorn of eyes... woo'd the slimy bottom of the deep', and of an ordeal of drowning, of belching, his soul seeking 'the vast and wandering air'. It needs little prompting to recognise these tiny prefigurations of the principal metaphors of *The Tempest* and of *Pericles*. In *Richard III* they shadow forth, however transiently, the existence of an imaginative world more spacious and elusive than that which Richard is managing, and its mysterious processes of transmutation and renewal, physical in themselves, seem haunted by a moral significance that receives in this play no sustained expression. Clarence is drowned in a malmsey butt, with little scope for allegoric tempest to his soul.

A history of Shakespearian metaphor might

pass readily from Clarence's 'reflecting gems' to Ariel's, 'Those are pearls that were his eyes'. The sea-change of *The Tempest* is a comprehensive metaphor, expressing those strange mutations that can come about in the moral and political world through the interventions of Prospero's magical skill. But natural processes, the metaphor reminds us, are themselves strange and unpredictable, particularly those that relate to death by sea. And in *The Tempest* the sea is a moral agent in itself, whether clearing the mud from the beaches (v, i, 79–82), or casting indigestible delinquents upon the shore:

> You are three men of sin, whom Destiny,
> That hath to instrument this lower world
> And what is in't, the never-surfeited sea
> Hath caus'd to belch up you.   (III, iii, 53–6)

Man's spiritual nature, it might be claimed from *The Tempest*, is made more comprehensible by Shakespeare's response to the nature of the sea, and by his command of verbal expressions of the sea's movements. And so it is in *Pericles*. *Pericles* is an old tale re-told within the comprehensive metaphor of the sea.

It is unfortunate that we may not be able to attend to the tale as Shakespeare first told it, for the text has, it seems, been sadly tempest-tossed. Assumptions about the nature of its transmission are apt to qualify one's account of the play, and there is therefore some need to say what they are.[2] Although attributed to Shakespeare when first published in Quarto in 1609, with five reprints following in the years to 1635, it was mysteriously excluded from the 1623 Folio and admitted only to the third in

[1] *Pericles*, ed. F. D. Hoeniger, Arden Shakespeare (London, 1963), pp. lxxxvii–xci.

[2] In what follows I have expressed a disposition but abstained from arguing a case. The relevant data are very fully set out in *Narrative and Dramatic Sources of Shakespeare*, VI (London, 1966), edited by Geoffrey Bullough, and also discussed by Kenneth Muir, *Shakespeare's Sources*, I (London, 1957).

1664. Rowe omitted it but Malone with reluctance included it. Modern editors and critics have largely agreed in finding the first two acts less authentic than the last three, but they have differed in their diagnoses. It has been argued that the text is wholly a reported one, with one reporter (with a poor memory but a stickler for form) responsible for the first two acts, and another (with a better memory but careless of form) responsible for the last three.[1] Rival hypotheses see the play as divided in authorship, with Shakespeare responsible for the last acts and a minor figure for the first two. The slender and inadequate evidence allows us to believe alternatively that Shakespeare took up an old play and intervened with quickening interest and confidence until, by the time he reached the third act, he was virtually re-writing it; if the text were a good one we would need to accept as Shakespeare's responsibility both what he wrote and what he left, but as at several points the text is manifestly corrupt, our acceptance must remain discontented. I find it convenient to acquiesce in the notion of an old play re-written, because it consorts well with the impression that Shakespeare is offering an old tale re-told. When the play lapses from,

> The blind mole casts
> Copp'd hills towards heaven, to tell the earth is
> throng'd
> By man's oppression, and the poor worm doth die for't
> (I, i, 101–3)

to

> So puts himself unto the shipman's toil,
> With whom each minute threatens life or death
> (I, iii, 23–4)

we may assume either that the text is scarred by the reporter's memory, or that Shakespeare has allowed some voice other than his own still to be heard. But we may also believe that these 'inferior' lines come between the manner imitated from Gower:

> The lady shrieks, and, well-a-near,
> Does fall in travail with her fear
> (III, Chorus, 51–2)

and what the mature Shakespeare will make of it:

> This world to me is as a lasting storm,
> Whirring me from my friends.
> (IV, i, 19–20)

In some areas Shakespeare retails the wide-eyed gaucherie of his romance sources, and in some he transmutes it to a revelatory simplicity.

Significantly enough, the play that was once a story was apparently turned again to story by George Wilkins in *The Painfull Adventures of Pericles Prince of Tyre* and its title-page tells us with satisfaction that it was 'excellently' presented in the theatre by 'the worthy and ancient Poet John Gower'. Whatever the history of the text there is little doubt that Shakespeare was either content to take over the theatrical figure of Gower or that he invented him. He is used to mediate between the sophistication of the audience and the naivety of the tale. Ben Jonson, skilled in the kind of comedy that by deftness of wit, subtlety of observation and controlled caricature, recalls us to norms of responsive social conduct, found nothing to admire in the 'mouldy tale' raked 'into the common tub' to 'keep up the Play-club'. Remembering what Samuel Johnson said of *Cymbeline* about wasting criticism upon 'unresisting imbecility', we must acknowledge that *Pericles* offers comparable resistance to good sense. The stage Gower could not appease everyone. Yet he is meant to appease; to disarm criticism, to invite the acquiescence of the modern intellect in an old eloquence. 'Thought with affection' (to adapt a phrase of Blake's) may take the play as Shakespeare took the verse of Gower and the prose of

[1] By Philip Edwards, *Shakespeare Survey 5* (Cambridge, 1952), pp. 25–49.

Laurence Twine, responding to its innocence and tolerant of its inconsequence, for these qualities seem here invincibly related; there are certain truths, Shakespeare seems to claim, that can only be conveyed in this archaic mode.

In a manner less conspicuously artless Shakespeare returns to a similar mode in *The Winter's Tale*. There is no story-teller, but the chorus and the wry and wondering allusions in the dialogue, remind us that we are attending to an old tale:

> 2 *Gentleman.* What, pray you, became of Antigonus, that carried hence the child?
> 3 *Gentleman.* Like an old tale still, which will have matter to rehearse though credit be asleep and not an ear open: he was torn to pieces with a bear.
>
> (v, ii, 57–61)

And a space is opened between what is true and what is credible:

> This news, which is call'd true, is so like an old tale that the verity of it is in strong suspicion.
>
> (v, ii, 26–7)

Shakespeare's disposition to tell old tales was not, of course, a merely personal one. He had participated and collaborated (see *The Two Noble Kinsmen*) in a Blackfriars fashion for revived romance. For it happened at the beginning of the seventeenth century, and would happen again at the end of the eighteenth, that a society with a highly complex and civilised literary culture looked back to old tales and to the Middle Ages in search of rich simplicities, expressible in innocent speech and show. Shakespeare's Gower is an artefact corresponding to Chatterton's Rowley, and testifies to a similar nostalgia for an unspoiled innocence of imaginative understanding:

> To sing a song that old was sung,
> From ashes ancient Gower is come,
> Assuming man's infirmities,
> To glad your ear and please your eyes.

> It hath been sung at festivals,
> On ember-eves and holidays,
> And lords and ladies in their lives
> Have read it for restoratives.
>
> (1, Chorus, 1–8)

I have no difficulty in believing Shakespeare well pleased with such an opening. It is close to what literary history would invite us to call the Romantic response to romance. The old songs, sung at festivals and read by lords and ladies for restoratives, are those that Chatterton taught Keats to admire and in his own way to emulate.

When Keats exclaimed upon 'The Floure and the Lefe',

> Oh! what a power hath white Simplicity!
> What mighty power has this gentle story!

he was acclaiming qualities that Shakespeare may have recognised in the sources of *Pericles*. If we ask of the play, as Pericles asks of Marina, 'how achieved you these endowments, which you make more rich to owe?', we might find answers from the *Gesta Romanorum*, the *Confessio Amantis* and *The Patterne of Painfull Adventures*. These are the principal literary versions for Shakespeare of a tale that had, and still has, live currency in the oral traditions of Mediterranean Europe. How does Shakespeare discover or confer the 'power of white simplicity'? Apollonius in the story solves the incestuous riddle of the King of Antioch, takes to the seas in fear of revenge, finds a wife at Pentapolis, loses her in childbirth at sea, leaves the child at Tarsus and returns years later to learn that she has died; desolate and despairing he nevertheless clings to life to be miraculously reunited with his daughter, unspoiled by the pirates and the brothels, and with his wife, votaress of Diana at Ephesus. Shakespeare's interventions in the narrative are slight: he abbreviates the incest at Antioch, adds a second and third fisherman to greet Pericles from the sea, contrives the tournament for Simonides' daughter and enlarges the brothel episodes at Mytilene. More marginally, the name of Apollonius is changed to Pericles (recalling the Athenian Pericles from Plutarch, it has been suggested, and chiming with *periculum* for the sake of the dangerous voyaging); the daughter's name, Thaisa, is given to the mother to make way for the more precise and evocative 'Marina'. But the play's closeness to the narrative in structure and manner startle more than its divergencies of detail. The deaths of Antiochus and his daughter, for example, are reported with comparably brisk moral expedition in the play and the tale, and are not featured like the similar event in *A looking Glass for London and England*. Gower's effacing, transparent fluency is sympathetically imitated by the play (if a little transposed into the manners of self-indulgent old age) and it offers the ground for the Shakespearian variations.

We may say of all Shakespeare's 'Last Plays' that each is about the renewal of creative life in an afflicted state of society. In each a miraculous providence works, through different agencies, to saving purpose. But in each an element of self-confessed artifice qualifies the auspicious outcome to remind us that the ultimately reassuring moral order that can be displayed to us in the theatre is indeed theatre; it cannot be transposed too promptly into 'fact' – the verity of it is under suspicion. *Pericles* is so contrived; its scenes of recognition and reunion that are the vehicles for the most expressive movements and metaphors of the poetry, are 'framed' in an old tale, by a particular technique of presentation. It is a technique that delights in spectacle and evades one kind of human reality in order to express another. We may take our cue from the stage Gower again:

> What pageantry, what feats, what shows,
> What minstrelsy and pretty din,
> The regent made in Mytilen,
> To greet the King.   (v, ii, 6–9)

The play opens as a pageant, a feat and a show, with Gower to display the ranked heads of dedicate but uncomprehending princes; we must not ask why they failed to read so transparent a riddle – the convention of an antique tale will not stay to be questioned, but must be satisfied with the sudden moral dismay of the Prince who finds that 'she who comes apparell'd like the spring' is an 'eater of her mother's flesh'. The dismay is present enough for the purpose of the tale but it is not tragically realised; Gower's language could not have explored it, and the play's does not attempt to. Nevertheless, play and tale alike open with a blight upon a father and daughter relationship and end after many ordeals with such a relationship miraculously perfected 'in very sanctity'.

Without betraying Gower's large design, however, the play gathers little by little its own range of intensities and significances. The second scene opens with what might have been a self-questioning soliloquy in the manner of Hamlet, with the Prince musing upon the prevailing sins of the world and assuming a vicarious burden of tragic guilt. But it is not sustained – not, at least in the version of the scene that reaches us through the eccentricities of transmission. The Lords of the Quarto bid farewell to Pericles before they can know that he is leaving and are promptly and inexplicably reprimanded for flattery. It may be that the authentic text provided a more decorous departure; as it is the play keeps the tale's peremptoriness ('Our Prince...Thus sodein-liche is fro ous went'[1]) while insinuating a more generous motive for flight than that he 'wolde his deth eschuie'. Pericles is moved by love for his subjects to evade the wrath of Antioch, to 'stop this tempest ere it came', and therefore 'puts himself into the shipman's toil'. The play is quick to initiate its dominant structural rhythm, its movement from the coast,

[1] Gower, *Confessio Amantis*, ed. G. C. Macaulay (Oxford, 1901), Liber Octavus, 1.494.

109

the several territories of the 'mortal shore', to the high seas and back again.

The inconsequence and waywardness of the play, however accidental it may be, does nothing to diminish its consonance with the romance, and it a little enhances its continuity with miracle play. Antioch is a scene to exemplify one condition of life – where courtesy and grace are the masks of vice. Tyre exemplifies another, where lords in council about a good king seek his safety and that of the state. Tharsus is the opulent and proud society humiliated and brutalised by famine:

> All poverty was scorned, and pride so great
> The name of help grew odious to repeat...
> Those mothers who to nouzle up their babes
> Thought nought too curious are ready now
> To eat those little darlings whom they lov'd.
>
> (I, iv, 30–1, 42–4)

Pericles comes from the sea 'with attendants' bringing corn to the desolation of the streets. Oddly, though he speaks of going to Tharsus when he leaves Helicanus, Pericles does not then speak of the famine he means to relieve. Human purposes of that kind are not sustained in the play or in the tale; the circumstances of the story make the Prince bountiful, and bounty becomes his natural attribute, an aspect of his royal virtue. It is not necessary to claim that the Digby play of *Mary Magdalene* is a source, but F. D. Hoeniger is right to see it as an analogue: *Pericles* is a sequence of pageant episodes that attends as much to divine as to human purpose.

The second act opens with the narrative and the dumb-show that take Pericles from Tharsus and have him wrecked on the coast of Pentapolis. The dumb-show, which takes little time in the reading can take much in the playing:

Enter, at one door, PERICLES, *talking with* CLEON; *all the* Train *with them. Enter, at another door, a* Gentleman *with a letter to Pericles; Pericles shows the letter to Cleon. Pericles gives the Messenger a reward, and knights him. Exit Pericles at one door and Cleon at another.*

The symmetrical entrances and exits ('all the train with them') and the ceremony of knighting, together no doubt with 'minstrelsy and pretty din' keep the ugly facts at a distance without disguising them. It is hard to realise that one king is seeking to murder another; the greater reality is the voyage and the storm, the sense of an odyssey, of a continuing pilgrimage.

We need not confine ourselves to those suggestions that the analogue with miracle play might prompt (the voyages of St Paul and of the King of Marcylle). Keats in a celebrated letter speaks of the world as 'The vale of Soul-making'.[1] 'Do you not see', he asks, 'how necessary a World of Pains and troubles is to school an Intelligence and make it a Soul?' Man is formed by circumstances, says Keats, and circumstances are the touchstones and provings of the heart that give *identity* to the intelligence that in itself has none. So it is in *Pericles*. The sea and the coast of Pentapolis test and find men, give identities to their intelligences. The Prince comes, wet, to the three Fishermen. The Fishermen are what they are because of the ordeals of their working lives, and Pericles what he is because of his exposure to the storm. This, surely, is a scene of Shakespeare's making – yet it keeps its continuity with what has gone before:

Pericles. May see the sea hath cast upon your coast –

2 Fisherman. What a drunken knave was the sea to cast thee in our way!

Pericles. A man whom both the waters and the wind
    In that vast tennis-court hath made the ball
    For them to play upon entreats you pity him;
    He asks of you that never us'd to beg.

1 Fisherman. No, friend, cannot you beg? Here's them in our country of Greece gets more with begging than we can do with working.

2 Fisherman. Canst thou catch any fishes, then?
Pericles. I never practis'd it.

[1] *The Letters of John Keats*, ed. M. Buxton Forman (Oxford, 1947), p. 336.

2 Fisherman. Nay, then thou wilt starve, sure; for here's nothing to be got now-a-days unless thou canst fish for't.

Pericles. What I have been I have forgot to know:
But what I am want teaches me to think on:
A man throng'd up with cold.   (II, i, 56–71)

It is a tableau to be wondered at ; Shakespeare musing again on unaccommodated man, with a naked king submitted to the resurrecting violence of the elements:

Wind, rain and thunder, remember earthly man
Is but a substance that must yield to you;
And I, as fits my nature, do obey you.
Alas, the sea hath cast me on the rocks,
Wash'd me from shore to shore, and left me breath
Nothing to think on but ensuing death.
                                                    (II, i, 2–7)

King and armour are belched from the sea (the 'wat'ry grave'), symbols of a harsh solicitude. But it is not merely tableau. Pericles is resurrected to the life of Pilch and Patchbreech. In the tradition that makes the lively talk of the shipman and his boy in the *Magdalene* play,[1] and in the track of the romance reports commending the 'fisher' for his 'great pity', Shakespeare allows the affections to prevail in a state of desolation; on this occasion, the good-humoured, neighbourly affections expressed by the Fishermen's readiness to let Pericles share their lives. Life, to put the point solemnly, is renewed from a condition of death; the Fisherman puts it otherwise:

Die quoth-a? Now gods forbid't! And I have a gown here! Come, put it on; keep thee warm. Now, afore me, a handsome fellow! Come, thou shalt go home, and we'll have flesh for holidays, fish for fasting days, and moreo'er puddings and flapjacks; and thou shalt be welcome.   (II, i, 78–82)

In another aspect the community of king and fishermen has a political significance. Simonides, says Pericles, 'is a happy king, since he gains from his subjects the name of good by his government'. The first acts return several times

to the responsibilities of kingship; yet they are acknowledged rather than dwelt upon. The qualities that Pericles ultimately embodies have little to do with government; they are constancy in endurance and constancy in the affections. These, we may say, borrowing the play's metaphor, are the jewels that survive the tempest.

Sympathetically regarded, the scenes that follow move deftly between the story and allegoric show. Where Gower tells of 'games' and Laurence Twine of the Prince's agility at tennis and his diligence in bathing the king, the play turns into a tableau and a tournament that have to do with the equality and the inequality of men. 'Every worth in show commends itself' and Pericles' sovereignty of nature is proved in honourable exercise. Shakespeare's gifts are not conspicuously present, but they seem to sound from far off:

Whereby I see that Time's the king of men;
He's both their parent, and he is their grave.
And gives them what he will, not what they crave.
                                                    (II, iii, 45–7)

Pericles' subdued patience in face of time and circumstance is foiled by the clamorous armoured dance by which the King awakes him from his melancholy, and by the love that Thaisa so eagerly bestows upon him. The Prince's 'voice celestial' and his skill upon the harp, much admired by Gower, are not demonstrated in the play as it reaches us, but they are reported:

I am beholding to you
For your sweet music this last night. I do
Protest my ears were never better fed
With such delightful pleasing harmony.
                                                    (II, v, 25–8)

It is likely that 'minstrelsy' did more than now appears to amplify the 'feats' and 'shows' of the first performances. As it is, music is much used both to superficial effect – the stage

[1] *The Digby Plays*, ed. F. J. Furnivall, E.E.T.S. (London, 1896), *Mary Magdalene*, II, sc. 40.

Gower's 'pretty din', and to profounder purpose, moving the imagination towards that moment when Pericles, his affections wholly reawakened and restored, hears the music of the spheres.[1]

The reawakening and restoring of the life of the affections after desolating loss is the continuing mystery, delight, preposterousness and satisfaction of the play. What is faintly pre-figured in the first two acts is marvellously accomplished in the last three, partly through the fuller realisation of the great central metaphor of the storm at sea, and partly through the exquisitely repetitious renderings of the tale of Marina – both are essential to the fulfilment of the play's dream of immortality.

The 'death' and burial of the queen at sea engage, as one might expect, the most generous resources of Shakespeare's art. When 'The sea-toss'd Pericles appears to speak', it is in a language whose sea-swell moves with formidable ease between cosmic awe and domestic intimacy, from, 'Thou god of this great vast, rebuke these surges, Which wash both heaven and hell', to, 'O, how, Lychorida, How does my queen?'. The exequy upon Thaisa finds its mysterious solace from a similar movement towards a more poignant solicitude:

> A terrible childbed hast thou had, my dear;
> No light, no fire. Th' unfriendly elements
> Forgot thee utterly; nor have I time
> To give thee hallow'd to thy grave, but straight
> Must cast thee, scarcely coffin'd, in the ooze;
> Where, for a monument upon thy bones,
> And aye-remaining lamps, the belching whale
> And humming water must o'erwhelm thy corpse,
> Lying with simple shells. O Lychorida,
> Bid Nestor bring me spices, ink and paper,
> My casket and my jewels.   (III, i, 56–66)

'A terrible childbed hast thou had, my dear', might be disarming domestic tenderness, and 'No light, no fire' could be the simple deprivations of birth at sea in a storm; but the terror and deprivation become momentous and

cosmic with, 'Th' unfriendly elements Forgot thee utterly', and by the submission of the sentiments to an implacable rhythm. Yet there is no despair. The protest is muted by the acceptance of necessity, and that necessity is made acceptable by the fuller recognitions of the sea's nature – the ooze, the belching whale, the humming water, the simple shells. The word 'ooze' gathered a rich significance in the later plays – Alonso in *The Tempest*, 'Therefore my son i'th'ooze is bedded', and Antony talking to Caesar about the Nile, 'as it ebbs, the seedsman Upon the slime and ooze scatters his grain, And shortly comes to harvest.' The 'ooze' is at once the end of life and its source, and to revert to it, we are made to feel, is almost a privilege. After touching in the fullness of its motion the huge elemental activities and sonorities of the sea – the belching whale and humming water – the verse comes to rest, with the dead Thaisa, in what is felt to be a condition of arrival – 'lying with simple shells'. As John Danby has said, it is the absolute *apathie* we both long for and disdain.[2] We may notice again the strange contiguity with the dream of Clarence. The 'aye-remaining lamps' here belong to the monument side of the metaphor, alluding to Roman sepulchres, but the lamps and the bones are not too remote from the 'in scorn of eyes, reflecting gems' of the dream, and it is fitting that Pericles should consign the jewels to Clarence's visionary slime.

The play's metaphor is elemental and its story elementary. We are fashioned from the elements, we are exposed to them, and we revert to them; hence the birth by sea, the many voyages, and the apparent death. Acceptance of the great elemental cycle is passingly expressed by Helicanus in an early scene:

[1] For a discussion of the music of *Pericles* and its analogues, see F. W. Sternfeld, *Music in Shakespearean Tragedy* (Oxford, 1963), pp. 244–9.

[2] In *Poets on Fortune's Hill* (London, 1952), p. 95.

We'll mingle our bloods together in the earth,
From whence we had our being and our birth.
(I, ii, 113–14)

But the process of Pericles' acceptance is more arduous; he must be schooled in patience:

Lychorida. Here is a thing too young for such a place,
Who, if it had conceit, would die, as I
Am like to do. Take in your arms this piece
Of your dead queen.

Pericles.   How, how, Lychorida?

Lychorida. Patience, good sir; do not assist the storm.
Here's all that is left living of your queen –
A little daughter. For the sake of it,
Be manly, and take comfort.   (III, i, 15–22)

The human simplicities prevail, but under protest:

Pericles.   O you gods!
Why do you make us love your goodly gifts,
And snatch them right away? We here below
Recall not what we give, and therein may
Use honour with you.

Lychorida.   Patience, good sir,
Even for this charge.   (22–6)

In the literary history of the story and its analogues, Pericles' protest sounds like a check to the reassuring theology of the *Golden Legend*. There, Saint Peter tells the stricken King of Marseilles to 'be not heavy if thy wife sleep, and the little child rest with her, for our Lord is almighty for to give to whom he will, and to take away that he hath given, and to re-establish and give again that he hath taken, and to turn all heaviness and weeping into joy'.[1] Without the miracle there is no reassurance, and Pericles' response depends not upon the 'gods' but upon Lychorida's affective human plea and invocation:
                    Now, mild may be thy life!
For a more blusterous birth had never babe;
Quiet and gentle thy conditions!...
Thou hast as chiding a nativity
As fire, air, water, earth, and heaven, can make,
To herald thee from the womb. [Poor inch of nature!]

Even at the first thy loss is more than can
Thy portage quit with all thou canst find here.
(III, i, 26–8, 32–6)[2]

It is apparently a generous patience, valuing his child's survival more than his own, for when the sailors ask, 'What courage, sir?', he can answer:

Courage enough. I do not fear the flaw.
It hath done to me the worst. Yet, for the love
Of this poor infant, this fresh-new seafarer,
I would it would be quiet.   (39–42)

Yet the worst of the ordeal is still to come, and 'patience' is not the only quality that will characterise the intelligence as it is fashioned into a soul.

If we ask what in the play assists in the recovery of life out of loss, we may take from it a diversity of answers: the sea, that casts up naked men, rusty armour and caskets; the skill of Cerimon at the miraculous first-aid post of Ephesus; the therapies of art and music; the human virtues of honour, fidelity, and bounty exercised by several minor characters; and the astonishing powers of acceptance and endurance displayed by Pericles, hirsute and atrabilarian, upon the barge. But supremely, there is the buoyant and creative grace, wit, ferocity and patience of Marina in the brothel world of Mytilene. Mary Magdalene in the old play is seduced by the devil with the help of a taverner, 'luxsurya' and a 'galaunt'.[3] Shakespeare's scenes have comparable vitality but an incomparably richer moral and theatrical impact – it is as if the saint herself (and not her frail unredeemed counterpart) were exposed to the luxurious energies of the fallen world:

The nobleman would have dealt with her like a nobleman, and she sent him away as cold as a snowball; saying his prayers too.   (IV, vi, 138–40)

[1] William Caxton, *The Golden Legend*, Temple Classics, ed. F. S. Ellis (London, 1900), IV, 80–1.

[2] I have followed Hoeniger in adapting from Wilkins the apostrophe in square brackets. See Hoeniger's note, Arden Shakespeare, III, i, 34.

[3] The Digby play of *Mary Magdalene*, I, sc. 8.

Her qualities are not wholly of the passively resisting kind but receive a spacious testament, both in her own words,

> Proclaim that I can sing, weave, sew, and dance,
> With other virtues which I'll keep from boast;
>
> (IV, vi, 182–3)

and in the stage Gower's,

> She sings like one immortal, and she dances
> As goddess like to her admired lays;
> Deep clerks she dumbs; and with her needle composes
> Nature's own shape of bud, bird, branch, or berry,
> That even her art sisters the natural roses.
>
> (v, Chorus, 3–7)

Her attributes may look back to the sense of wonder that created the miracle plays and look about to the immediately contemporary Jacobean England, celebrated for its music and its embroidery; but they are mediated to Pericles, unwashed, hairy and dumb upon his barge, by the tale and its re-telling.

One of Keats's favourite speculations, he tells Benjamin Bailey, is 'that we shall enjoy ourselves here after by having what we call happiness on Earth repeated in a finer tone and so repeated'.[1] The play affords many repetitions (not always of happiness), and Marina's tale is several times told – by the stage Gower, by Shakespeare in the act of showing it, and by Marina within the play when she meets her father. The repetition is essential to the play's gathering significance, moving us away from Gower without losing touch with 'the power of white simplicity'. Gower's craft is as innocent as his burden:

> The unborn event
> I do commend to your content;
> Only I carry winged time
> Post on the lame feet of my rhyme.
>
> (IV, Chorus, 45–8)

Events are 'commended', 'born' and, in recollection, born again. Repetitions return us to the central episodes with a transfiguring intensity, to be reflected on, wondered at, or

energetically re-created. When Marina comes with violets and marigolds to the grave of Lychorida, her self-pity finds solace in poignantly stylised recollection:

> Ay me, poor maid,
> Born in a tempest, when my mother died,
> This world to me is as a lasting storm,
> Whirring me from my friends.
>
> (IV, i, 17–20)

As her 'death' approaches at the hands of Leonine (we know of it but she does not) the reminiscences, owed no doubt to Lychorida but testifying to the presence of the past in her quick imagination, grow more circumstantial:

> When I was born,
> Never was waves nor wind more violent,
> And from the ladder-tackle washes off
> A canvas-climber.   (58–61)

When Marina comes at last to tell her tale again to Pericles it is in a language capable of immense perspectives, touching fortune, time and breeding, and great moral authority:

> She speaks,
> My lord, that, may be, hath endur'd a grief
> Might equal yours, if both were justly weigh'd.
> Though wayward fortune did malign my state,
> My derivation was from ancestors
> Who stood equivalent with mighty kings;
> But time hath rooted out my parentage,
> And to the world and awkward casualties
> Bound me in servitude.   (v, i, 86–94)

The tale as Marina tells it literally awakens Pericles from his long trance.

'The Imagination', says Keats, 'may be compared to Adam's dream – he awoke and found it truth.' Keats's eager speculations are not, in his own terms, to be known for truth by consecutive reasoning. Yet they offer insights consonant with our experience of the play:

Adam's dream will do here and seems to be a conviction that Imagination and its empyreal reflection is the same as human life and its Spiritual repetition

[1] *Letters*, ed. Forman, p. 68.

. . . the simple imaginative Mind may have its rewards in the repetition of its own silent Workings coming continually on the Spirit with a fine suddenness.

In the impulsive sentences that follow Keats speaks of being 'surprised with an old Melody – in a delicious place – by a delicious voice' and of the image persuading him that 'the Prototype must be here after'. Forgiving the lapse into a sentimental mode (so much is 'delicious') and recalling the more tragic perceptions of the letter about the 'vale of soul-making', we may see in *Pericles* an answering experience. Pericles awakens to find his dream true, the silent workings of his mind (for much is made of his dumbness) surprised with a fine suddenness:

I am great with woe, and shall deliver weeping.
My dearest wife was like this maid, and such a one
My daughter might have been: my queen's square
                                brows;
Her stature to an inch; as wand-like straight;
As silver voic'd.   (v, i, 105–9)

It is not that Pericles believed wife and daughter to be alive still, but that Marina's presence in his imagination meets her presence in fact, with a rapture of recognition. The reality does not betray the dream but fulfills it – the paradisal experience that is denied to Lear when he awakens from his phantasmagoric hell at Dover, bound upon a wheel of fire and tears scalding like molten lead. Recognition is a principal element in the story and the story is the vehicle of recognition; Pericles asks for more circumstance, and Marina tells him:

If I should tell my history, it would seem
Like lies, disdain'd in the reporting.
                    (v, i, 118–19)

The realisation (and how inescapable that word is) of Pericles' waking vision is exquisitely phased, for the tale offers an order of verities, attested by the beauty and virtue of the teller, and by her life in the affections:

                    Prithee speak.
Falseness cannot come from thee; for thou lookest
Modest as Justice, and thou seem'st a palace
For the crown'd Truth to dwell in. I will believe thee
To make my senses credit thy relation
To points that seem impossible; for thou lookest
Like one I lov'd indeed.   (119–25)

The verities range from the remotely formulated kind, through the humane and intimate ('Modest as Justice'), to the satisfaction of the senses – both critical and physical. It is as if in all territories of experience the play had found the perfect voice and perfect auditor of its own story:

             Tell thy story;
If thine consider'd prove the thousand part
Of my endurance, thou art a man, and I
Have suffered like a girl. Yet thou dost look
Like Patience gazing on kings' graves, and smiling
Extremity out of act.   (134–9)

The patience-upon-a-monument metaphor is a disquieting gloss on the spectacle just witnessed, for Pericles looks almost literally like one rising from the grave. But the moral discovery – distinguishing his own austere 'endurance' from the smiling 'Patience' of the 'fresh, new seafarer' is vital enough, and it is completed as the circumstance of the story is repeated in, as it were, 'a finer tone'. The climax of the revelation, a spiritual and sensual delirium, is expressed again by the sea metaphor, with drowning now become an ecstasy:

          put me to present pain,
Lest this great sea of joys rushing upon me
O'erbear the shores of my mortality,
And drown me with their sweetness   (191–4)

and by a transparently riddling statement of the elements of the tale:

        O come hither
Thou that beget'st him that did thee beget;
Thou that was born at sea, buried at Tharsus,
And found at sea again!   (194–7)

These truths attained, the story recedes into that music of the spheres that Pericles (and the theatre audience) alone can hear. It entrances him into the sleep in which Diana appears, commanding him to give his 'crosses...repetition to the life', and to 'Awake and tell thy dream'. By the theatrical device of a vision the story is formally given what the poetry and the music have already conferred upon it – a supernal and subliminal authority. There is little left for the poet to do when Pericles goes to Ephesus, but he finds for Thaisa the quintessential formulation of the tale's mystery:

> Did you not name a tempest,
> A birth and death?   (v, iii, 33–4)

and the play is allowed to end with Pericles longing 'to hear the rest untold'.

It would be wrong to claim that *Pericles* as it reaches us is a consistently finished work of art, but it does fully express the potential of the material and tradition from which it was made; it rises higher than its sources and it does not muddy them. When the queen in Gower's story is retrieved from death, we are told how piteously,

> Sche spak and seide, 'Ha, where am I?
> Where is my lord, what world is this?'[1]

The play retains her words precisely, but with a transfiguring prelude, in which the most natural and spontaneous of effects – 'See how she gins to blow Into life's flower again', is conjoined with the most artificial – 'the diamonds Of a most praised water do appear, To make the world twice rich'; it is a conjunction of eternity with life.

As for the play's experiential as distinct from literary sources, Keats a short while before his death wrote to Charles Brown a letter that intimately conveys the kind of human ordeal to which *Pericles* is foil:

I wish for death every day and night to deliver me from these pains, and then I wish death away, for death would destroy even those pains which are better than nothing. Land and Sea, weakness and decline are great seperators, but death is the great divorcer for ever...Is there another Life? Shall I awake and find all this a dream? There must be we cannot be created for this sort of suffering.[2]

Pericles offers its reassurances, creating a world in which death is an illusion and the dream of immortality is appeased without the postulate of an after-life.

T. S. Eliot, who found in *Pericles* 'the finest of all the "recognition scenes"',[3] was clearly thinking of Thaisa's waking words when he chose his epigraph for 'Marina' from the *Hercules Furens: Quis hic locus, quae regio, quae mundi plaga?* In conjoining the tragic *anagnorisis* (Hercules awakens from his fury to find that he has slaughtered his family) with the infinitely auspicious recognitions of *Pericles*, Eliot puts both plays and poem into a vast perspective; one in which the crucial questions about death are not questions about survival, but questions about the ultimate awarenesses that the life lived enables and necessitates:

> What images return
> O my daughter.

In its 'sense of life' the poem's allusion to *Pericles* acknowledges a profound debt and that to Seneca measures a profound distance. For 'Marina' is an intense but muted response to the play – the woodthrush sings 'through the fog', the protagonist's expectations are held this side of ecstasy:

> let me
> Resign my life for this life, my speech for that
>   unspoken,
> The awakened, lips parted, the hope, the new ships.

Pericles is vital in comparison, for it creates deaths that in the theatre can be 'lived through' to a gay and imaginatively satisfying outcome. It smiles extremity out of act.

[1] *Confessio Amantis*, bk VIII, ll.1207–8.
[2] *Letters*, ed. Forman, p. 520.
[3] In the second unpublished lecture, 'The Development of Shakespeare's Verse', given at Edinburgh, 1937.

© J. P. BROCKBANK 1971

A NECESSARY THEATRE:
THE ROYAL SHAKESPEARE SEASON
1970 REVIEWED

PETER THOMSON

In 1970 the Royal Shakespeare Company presented at Stratford new productions of eight plays. Of these *The Tempest*, directed by John Barton and with Ian Richardson as Prospero, opened too late for review here, and *King John* and *Doctor Faustus* were prepared for the touring Theatregoround group, whose requirements are necessarily at occasional odds with those of the Memorial Theatre stage. Such a repertoire is, by any reckoning, ambitious; for the actors mighty gruelling – an extreme test for the company spirit which Peter Hall set out to foster in 1960. The achievement of the sixties was, of course, uneven, but the spectacle of Peter Hall's bold vision boldly enacted has been a splendour of the British theatre that could be missed only by the impercipient. Trevor Nunn in 1970 must have been uncomfortably aware of the inevitable comparison with Peter Hall in 1960. What are the prospects now? There is a company unique in the British theatre, an audience unique anywhere, and an international reputation which can as well diminish as increase. Above all, after the daring of the previous decade, the conditions are right, for the first time since the Restoration, for the establishment of an English ensemble theatre with a style of its own and an aim in view.

The 1970 season has left all the roads open. Trevor Nunn's decision has been not to decide. Each of the first seven plays had a different director; there was no evident linking of the repertoire; there were as many designers as directors; no clear message for the seventies emerged. The confirmed existence of a Royal Shakespeare *Company* has, for several years, tempted speculation about a 'company style'. Over the season I observed none that could be usefully separated from the actors' individual expression of their variable sameness. There is no master method of voice production that can link Sebastian Shaw's habit of hesitating among words with Ian Richardson's masterful summoning and dismissal of them. There is no single rigorous leadership seeking to expose to these two actors their tendency to discover in each character they play a psychological reason for speaking as they most naturally and confidently speak. There is no new uniformity in the verse-speaking, though the 'pushing and chopping technique' which Gareth Lloyd Evans described in *Shakespeare Survey 22* is still prominent. There is no doubt, nor *need* there be any regret, that the Royal Shakespeare Company in 1970 continues to accommodate more ideas than it defines.

It is, I think, a pity that this production of *King John* took place at all. Its flippancy was ill-judged and often puerile. Buzz Goodbody, who directed the play, imposed on it a single simplified view of politics as a dangerous game incompetently played by caricature kings and councillors who can give or take a giggle but defy respect. Patrick Stewart was required to play John as a smirking monarch whose development had been arrested at the nursery stage. He followed the order for the march on Calais (III, ii, 73) with a whooping rocking-horse gallop round the stage. He prefaced the opening lines of IV, ii:

Here once again we sit, once again crown'd,
And look'd upon, I hope, with cheerful eyes...

with sufficient farcical by-play with crown and throne – both of these props were used throughout to provoke hilarity – to excite an outburst of obligatory audience laughter. His death, a gay and giggly affair, drowned the Bastard's news of the Dauphin's march with a louder roar of amusement. Not surprisingly. Stewart contrived, by a rigid slide down the throne and on to the floor, to dislodge the golden cushion and bring it with a gentle plop over his dead face. I felt sorry for the actor, never for the king. And sorry, too, for Norman Rodway and Sheila Burrell. It may be that Rodway lacks the gusto of a really fine Faulconbridge, but he didn't deserve to be made redundant by the director's insistence that *she*, not *he*, should expose the 'Mad world! mad kings! mad composition!', nor to be forced, against the text, into playing the unobtrusive straight man on a stage swamped by the Crazy Gang. It may be that Sheila Burrell overstretches her voice as Constance, but who can blame her, playing act II to an audience that is expecting to laugh all the time? In both v, i and v, ii Miss Goodbody reinforces her misinterpretation by introducing passages from *The Troublesome Raigne*. The second of these additions, in which the Dauphin tells Melun of his plan to kill the turncoat English lords and then has them swear loyalty on a grotesque silver stage Bible, allows her to establish a picture of Lewis as a sneering, narcissistic young puppy, but denies any credibility to his subsequent mastery of Pandulph. Philip Locke's well-spoken, menacing Cardinal should have been more than a match for this priggish pansy. Astonishingly, the pathos of IV, i survived the

massacre of the play. Anthony Langdon's Hubert was physically eloquent, carrying the dignity of honest acting on to a stage that seemed determined to mock that commodity too. That was, perhaps, the saddest thing. Playing *King John* as if it were *Ubu Roi* led, not to a parody of the business of politics, but to a parody of the business of acting. It is not politicians who are mocked when actors 'pass over the stage' for laughs or form in straight downstage lines, facing front, to speak their words as foolishness. The chief, perhaps sole, victim of this production's crude assaults is the theatrical profession.

In three more plays during the season I was made to feel this confrontation of the theatre with itself. It was implicit in Terry Hands's wish that Norman Rodway should play Richard III 'Like to the old Vice', and explicit in the inset plays of *Hamlet* and *A Midsummer Night's Dream*. Rodway's performance pushed *Richard III* dangerously close to the theatrical parody of *King John*, but the other two proposed a clear alternative. The dignity and seriousness of Clement McCallin's First Player charged and challenged Hamlet's spiritual resources:

What would he do
Had he the motive and the cue for passion
That I have? (II, ii, 594–6)

In coupling 'motive' and 'cue' Shakespeare is approaching the paradoxical centre of acting, the simultaneity of emotional involvement and technical remove. It is this mystery that most excites Hamlet's interest in the First Player, and deepens the complex 'truth' of his own feigning. This was a troupe of actors deserving of a royal command. Peter Quince's troupe lacks all technique and, in many productions, all involvement too. The temptation is to turn their playing into broad burlesque of nineteenth-century 'stock' melodrama style. This is not Peter Brook's way. His mechanicals have a touching belief in the solemnity and importance of their play. It is important *to them*. It refines and releases their humanity. The loss of Bottom is a real deprivation, and his return a real delight, not because it saves their reputation but because it saves their play. In the terms laid down by Theseus they too deserve a royal command:

> For never anything can be amiss
> When simpleness and duty tender it.
> (v, i, 82–3)

The actors exhibit what Quince's prologue promises, 'good will' and 'simple skill'. Starveling's concentration is exemplary, Snug's involvement embarrassing chiefly to himself, Bottom's bombast subdued by a reverence for the words he speaks and the wonder of his speaking them. When the play is over, Bottom the actor can offer words of comfort even to the exalted:

No, I assure you; the wall is down that parted their
fathers. (v, i, 359–60)

In speaking these words, David Waller discarded the roughness of Bottom's voice, as though the experience of acting had transformed and elevated him. In their uncomplicated eagerness to perform, the mechanicals typify the attitude of the play's whole cast and present themselves as a model to any company of actors. Through them Peter Brook is speaking to the whole spiritually attenuated condition of the British theatre. The reading is not foisted on to Shakespeare, but discovered in him, and the discovery is both joyous and solemn. In confronting its own image the theatre is not often so demanding and so hopeful. The rehearsal and playing of 'Pyramus and Thisbe' was, for me, the high peak of the 1970 season.

Richard III was a disappointment. The problems began with the casting. Norman Rodway has a broad, honest face and an innocent solidity of build. He is a generous, self-effacing actor, whose rasping voice has no easy variability of pitch and tone. The volatile transitions of Richard are outside his normal physical and vocal range. I wonder whether his habit of bouncing as he talked was a result of the nervous strain of acting constantly *towards* rather than *inside* the character. Certainly it put him at a disadvantage with Ian Richardson's Buckingham. Richardson has a supreme ability to stand still. It gave him, in this production, all the sinister authority that Richard lacked. His 'Have done, have done' at I, iii, 279 silenced an unruly stage, and it was entirely he who engineered the league with Richard. It came about like this. Having received and dismissed his mother's blessing (II, ii, 109–11), Richard was stopped in mid-exultation by Buckingham's 'Tch...tch...tch'. He turned, and Buckingham stepped icily towards him, removed his own left glove, transferred it to his right hand, lifted it slowly over his right shoulder – was he about to strike Richard with it? – and then held out his bare left hand towards Richard's good arm. The shaking of the hands was a sealing of Buckingham's (and Richardson's) authority. There was, I think, no craft in this Richard's assurance that,

> I, as a child, will go by thy direction.
> (II, ii, 152)

It was an aim of Terry Hands's production to divert to the title role the jeremiad of 'Woe to that land that's govern'd by a child'. There was some confusion here. Richard was to be both child–man (a favourite, frolicking uncle to the young Princes, playing politics with the 'bang, bang, you're dead' insouciance with which he played horses in III, i) and prankish Vice; but how far can you expect an actor to step in and out of psychological creation? I heard only one voice, albeit a very valuable one, in praise of Rodway's performance; but much of the fault was the director's. He had laid down two contradictory lines for his leading actor. His larger intention was, I suspect, to apply to the play the 'fresh, unrealistic treatment' for which Professor Sprague has interestingly called.[1] So it was that the opening soliloquy was spoken skippingly, that a red 'Olivier' wig was donned for comic effect in I, iii in overt disavowal of a great tradition, that Richard's acting in III, vii, cynically presented by Buckingham as a play-within-a-play, was not designed to convince but offered as a party-joke, that the Battle of Bosworth was a slow-motion ballet played upon by lighting, and that Richard was killed, not by Richmond, but by Death, who then led him off with the ghosts of his victims in a *totentanz*. But the damaged mind of the child–man was allowed to intrude. There was a spine-chilling moment in III, i when the tantrum-prone Prince Richard leapt on to his uncle's deformed shoulders to be spun convulsively off by a man in sudden anguish. Again, at the end of III, v, awaiting Buckingham's return, Richard gestures to his attendants to turn away while the racking pain of his body produces in him some kind of fit. The uneasy combination of these two styles reduced Richard to petulance and the play to formlessness. It was in this production that I felt most strongly the shortage this season of experienced actors. Only ten of the company's thirty-eight associate artists were in Stratford. A greater authority in the cast might have helped Terry Hands to miss some of the holes into which he fell. The difficult women's roles, including that of a speaking Jane Shore, were well acted, but the play's transitions were inadequately marked off. This may have had something to do with Farrah's set – large, mobile screens, back-lit for the splendour of a stained-glass effect. The reliance on black-outs, which broke and lengthened the play, argued a lack of faith in the design. Why should we not see the sudden filling of the stage in I, ii, or its sudden clearance for Clarence's cell?

The secret scene-changing gave the play an old-fashioned gloss. It was a long way from the basic unit-settings of the other plays, and if it had its triumphs – the scene of Buckingham's rejection, the lit corridor of wailing women in IV, iv – it had also the defect of over-dominance.

Daphne Dare's set for *The Two Gentlemen of Verona* had a ramp and steps from mid-stage leading up to three large screens, with a heavy diving-board scaffold mid-stage left and a small pool downstage right. The forest was created by the dropping of a single batten of ropes from the flies and a dappling of the light. The costumes were basically, but not consistently, modern. It was a curiosity that the sun-drenched impression created by the clothes and emphasised by the use of sun-glasses was contradicted by a chilly lighting-plot. This was a production that opened amid ominous rumours of company quarrels, last-minute changes and threats of withdrawal. In the event it was kindly received. I found it an unresolved combination of quick-witted inventiveness and ponderous point-making. It opened with a tableau of the lovers in silhouette and a recorded echo-song, 'Who is Silvia? Who is Valentine? Who is Proteus? Who is Julia?', but addressed itself, in the main, to a clarification, along plausible psychological lines, of Proteus's misconduct. The initial exchange had an athletic Valentine, stripped for the lido, doing exercises with a beach-ball to the admiring envy of a comparatively puny Proteus, the sort of man who would never dare take off his shirt in the face of such competition. With Valentine's exit, Proteus deprecatingly felt his own muscles. The vanity and disloyalty of Proteus has, then, its origin in his sense of his own inadequacy. It is exaggerated self-awareness that impedes his farewell to Julia and, presumably, limits his capacity to love.

[1] A. C. Sprague, *Shakespeare's Histories: Plays for the Stage* (London, 1964), p. 141.

This Proteus is a man who reads books, but only because he isn't good at games. Ian Richardson finds a precise comic image of Proteus's search for physical grace when he throws his strapped bundle of 'books for the voyage' over his shoulder in a gesture of careless abandon that Valentine might have admired, but fails quite to restrain a wince when the strap brings them round in an arc to clobber him on the left buttock. In Verona Proteus is constantly tense. In Milan he relaxes, finding Valentine reduced to love. The betrayal is confident, and Ian Richardson's 'comforting' of the banished Valentine is almost complacent. But here a director's point turns the tables. Valentine interrupts Proteus's account of Silvia's imprisonment by slapping him hard on the cheek. The blow is not well motivated, but its consequence is interesting. For the rest of the play, Proteus feels the horror of his deception in his stinging cheek. At III, ii, 89, when Thurio pinches his face in a patronising gesture of thanks, he pulls away in pain. On other occasions he soothes his cheek nervously. Only when Valentine forgivingly kisses him exactly where he had struck him is this Proteus free of his confining self. In new delight the lovers pair off and tousle on the forest floor. Valentine's 'Forbear, forbear, I say; it is my lord the duke' (v, iv, 122) is addressed, not to the outlaws, but to Julia and Proteus – 'do her up quick. It's Silvia's father!' – but the gaiety of this trick is not sustained. The play ends with a tableau, set against a reprise of the opening echo-song and following Valentine's portentous delivery of the final speech. He phrases the last line in such a way as to cast doubt on the prospect it promises:

One feast, one house, one mutual (*pause*) happiness (*with an interrogatory vocal rise*).

Robin Phillips, the director, brought to the play a sense of humour and a dangerous desire to analyse its presentation of adolescent sexual confusion. Hence the combination of inventiveness and point-making. The invention was generally superior to the analysis. Thurio was aptly portrayed as an amorous narcissist with sun-glasses and an Italian accent, Eglamour as a sad old scoutmaster, who brought an ordnance survey map to aid in Silvia's escape; and the difficult I, iii was turned into a theatrical triumph by having Antonio, a bloated, cigar-smoking capitalist, plunge into his private pool, leaving Panthino to hold his smoking cigar and monogrammed beach-wrap. Phillips saw the play in a context of leisured society, sun-bathing and beautiful bodies. Verona was a high-class resort, Milan an open-air university, with the Duke as its avuncular Vice-Chancellor. The tone-painting was ingenious and acceptable, the analysis tendentious and speciously plausible. Julia sucked chewing-gum in I, ii, her thumb in II, vii, and rolled on to her back to say,

Now kiss, embrace, contend, do what you will.
(I, ii, 126)

Silvia revealed a modern willingness to take the initiative in embracing her men, but escaped from Proteus's attempted rape to the comforting arms of Sebastian/Julia rather than to Valentine's. (Why?) It was in the interpretation of Launce that the dangers of a production insecurely anchored to the text were most apparent. Phillips seems to have felt the need for a sentimental counter-balance to the blissful ignorants. His Launce knew, and could endure, everything. Patrick Stewart played him (well) in ragged black, a dour northerner against Speed's jaunty cockney. From the opening tableau, when he threaded his way among the still lovers in a springless stroll, to the curtain-call, when he stood downstage of the main group, separated by his knowingness, Launce was the unmoved observer, tearless throughout and tolerant, a man who never expected much. The play ran for 160 minutes. That is too long.

Trevor Nunn's production of *Hamlet* was interestingly divided by its two intervals. The first came after act I, the second not until the end of IV, iv. Nunn has explained that 'the whole fascination of the centre part of the play to me, and to Alan Howard, were [*sic*] the shifts between real madness and performed madness unknown to the person in the middle of it all'.[1] The chosen intervals defined the interpretation. Act I carries Hamlet to breaking-point in confrontation with his father's ghost, this act II contains the 'shifts between real madness and performed madness' for which the players provide a major impetus, and this act III completes the story *after* Hamlet has recovered his self-control. The lightening of Hamlet's tone (and costume) in this last act, the evident sea-change wrought by the voyage, is this production's most radical assertion. The special burden of Alan Howard's Hamlet is certainly not the charge to kill Claudius – that seems never seriously to engage him – but the mental disorder into which his thudding thoughts throw him. The end is almost restful. The dialogue with Osric is jocular banter, the duel with Laertes is finely and gracefully fought, even Gertrude's death is bearable; and Hamlet who would not kill Claudius praying in III, iii now flicks his ear with the poisoned sword despite the fact that he is kneeling in prayer beside his dead wife. From the outset this Hamlet is vulnerable to nothing but his own thoughts. He is unthreatened by the court-bully Claudius of David Waller or the endearingly (but over-) bumbling Polonius of Sebastian Shaw; but he is at the mercy of memories that he tries vainly to shut out of his head. The stress falls on 'Heaven and earth! Must I *remember*?', on the Ghost's 'Hamlet, *remember* me' and on 'for there is nothing either good or bad, but *thinking* makes it so'. The Players fascinate him because they offer feigned madness as a lively alternative to the real madness that threatens him, and that over-

takes him in, for example, the frenzied stabbing of Polonius. It is the sea-voyage that restores him, for reasons that the playing never really made clear to me. That, I believe, was the production's main through-line of action, and the line that Alan Howard played with some virtuosity. His voice is neither strong nor resonant, but surprises by its range and suppleness, his charisma is of the matinee idol kind, a coming together of confidence and sex appeal, his chief weakness a playing *off* rather than *with* other actors. He was out of contact with Brenda Bruce's Gertrude in III, iv, but elsewhere made a virtue of his solipsism. Not a great Hamlet, but not a negligible one. The same might be said of the production. Trevor Nunn is a thoughtful director, who likes to use his intelligence responsibly. Like John Barton, he persuades an audience that he has done nothing that he could not explain. Thus, the off-white boards of the stage-floor leading up to four off-white screens across the back wall and broken intermittently with off-white furnishings, together with the rich flecked-white costumes of the Danish court, have, for Nunn and his designer Christopher Morley, a simple explanation: 'I wanted to present something believably Scandinavian in terms of climate and practicality. I also wanted to show that the Court was in celebration rather than mourning.'[2] And yes; boldly and evenly lit, the stage has an icy glitter that may tire but doesn't bore the eye. Certain features of the production might be of interest to stage historians:

(i) I, iii begins with Laertes giving Ophelia a lute lesson. The tune they play is movingly recalled in IV, vii when the mad Ophelia plays it again, and Laertes joins in the singing in a desperate attempt to penetrate her madness.

[1] In an interview with Peter Ansorge reported in *Plays and Players*, vol. 17, no. 12 (September 1970), pp. 16–17 and 21.
[2] From the same interview.

(ii) III, i is set in a chapel. Ophelia sits on a long pew, placed parallel to the proscenium, Claudius and Polonius hide in a confessional a little upstage right of it, and Hamlet speaks 'To be, or not to be' downstage right. Alan Howard was fine and frightening in this scene. His departure left Ophelia slumped on the pew like one recently raped, whilst Claudius and Polonius muttered downstage, conspiring when they ought to sympathise.

(iii) III, ii began with a short, interpolated scene of Hamlet rehearsing the players in the mime. 'The Mouse-trap' was acted on a portable booth-stage, with Gertrude and Claudius beside it facing Hamlet and Ophelia downstage of it.

(iv) III, iii was continuous with III, ii, and Hamlet, hiding behind the curtains of the booth-stage, must have overheard Claudius's plans to send him to England. It is on the booth-stage that Claudius prays, and Hamlet creeps up behind him wearing a black cowl from the Players' wardrobe.

(v) In IV, ii the captured Hamlet, still in the cowl, is brought to Claudius, presumably in a cloister of the palace, where a group of black-cowled monks is gathered. Hamlet makes an impish attempt at escape by joining their ranks, and the audience's laughter is cut suddenly short when Claudius strips him down to a pair of black jockey-shorts and punches him in the belly. (Where is the indirect, deputing Claudius? I have a worried impression that this stripping of Hamlet was intended to be the beginning of his recovery.)

(vi) The mad Ophelia was petulant, stamping her feet when her songs were interrupted. It was the reverse of her submissive sanity.

(vii) Claudius took the poisoned drink from Hamlet, and drank it of his own volition.

It is a general point of some accuracy that this was a *Hamlet* produced more as a problem play than as a tragedy.

Nothing unthought happens in a play directed by John Barton. The Duke's desk, in the opening scene of *Measure for Measure*, is piled high with dusty books, probably the overspill of this endearing eccentric's untidy library. Angelo uses the same desk in II, ii, but there are no books on it. He loves neither dust nor scholarship. The desk has become a judgement table. Angelo is busy at it when Isabella is first admitted. 'You're welcome' he announces tonelessly, then looks up, *sees* her, and continues, 'what's your will?' The pause is not a long one, but a lot of work is done in it. The process begun there is confirmed in II, iv when Angelo, admitting his lust, moves from behind the judgement table impulsively towards Isabella, and she, in escaping, replaces him. Isabella, at that moment, judges Angelo. (It was, I think, at II, iv, 125.) There is some danger that, in the pursuit of significant detail, Barton will shy away from Shakespeare's larger gestures. There is nothing certainly wrong in having Claudio (in a blonde wig suggestively similar to Angelo's) eat a prison meal whilst the Duke exhorts him to 'Be absolute for death', but, in offering an alternative object of attention, such an action is, I think, false to the text. Such falseness is less obvious where the pursuit of truth is less meticulous; and it should be stressed that this *Measure for Measure* is serious, intelligent, and sometimes dull. The dullness gathers around Sebastian Shaw's Duke. To the Shakespeare Conference, John Barton described the Duke as a 'complex, inconsistent man', adding that 'the *point* of the part is its inconsistencies'. Shaw spoke it like a man conscious of his own complexity and willing to keep slow pace with it. He found prose rhythms even in the octosyllabics of III, ii, but only by blurring stress and unstress and placing the words round pauses. If the pipe-smoking eccentric of I, i seemed wise, it was partly because his sniggering councillors behaved foolishly; and if the good humour remained with him, even embracing a quizzical fondness for Lucio, it wasn't always distinguishable from simple-mindedness. Certainly the gravity with which this Duke followed his own thought processes exposed more triteness than sagacity in his pronouncements. At the end of the play Isabella was left alone on stage, puzzled still for an answer to the Duke's proposal. Such an ending is, of course, a rejection of comedy convention in the pursuit of psychological consistency – unnecessary but not uninteresting. Estelle Kohler's Isabella was always imperfectly aware of her real feelings. I am uncertain whether Miss Kohler was acting the character's uncertainty or making drama out of her own uncertainty about the character. Something was missing, although a lot was there. Neither the Duke nor Isabella held me as Mariana and Angelo did. Watching Sara Kestelman this season, as Jane Shore, Mariana and Hippolita/Titania, I have felt in touch with future greatness. Mariana is given unusual prominence in this production. She is, writes Anne Barton in a programme note, the one character who 'exists as an uncriticized absolute', and, by placing the interval immediately before the play's move to the moated grange, John Barton has reinforced his view that *Measure for Measure* undergoes a radical shift of emphasis with the introduction of Mariana. Hers is the dominant presence in act v (should it be?), a pale, auburn-haired, pre-Raphaelite beauty whose dejection has produced in her no hesitancy. Angelo was given a less helpful introduction. The Duke's announcement of his deputy was met with concerted chuckles by the assembled officers. (Even stranger was the giggle with which Friar Thomas greeted the Duke's,

> hence shall we see,
> If power change purpose, what our seemers be.)

I was disturbed by this. Right government was *not* a serious issue in I, i, so that Claudio's subsequent condemnation lacked political definition. It seemed as peripheral as the trial of Froth and Pompey, a scene that was neither funny nor controlled in this production. It was left to Ian Richardson to establish his own authority as Angelo. Richardson's individuality is strongly marked in this company. Dangerously so, perhaps. Buckingham, Proteus and now Angelo stood out as cold-blooded, precise figures whose disdain for baser men was signalled in the carriage of the head, the subtle modulation of the voice, and the sparse, carefully expressive gestures. All accurately acted, they were all improbably similar. But the theatrical delight of such accomplished playing is irresistible – the greeting of Isabella in II, iv when, seated on his desk, he pulls a chair towards him with his foot and indicates with a flick of the right hand that she should sit; the distaste with which he handles the Duke's dusty books in I, i; the fastidious wiping of his fingers, which becomes an image of his misanthropy, later to be parodied in the Abhorson/Pompey scene; the desperate phrasing of,

> Would yet he had liv'd!
> Alack! when once our grace we have forgot,
> Nothing goes right: we would, and we would not.
>   (IV, iv, 35–7)

There must be some questioning of so physically 'beautiful' an Angelo, and of Barton's decision to have him seize Isabella's hair in II, iv to pull her down on to the judgement table and stroke her body from breast to groin, but there is no doubt of the continuing control of Richardson's performances. John Barton suggested to the Shakespeare Conference that *Measure for Measure* is 'Isabella's play'. Timothy O'Brien's set pushed it further towards Angelo. The wall-blocks of panelled wood indicated, but did not complete, a box-set. Continued into semi-parquet flooring and slung, wooden ceiling, they had a clinical (puritannical?) cleanliness and a forbidding solidity. But the perspective was sharply exaggerated, a distortion of the geometrical form it adumbrated, and a realisation almost of Angelo's mentality. It must have been a beautiful model. Full-size, it tended to crush the play.

When Peter Brook directed *Measure for Measure* at Stratford, he illustrated Pompey's account (IV, iii, 1–21) of the inmates of the prison by bringing them on in a hideous parade of corruption and disease. John Barton followed the idea in 1970, but his gathering of felons became a jolly thieves' kitchen with a *Beggar's Opera* tunefulness. Peter Brook and John Barton could scarcely be more different. Barton looks for ways of revealing theatrically what he has discovered in reading a text. Brook prefers to make his crucial discoveries in rehearsal, believing that theatrical revelation must not be anticipated but 'risked'. The opposition of an 'intellectual' and a 'spiritual' theatre might be argued from their differing approaches. Peter Brook's production of *A Midsummer Night's Dream* is the sensation of the 1970 season. Those who did not respond to it will feel compelled to argue against it. Those for whom it was a uniquely joyful experience will regret the cribbed confinement of the cavillers, who lost the light for a handful of prejudices. I am decidedly of the second party, and can only with hesitation undertake to analyse an experience that came to me whole. I think I understand now what Brook means when he describes himself as a man 'searching within a decaying and evolving theatre'.[1] It is not enough that the Royal Shakespeare Company should serve Shakespeare. It must be prepared, from its position of privilege, to serve the British theatre, which finds itself, in 1970, threatened materially by, for example, a new minimum wage for actors, and spiritually by a loss of faith in the holiness of its art. One member of the *Dream*'s cast told me that

working with Peter Brook was 'fantastic. It changes your life.' England has a bad record in its treatment of wayward theatrical genius. Some of the attacks on Peter Brook ring like repeating history, but no one to whom I talked at Stratford was ready with outright condemnation of *A Midsummer Night's Dream*. One Shakespearian scholar confessed that he shut his eyes during the performance, loving the way it was spoken, hating the way it was presented. And yes, it was superbly spoken, despite the fact that Brook gave no textual notes throughout the rehearsal period.[2] I choose to believe that the actors spoke well because the director had renewed in them a generous anxiety to communicate with the audience. It was no accident that the programme notes featured Meyerhold's insistence that, 'There is a fourth *creator* in addition to the author, the director and the actor – namely, the spectator...from the friction between the actor's creativity and the spectator's imagination, a clear flame is kindled.' At the end of the performance Puck's 'Give me your hands, if we be friends', was taken as the cue for the actors to leave the stage and walk through the auditorium shaking hands with the audience. It was the culmination of a feast of friendship. I was moved.

The design by Sally Jacobs set the play among white walls rising to about eighteen feet and topped by a practical gallery from which actors not on stage were constantly surveying those who were, and contributing where necessary to the mechanics of the staging. Two upstage doors, much narrower than their Elizabethan counterparts but similarly placed, provided the only access at stage level, but there were ladders at the downstage end of both the side walls, and trapezes slung from

---

[1] Peter Brook, *The Empty Space* (London, 1968), p. 100.

[2] My informants on this point were John Kane and Ben Kingsley, Puck and Demetrius in this production.

the flies could lower and raise Oberon, Puck, Titania and the four fairies. The costumes were vivid, of no single period, aiming at beauty and the actors' comfort. Puck was in a glossy yellow clown-suit and blue skull-cap. Demetrius and Lysander wore smocks of the currently popular smudged pastel design over pressed white flannels, Helena and Hermia long, side-slit dresses with the same smudged pastel decoration. Oberon wore deep purple, Titania bright green, the Mechanicals the working clothes of British labourers in the age of austerity. The Fairies, unobtrusive amid the colour, wore practical suits of grey silk. Against white walls, costume stands out. So do properties. The trees were coiled wire mobiles, hung out from the gallery, which produced metallic music as they twisted and settled. Hermia, waking alone at the end of II, ii, was threatened and snared by them in a nightmare realisation of 'the fierce vexation of a dream'. At the amazing end of III, i (immediately followed by the interval), the stage was a bedlam of flying plates and flashing tinsel darts, the wild confetti for the 'marriage' of Titania and Bottom. The play's magic was replaced by circus tricks. Brook has described the reasoning:

today we have no symbols that can conjure up fairyland and magic for a modern audience. On the other hand there are a number of actions that a performer can execute that are quite breathtaking. So we went to the art of the circus and the acrobat because they both make purely theatrical statements. We've worked through a language of acrobatics to find a new approach to a magic that we know cannot be reached by 19th century conventions.[1]

I am not convinced of the necessity for the substitution, but its effectiveness in the theatre can be assessed only in the theatre; and even there not argued, only perceived or denied. At II, i, 246, Puck swings down on a trapeze, spinning a plate on a rod. Oberon, on a lower trapeze, looks up to ask,

Hast thou the flower there? Welcome, wanderer . . .

and Puck leans over to tip the still spinning plate on to Oberon's rod – 'Ay, there it is'. The plate does not *become* the flower. Instead, the act of passing it becomes the *magic* of the flower. In order to harry Lysander and Demetrius in III, ii, Puck climbs on six foot stilts and darts around the stage in a new-established convention of invisibility that makes stage poetry out of a scene normally surrendered to a dead convention. I feel no inclination to defend any of Brook's decisions. I doubt whether the play could have been so well spoken if it had been seriously falsified. It should, however, be recorded that there was doubling of Theseus and Oberon, Hippolita and Titania (the change at IV, i, 102 was simply managed, though with remarkable poignancy, by having Oberon and Titania walk up to the stage doors, don cloaks and turn to walk downstage as Theseus and Hippolita), Philostrate and Puck, Theseus' courtiers and the fairies, so that the lovers carried with them into their dream all the familiar faces of the Athenian court. And it should also be admitted that a man more musically accomplished than I would annotate the variety of Richard Peaslee's score where I can only applaud it. More than anything I have ever seen, this production declared its confidence and delight in the art of performance. In doing so, it went, for me, beyond the meaning of the play to a joyous celebration of the fact that it was written. And it did all its work in full view of the audience. I am reminded of another of Peter Brook's stated beliefs: 'This is how I understand a necessary theatre; one in which there is only a practical difference between actor and audience, not a fundamental one.'[2]

[1] Quoted in an excellent discussion of the production by John Barber in the *Daily Telegraph*, 14 September 1970.
[2] Brook, *The Empty Space*, p. 134.

© PETER THOMSON 1971

FREE SHAKESPEARE

JOHN RUSSELL BROWN

Shakespeare is unique and those who present his plays in the theatre should try to take this into account: usual ways of working may be quite inappropriate.

Matthew Arnold's description of Shakespeare's special qualities has become proverbial:

> Others abide our question. Thou art free.
> We ask and ask: Thou smilest and art still,
> Out-topping knowledge.

In our own words, most of us would agree that we cannot nail down his purposes or be sure that we understand. Returning to a play after a few years, we realise that we have seen only what we had looked for, and that as we have changed so, it seems, has he. But we are also aware of a direct, involving engagement and, like Keats, we will not sit down to read *King Lear* again without some prologue, at least a moment of adjustment:

> once again the fierce dispute,
> Betwixt Hell torment and impassion'd Clay
> Must I burn through . . .

Shakespeare seems to draw us into his creation, into fresh discovery and active imagination: we 'burn through' a re-creation of the play in our own minds.

Standing further back from individual plays, we, like Dryden, wonder at the range and power of his mind: 'He was the man who of all Modern, and perhaps Ancient Poets, had the largest and most comprehensive soul.' Coleridge was later to call him 'myriad-minded', in that phrase catching the bafflement

that mixes with our admiration. The apparent ease with which he wrote is at once the most attractive and most astonishing of his qualities. Dryden called it 'luck': 'All the Images of Nature were still present to him, and he drew them not laboriously, but luckily . . .' But while Ben Jonson praised the naturalness of his writing –

> Nature herself was proud of his designs,
> And joy'd to wear the dressing of his lines,

he also knew that the 'joy' depended on craftsmanship, each line being 'well turned and true filed' as in a blacksmith's forge.

Besides these old encomiums, scholars and critics today have added to our appreciation, showing verbal complexity, theatrical variety, social awareness, psychological perception, intellectual grasp and scepticism. No theatre producer could read all that has been written, let alone judge each opinion and find means to reflect what he has thought in theatrical productions. The readiest response is to stage Shakespeare according to current theatrical methods and the perception of the moment, and trust Shakespeare to survive. So we should go to the theatre to see new facets of his plays, knowing that in five years' time we shall see still more.

I have long supposed that this was the only sensible course for playgoers or for producers. But to spend one's time wholly in the pursuit of 'something new' is to run the risk of being 'too superstitious', as the apostle Paul told the men on the Hill of Mars. If the Shakespeare devotee is able to build up a composite impression of the plays from the many partial renderings he has seen, must every play-goer go through the same progression? Must each view be limited by another man's momentary perception? Journalistic criticism of Shakespeare productions reflects the interest which is centred today on the task of deciphering the 'director's intentions' in a production.[1] A director describing his work will explain what is 'the whole fascination of the centre part of the play to me', and how that has influenced his staging.[2]

The history of Shakespeare in the theatre shows how each age has, indeed, seen the plays only through the various filters of individual interpretive artists. But in the present century there is a new situation, for now the filter is more likely to be provided by a director than by an actor: we talk of Peter Brook's *Dream*, Peter Hall's *Dream*, or Zeffirelli's *Romeo*. The nature of the intervening filter is changing, for while an actor has to bring himself along with his interpretation and work out his recreation of Shakespeare's character in daily contact with Shakespeare's words and with his own complete personality, the director never has to live with what he has created. Good directors do respond widely to the text, will 'live' through the rehearsals using all their experience of life and all their intuitive responses as well as their intellectual grasp of the play and their verbalisation of the fascination that the text has for them; but this is not the same kind of engagement as an actor's, working on a single play with other actors over the course of months or, perhaps, of whole years. Moreover the director has much greater power over the play than any one actor. He can, with his designer, reduce individualised characters to an almost uniform appearance through which the actors would have to work crudely to make any individual impression: see, for example, the all-red costumes for a recent Stratford production of *Much Ado* (1968) in which

prince and soldier were scarcely distinguishable, or the current *Hamlet* (1970) where the whole court is dressed in regulation white, trimmed with fur, and boots. The director can set the play in a period that forces the actors to assume a range of mannerisms which limits their rhythms, tones and responses, and this assumption of a period may well take their attention away from more basic aspects of their task: see, for example, the current version of *The Merchant of Venice* (1970) at the National Theatre in London, which is set in Victorian streets and drawing rooms.

Today Shakespeare does not 'abide' the question of audiences. Directors are working all the time to make their own *answers* abundantly clear, by underlining with all the contrivance of set, costume, lighting, sound and the drilling of actors (and invention of improvisations); by placing of visual emphasis; by grouping and movement; by verbal emphasis and by elaborate programmes and public-relations operations. Shakespeare is not free; he is not still. We do not 'ask', for all the time we are being 'told and told'. Nothing much happens 'luckily', and if it does, it is assimilated into the defined and high-powered presentation of a particular 'interpretation'. What is forged in the smithy of the rehearsal-room is nothing 'natural', but a clear, surprising, challenging, unavoidable interpretation of Shakespeare: 'something new'.

The 1970 productions at Stratford and *The Merchant of Venice* in London offer many examples of the director getting the better of

[1] See an analysis of criticisms of two Shakespeare productions, in my 'English Criticism of Shakespeare Performances Today', *Deutsche Shakespeare-Gesellschaft West Jahrbuch* (1967), pp. 163–74.

[2] Trevor Nunn reported in *Plays and Players*, vol. 17, no. 12 (September 1970), pp. 16–17 and 21; this report is quoted in Peter Thomson's criticism of the ensuing production in this volume of *Shakespeare Survey*, p. 122 above.

A

B

I A   Portrait of Talma as Ducis's Hamlet

I B   Lithograph of Talma and Mlle Duchesnois as
       Hamlet and Gertrude in Ducis's Closet Scene

I C   Portrait of Ducis

C

II *Hamlet*, Royal Shakespeare Theatre, 1970. Directed by Trevor Nunn, designed by Christopher Morley, with music by Guy Woolfenden. The Duel Scene (foreground, l. to r.): Christopher Gable as Laertes, Peter Egan as Osric and Alan Howard as Hamlet

III   *Measure for Measure*, Royal Shakespeare Theatre, 1970. Directed by John Barton.
A (above), Ian Richardson as Angelo;   B (below), the prison scene

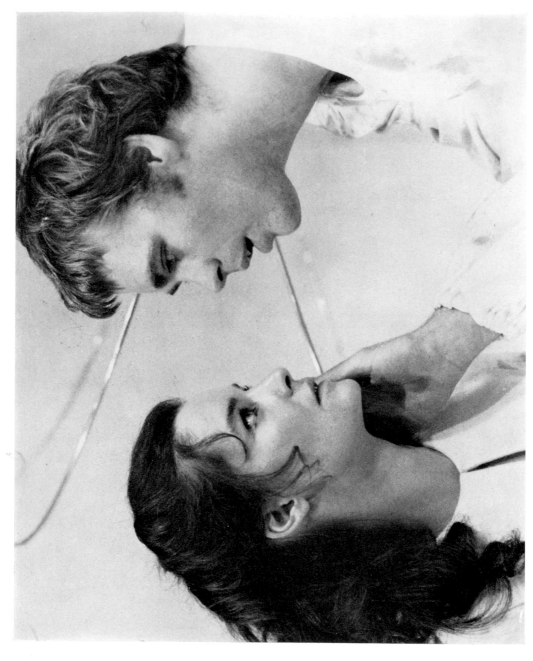

IV *A Midsummer Night's Dream*, Royal Shakespeare Theatre, 1970. Directed by Peter Brook, designed by Sally Jacobs, with music by Richard Peaslee. Mary Rutherford as Hermia and Christopher Gable as Lysander

V *A Midsummer Night's Dream*, with (l. to r.) Alan Howard as Theseus, Sara Kestelman as Hippolyta, Mary Rutherford (Hermia), Christopher Gable (Lysander), John Kane as Philostrate, Frances de la Tour as Helena and Ben Kingsley as Demetrius

VI *A Midsummer Night's Dream*, with (above, l.) Alan Howard as Oberon and (above, r.) John Kane as Puck; (below) Sara Kestelman as Titania and David Waller as Bottom

VII *The Merchant of Venice*, National Theatre, 1970. Directed by Jonathan Miller and designed by Julia Trevelyan Oman. Anna Carteret (l.) as Nerissa and Joan Plowright as Portia

VIII *The Merchant of Venice*, with (l. to r.) Joan Plowright (Portia), Jeremy Brett as Bassanio, Benjamin Whitrow as the Duke of Venice, Laurence Olivier as Shylock and Derek Jacobi as Gratiano

the textual material in order to force the audience to notice his interpretation. Most obvious are the occasions when silent incidents are interpolated into the plays. In *Richard III*, the director, Terry Hands, cut the Scrivener scene (III, vi) and kept Richard on stage, silent: he feels pain in his deformed leg; there is a long silence as he struggles for control; he becomes fretful and childish. The director has decided to make the audience consider the grounds of motivation at this point: the Scrivener, who shows both a man and common humanity, morality and cynicism, perhaps pathos, and certainly irony, is sacrificed in order to build up a particular view of the central character. Earlier, as Edward IV leaves the stage after hearing of the death of Clarence, he speaks a line that might imply self-awareness or pity, or resolution, or fear, or the mere putting of an unpleasant thought out of mind – 'Come, Hastings, help me to my closet. Ah, poor Clarence!' (II, i, 133). At this moment, Terry Hands directed that the King pushes over a tub from which rolls a heap of skulls. It had been placed downstage centre, not by necessity of words or of action implicit in the text, but by the director who is intent on one unambiguous effect, a reminder of mortality. (The trouble is that even a play-goer accustomed to theatre ways may be more impressed by the intrusive novelty than by anything else.)

In making such simple additions to the plays, directors are often less resourceful than their texts, and fall into clichés. The delayed exit is one of these. In John Barton's production of *Measure for Measure*, Isabella does not go out with duke or brother at the close of the play, but remains for a silent soliloquy, which marks her undeniably as the odd one out. At the end of *The Merchant of Venice* both Jessica and Antonio are left on stage after the group *exeunt*, each reading the letter Portia has just given them; Jessica takes longer than the Merchant to leave, and as she goes, sadly, a voice is heard singing offstage. Jonathan Miller, the director, has insisted that the audience goes away counting the cost of happiness, despite the fact that the text of the play ends with a bawdy joke from Gratiano. Robin Phillips's *Two Gentlemen* ends with a silent tableau as all the characters remain on stage where Shakespeare's text asks for an *exeunt*; at this point the director introduced a further character, a silent, black-visaged Launce who slowly threads his way through the silent figures.

The designer is the strongest ally of the director. When Terry Hands wished to stress the nightmare quality of the end of *Richard III* and extend its influence over previous acts, his designer provided grotesque costumes for the coronation scene (IV, ii), Richard having a large boar's head growing on his shoulder and Ann a vast ruff and a costume so apparently heavy that her arms were supported with crutches as she held the symbols of queenship in her hands. For John Barton's production of *The Tempest*, Prospero was dressed in plain beige, his magic cloak offering no contrast and suggesting no formality; there was no apparent need to ask Miranda to help 'pluck' it off (I, ii, 24). The effect was to get the audience to see Prospero as a man feeling his way through a crisis, not as a strange, powerful magician. The banquet and masque were staged with scarcely any pomp or explicit meaning, with scarcely any costumes and the fewest, all-male performers. The text speaks of a 'most majestic vision' and of 'revels' (IV, i, 118 and 148), but designer and director had ignored these clues to achieve their clear-cut objective. In the National Theatre *Merchant*, Sir Laurence Olivier appears as Shylock in frock-coat and top hat, so that an unmistakable contrast is made when he dons a Jewish woven robe before calling on Tubal to meet him at 'our synagogue' to prosecute his revenge (III, i,

111): no one in the audience would doubt the religious and racial motivation of that exit, although in the text his words are also full of murder, money and merchandise.

In his handling of actors, the director's aim is often to remove ambiguity and to enlarge those incidents or words that seem most relevant to his own 'view of the play'. How much can be achieved in this way may be seen in Buzz Goodbody's production of *King John*. Here the characters frequently enter like marching toy soldiers, smirk, giggle and repeat phrases in chorus: they pray in unison with mechanical gestures and toneless voices. Blanche's wedding is proposed with humorous over-emphasis and, at the end, a comic 'phew'. For his death-scene, the King is carried on stage lumped unceremoniously over a Lord's back. The director wished to stress the repetitions, self-satisfaction and self-interest of politics, and does so with wearying completeness, so that suffering, uncertainty, passion and moral considerations, so often suggested by the text, are crowded out, submerged in what the director is telling us. The Bastard mocks behaviour that is all the time being mocked by the actors.

In *Hamlet*, Trevor Nunn has Alan Howard, as the Prince, kneeling in church for 'To be, or not to be': and at the end of this he looks round as if not knowing where he is. So the soliloquy becomes an activity that starts as an assumed seriousness, and clearly it occupies only a part of his conscious mind. In the following scene with Ophelia, she tries to kiss him and there is a long pause before Hamlet exclaims with strength: 'It hath made me mad' (III, i, 147). The director has said that he is examining the 'shifts between real madness and performed madness unknown to the person in the middle of it all': and so 'enterprizes of great pitch and moment', relationships with others, suspicion, guilt, philosophical concern with the nature of human existence, all of

which can be seen in the text, are allowed no representation; they must not challenge the clear 'line' through the play's action that director has chosen. After the closet-scene with his mother, Hamlet is made to appear almost naked, and the King gives him two forceful blows in the crutch: the reasons for this change of dress and sudden brutality are harder to discern. Perhaps Hamlet finds himself making an obscene gesture or exposure: perhaps he is trying to find a new activity by shedding his mourning and Claudius is taking the nearest way to stopping him for the moment. The director has clearly turned Shakespeare's ironic, challenging, uneasy scene into some sort of physical, man-to-man opposition. He is interpreting the scene in the light of his own 'fascination' with the possibilities of the text and has found a physical way of making an unprecedented statement; whatever that statement is meant to say, it overwhelms anything that is actually said or merely implied.

John Barton is particularly fond of enforcing his view of the play by breaking speeches with silences, or by heavy emphasis on a few words or by some eye-arresting gesture accompanying them. Sometimes this underlines what is already plain enough, as in Angelo's reply to Isabella's departing, 'Save your honour!' (II, ii, 161). The text reads, 'From thee; even from thy virtue!', which could be said within the same iambic verse-line. Ian Richardson, however, speaks it with a long pause after 'thee'; this stresses an opposition between the instinctive 'thee' and the more demanding 'virtue' of Shakespeare's text. At the end of *The Tempest*, John Barton found more that he wanted to emphasise in Prospero's farewell to Ariel, than in Shakespeare's conclusion which has Prospero asking the courtiers to 'draw near', implying a general *exeunt*. So the words are transposed, and after a pause as Antonio and Sebastian *leave* Prospero, the farewell to the spirit is gravely and slowly said as the new conclusion to the play.

In the National Theatre's *Merchant of Venice*, Portia was presented against a background of Victorian comedy, playing in idleness until becoming impatient with her manifestly absurd suitors. Here by-play speaks for the director: Arragon pulls a knotted handkerchief out of his pocket, sees the knot, can't remember what he should remember, and so moves on to the caskets; he drops a lump of sugar, a footman picks it up and swallows it, and the audience laughs again. Jonathan Miller has Portia assume a deep, false male voice when disguised as a lawyer to accentuate the change from frills and curls, and, more originally, has her maintain something of this deeper quality of voice when she faces Shylock across a table and finds herself face-to-face with a man (instead of fluttering with social niceties), pleading for the 'quality of mercy'; she is transformed by this experience, and so a clear line is given to her characterisation throughout the play. To this end the tricks are played earlier, Bassanio's casket-scene greatly cut, and Portia's yielding speech played rhetorically, rather than with response to the subtle rhythms, delicate hesitations and simplicities of the text.

The choice of a unifying idea for a production, and its expression in settings, costumes, interpolations, by-play, verbal emphasis, manner of performance, limits the presentation of what Shakespeare has written. It concentrates on one single meaning for almost every ambiguous line. It enlarges one incident and diminishes, or cuts completely, some other incident that is capable of contrary emphasis. The productions are not myriad-minded; Shakespeare is not free. If questioned about this procedure, I suspect that most directors would answer that to gain power, a production must be simple, must not dissipate its effectiveness, must lead in one way not several and must build up climaxes. They would also explain that Shakespeare is often difficult to understand and that their additions serve to clarify his obscurities.

To these usual attitudes, Peter Brook offers some contrasts. In company with Nunn, Barton, Hands and Miller, this director assumes an individual way of working. He refuses to 'take a categorical position' in approaching a production: 'I often drive people mad by not making up my mind, but I don't believe it's really a fault. In a work context, the eventual clarity I hope for comes not from any dogmatism, but an encouraged chaos from which the clarity grows.'[1]

The first step towards a production is a series of exercises for the actors, physical, vocal and improvisational, which aim at making the 'actors work more freely together as a group'. The next is to seek a 'collective understanding' of the play, by using specific acting methods to explore the text through voice and body, through experiment in action. Instead of thinking about the meaning of words, the actors are encouraged to see how they can speak them, represent, support or contrast them. They criticise each other's work and wait for something to come right. Peter Brook tells the story of experimental rehearsals for *The Tempest*, when:

A Japanese actor who, by approaching Ariel through his breathing and through his body, made Ariel something very understandable. A certain force became tangible in something which to the Japanese was easy to understand because in the basis of the Noh theatre, from which he came, there was a certain type of sound, a certain type of cry, a certain type of breath. The idea of that force was truly represented. It could be discussed because it had suddenly happened. There it was amongst us. It was no longer force, an abstract movement, it was *force*, a reality, something which could influence other people.[2]

[1] 'Showman Extraordinary', an interview with John Heilpern, *The Observer* (30 August 1970).
[2] 'Life and Joy', an interview with Ronald Hayman, *The Times* (29 August 1970).

By asking the actors to respond to the text and to various tasks of the director's invention, different ways of presenting characters and incidents are evolved in random patterns. From these the most 'forceful' are chosen, and so, 'in place of a lack of an intention, an intention appears'.[1]

Is this 'new' way of directing the means to 'free' Shakespeare, to avoid fixing a production according to a director's 'interpretation' or 'view'? Peter Brook's *A Midsummer Night's Dream* in the 1970 Stratford season has been hailed as a revelation by many playgoers: does it provide hope for a specially appropriate production method for Shakespeare?

In the acting some results are obvious. Peter Thomson reports in this issue of *Shakespeare Survey* that the actors found their work 'fantastic',[2] but it is noticeable that this is because they are working 'with Brook', not with Shakespeare. At least half of their task must have been getting accustomed to the trapezes, coiling wires and stilts, and to the wayward percussive music and sounds that all derive from Brook's decision to work as in a circus, whenever possible. This idiom seems to have been chosen to encourage a 'display of physical virtuosity – an expression of joy'.[3] However, in these skills the actors remained amateurs, and nothing was attempted like the silence that falls in a circus as danger is confronted. The revealing all-white stage seemed suitable for a ballet or gymnastics, but only a sporadic attempt was made to move with dancer-like precision or authority. The technical hurdles have been introduced to thrust the actors into unknown territory so that they court discovery, rather than to display the effortless skill of artistic achievement. Variety of style seems to have been pursued for much the same reason. Movement varies from solemn simplicity (and often cliché) to novel ingenuity. On occasion the speaking is noticeably slow,

especially when the words are about death or virginity, or about the actor and his art, dream and reality. At times movement and noise obliterate speech, or make so strong a counter claim for the audience's interest that words can scarcely be followed. At other times, the drama seems to be going on inside the minds of motionless and inexpressive performers, and the pace is so slow that either the audience loses interest or is forced to find it for itself in general curiosity.

The production met with such good-will that many of the audience seemed wholly satisfied. When Peter Thomson writes: 'I feel no inclination to defend any of Brook's decisions. I doubt whether the play could have been so well spoken if it had been seriously falsified', he sounds as though he is accepting a piece of novel showmanship entirely in its own terms. He goes on to say: 'More than anything I have ever seen, this production declared its confidence and delight in the art of performance. In doing so, it went, for me, *beyond the meaning of the play* to a joyous celebration of the fact that it was written...'[4] This is not criticism, it is capitulation. But it does suggest that Shakespeare's play might have become open to the audience, with no directorial interference of note, beyond the surface interest of the performance itself.

But if we wish to ask how the production served the play, we must go beyond recording pleasure or distaste. Nor is this difficult, for certainly a single interpretation had been found during the actors' explorations under the director's guidance, and this has been unambiguously presented. Time and again, the audience is forced to take the play in one comparatively simple way. Helena and Theseus

[1] 'Director in Interview', with Peter Ansorge, *Plays and Players*, vol. 18, no. 1 (October 1970), pp. 18–19.
[2] See above, p. 125.
[3] *Plays and Players*, p. 18.
[4] See above, p. 126; italics are mine.

hold fixed kneeling positions for soliloquies and so contradict the energy and light rhythmic variety of the writing. The Mechanicals parade on to the stage accompanied with blaring noise that makes them far more broadly comic and assertive than the words alone imply, and quite alter the textual contrast (and similarity) between their speeches and Helena's preceding soliloquy. Certain words are chosen for repetition, usually by a listener, and so are underlined as they are not in the text. Laughter is provided on stage with no direct cue in Shakespeare's words, and while the audience remains silent. Helena's quarrel with Demetrius is made funny by the boy falling on to the floor, the girl crawling on to his back, and he trying to crawl from underneath. Bottom is carried off to Titania's bower accompanied by large phallic gestures and cries of triumph, when the concluding words in that incident suggest delicacy and silence:

> Come, wait upon him; lead him to my bower.
> The moon, methinks, looks with a wat'ry eye;
> And when she weeps, weeps every little flower,
> Lamenting some enforced chastity.
> Tie up my love's tongue, bring him silently.
>
> (III, i, 182–6)

Hippolyta and Titania, Theseus and Oberon, are openly doubled as if the actors' task was to make what likeness exists between the pairs as obvious and inescapable as possible, and to minimise the very considerable differences. Verbally certain phrases are given overwhelming importance by pauses and exaggerated enunciation, which only directorial decision could permit. One such item picked out for emphasis is 'cold...fruitless...moon' (I, i, 73), so that the incidental phrase becomes a posed invocation, at least an evocation, for which the pace of the action (and of the metre) must be suspended. The actors seeking 'force', 'clarity', 'reality', or 'something which could influence people', are not presenting a free Shakespeare. Above all, they are trying to

impress what they, themselves, have found, and Peter Brook has chosen.

Speaking after the rehearsals were complete, Peter Brook was obviously committed to one particular interpretation. While he quotes the text in his own support, it is noticeable how easily he contradicts it, or misrepresents it. Now he is far more concerned with what the experiments have thrown up, not only from the text but also from his own and his actors' experience, predilections and theatrical improvisation. So in an interview, he has said that: 'Theseus and Hippolyta are trying to discover what constitutes the true union of a couple...'[1], but what he should have said is that this issue came to interest the actors who had the task of presenting the two characters. I can find nothing in the text that suggests this concern, and it is quite as likely to derive from the fantasies of the experimenting and questioning actors as from the subtextual possibilities of the play. Speaking of Oberon, Brook put the dramatic point in extreme terms of 'total' love, whatever that means (it is not a Shakespearian phrase): 'a man taking the wife whom he loves totally and having her fucked by the crudest sex machine he can find... Oberon's deliberate cool intention is to degrade Titania as a woman'. The director has here left the text far behind. First, Oberon is a 'creature of another sort', a fairy not a man. Second, he does not choose a 'sex machine' of any sort, but expects Titania to have more general 'hateful fantasies' (II, i, 258) and is prepared for her to 'love *and languish*' for any 'vile thing' (II, ii, 27–34). When Oberon has enchanted Titania, he still does not know what she will 'dote on' (III, ii, 3), and hearing of Bottom's transformation says, specifically, that 'This falls out better than I could devise' (l. 35). Finally, the object of devotion is not an ass, but a man with an ass's head who never says a word suggesting an intention to fuck her,

[1] *Plays and Players*, p. 19.

crudely or otherwise. Bottom's first thought is of how to escape, his second of answering Titania's attendants with requisite courtesy. When Titania is seen 'coying' his cheeks and kissing his ears, he is irritated by an itch, feels hungry, and then announces simply – or perhaps ambiguously – that he is tired (IV, i, 1–42). The director, with his actors to help him, has discovered something that is not in the play-text at all, but in the reactions, predispositions, theatrical consciousness and fantasies of their own, and he enforces this upon the audience's attention with elaborate business, noise, vocal reactions and climactic placing at the end of the first half of the performance.

Most critics have proclaimed a new way of staging Shakespeare after seeing Brook's production, but what seems newest in his work is the theatrical playing with the text in order to invent business and discover an interpretation that suits his own interests and the actors with whom he is working. This is said to release the potential of the text, but in fact the 'chaos' with which rehearsals began led to a limited, eccentric, single-minded (and rather simple-minded) interpretation. Once more the director has fixed the production so that certain points are made without ambiguity and without any danger that the audience could overlook them.

Will anyone find a way of presenting Shakespeare freely? Could an audience be allowed to find 'meaning' for themselves, be struck with whatever force or reality that their own imaginations can observe? Could there be a direct audience contact with the stage and with Shakespeare's creation, or do the necessities of theatrical art, the need for preparation and obvious excitement, preclude this open-ended experience? Could theatrical craftsmanship be allied to a production which seemed as unstrained, as 'easy' and 'natural', as Shakespeare's writing? And as ambiguous, reflective, invitingly difficult, and alive?

To seek for such a way is, I believe, of utmost importance. It would not rediscover the 'essential' Shakespeare or explain anything in the plays for good and all. In no way would it lead to a museum production, seeking an elusive 'Elizabethan' accuracy of speech or behaviour. But it would bring Shakespearian qualities to the theatre, and allow audiences to respond in ways that are generally recognised as appropriate to Shakespeare's genius. The audience might become seekers – askers of questions, as Arnold would say – whereas, at present, they are invited to accept and share other people's answers.

The first step might be to place the audience in the same unvarying light as the actors, so that they can easily withdraw from the play and can look where they please. This would be a fundamental change, and it is, perhaps, no wonder that in an age of experiment this obvious one goes largely unattempted. Smallish theatres, in overall dimensions, and a thrust stage would probably be necessary to allow close contact with the actors and off-set the loss of scenic dominance. Composed and highlighted pictures with an obvious centre of interest would be replaced by a group of actors, viewed on all sides, expecting to be overlooked rather than displayed.

If the play were set in these conditions, the mere necessity of holding attention would enforce greater vitality and variety in the acting. A far quicker overall pace would be required and varied rhythms, but it is arguable that Shakespeare's iambic pentameters may well be made for such speaking, not for the silences, pauses, exaggerated stresses, slow pulse and explicit sententiousness that are common today. Two-and-a-half hours should be able to accommodate all but the longest plays, and here would be no more productions that wind on to three-and-a-half or four hours, as not infrequently today: this length of time is required only by reason of laboured points, interpolated business, and carefully arranged crowd and scenic effects in which the invention stems almost entirely from the director, not from the text.

Overlong group rehearsals should be avoided because they are the director's opportunity to create his own little dramas, and often dull the actors' responses and preclude repeated return with open eyes to the text. Actors could do much of their work alone, or in small groups, and they should not worry about ironing out all differences in approach or interpretation. If actors respond minutely to the varied potential of what they say, and remain open to renewed contact with Shakespeare's text and their own experience, their performances might remain constantly alert and variously suggestive, rather than definitive and limited. Options should be kept open, not decided by the director by the light of his own wit, or by his recognition of what, at the moment of one particular rehearsal, is the strongest of two or more opposing interpretations.

Movement should not be clearly fixed, because this limits an actor to certain rhythms and certain ways of confronting the other characters on stage. He should be free to discover new nuances, levels of meaning, contrasts, possibilities of physical action through his own skill, the changing context of the peopled stage, and his growing acquaintance with the text. If the actor remains free to discover, the audience may be encouraged to do so too: they would need to, because a clear line would not run through every incident for them to follow.

Costumes should not be limiting for the actor, nor relied upon to set the tone of a dramatic moment, or create striking contrasts at the cost of others. Both tone and centre of interest can come from the actors, if their physical and verbal performance is sufficiently dynamic. Except for necessary identifications and signs of rank or business, the costumes might well start as uniforms, and be modified as rehearsals and performances require.

The dangers of such freedom from a director's limiting conception and guidance to actors, would be confusion, ordinariness, reliance on mere luck, lack of power or variety, and boredom of the audience. To create a work of art is to exercise choice and limitation: the experiment would be to allow the dominating, fixed and limiting influence to be only the easy, natural and complicated words of Shakespeare's text and the presence on stage of the actors and business called for by that text. The advantages might be great: the audience's creative and necessary collaboration and the actor's continually renewed view of the play and the growth of their imaginative and technical powers.

The alternative to such radical departure from accepted practice would be to find a director who would maintain close contact with the text and seek to avoid limiting the actors' work by a single-minded interpretation. He would be courting failure, but also attempting to release Shakespeare's plays from confinement.

© JOHN RUSSELL BROWN 1971

THE YEAR'S CONTRIBUTIONS TO SHAKESPEARIAN STUDY

1. CRITICAL STUDIES

reviewed by NORMAN SANDERS

There is some indication that in recent years more critics are prepared to tackle the whole range of Shakespeare's achievement. The first two parts of what will ultimately be such a general critical account have appeared from Gareth Lloyd Evans.[1] The plan is to follow the dramatist's career more or less chronologically, with volume I being devoted to the years 1564–92, and volume II 1587–98. Together they represent about as good a commentary on the early and middle plays as one could find for the intelligent non-professional reader of Shakespeare. Certainly they aim at offering in a very readable manner the accepted state of scholarly knowledge; but at the same time they contain a very personal approach to the works which is based upon theatrical as well as classroom expertise and which never becomes merely eccentric.

In discussing the early plays, Lloyd Evans displays his critical strengths best in the essays on the *Henry VI* plays. He conveys well just how dramatically 'promising' these works are, demonstrating the way in which the larger political issues are located in single scenes and details of character, perceiving the thematic and theatrical relationships between Joan and Talbot or Cade and Gloucester, explaining with real insight the dramaturgical problems which faced Shakespeare in part 3, and in general managing to move gracefully between abstracted ideas and detailed analyses of particular passages.

The promise of excellence displayed in these early chapters is fulfilled in the later parts on the second tetralogy. The writing here clearly indicates that the critic's imagination has caught fire and there are rewarding passages on such matters as the romanticization of Falstaff, the distinction to be made between the Fat Knight as a play character and the national image he has become, and the critical problems presented by the character of Hal as Prince and as Christian king. The sections of both volumes concerned with the comedies and tragicomedies are less uniformly good and clearly reflect the author's personal response to different plays. In fact, for all his obvious enjoyment of these early and middle comedies, one gets the impression that Lloyd Evans is just not really convinced that comic profundity exists. If Lloyd Evans can blend the theatrical awareness shown in the essay on *Romeo and Juliet* with the insight, shown in his reading of the history plays, into how intellectual ideas can be given dramatic form, then his forthcoming work on the tragedies and problem plays may be anticipated with pleasure.

Two other general books command more attention for the names and reputations of their

[1] *Shakespeare I: 1564–1592* and *Shakespeare II: 1587–1598* (Oliver and Boyd, 1969).

authors than for any outstanding critical originality in their content. In *Motiveless Malignity* the novelist Louis Auchincloss offers a series of well-written essays 'connected only in their tendency to speculate on the lack of apparent motivation in some of Shakespeare's principal characters'.[1] He believes that Shakespeare had an enormously developed sense of the perverse and irrational in human nature, which deepened with his experience; and further, that much in the plays may be accounted for by reference to 'the deeper motivation, the human impulse to self-destruction'.

The critical approach is obtrusively character-orientated for much of the book. Iago is incredible, therefore he must be the evil in Othello, which renders this play the spectacle of a man destroying himself. Richard III fiendishly understands that all the silly world requires of him is that he act hypocritically a role that will lead to his damnation. Antony is the pathetic spectacle of a man attempting to equate his present performance in bed with his former conquest of the world.

Most of the major works are touched on in Auchincloss's presentation of this Shakespearian vision of human ruin. In the final section, Auchincloss offers his personal theory of the *Sonnets* (without much scholarly proof) as being concerned with two patrons, two young men, and the Dark Lady. This is a book which is a pleasure to read and is packed with fine phrasing, but which one suspects is more useful in the explication of the author's own novels than of Shakespeare's plays.

D. J. Enright's *Shakespeare and the Students*[2] has risen directly out of this distinguished poet's experience as a university teacher – an experience which has made him disturbed that we have been rescued from the smoke and fire of Romanticism only 'to be dropped into the hygienic incinerators of symbolism, imagery-computation, a curiously trite moral-

ising and philosophising of a sort so primitive as undoubtedly to have contributed to the discredit which literature has fallen into among the serious minded'. As a corrective to this state of affairs we are offered the sort of scene-by-scene commentary on *Lear*, *Antony and Cleopatra*, *Macbeth*, and *The Winter's Tale* which many teachers adopt as a classroom method, with its modern paraphrasing of important and difficult passages, the singling out of the line of narrative development, the controverting or supporting of the remarks of outstanding critics, and some humane comment in the light of real-life experience. Enright does all of these things entertainingly and well; and at the end of the book, one is convinced that he is a very good teacher indeed and that the students who read the plays with his help were very fortunate. But one wonders whether this is quite the form best suited to the publication of a poet's reading of four of Shakespeare's major plays.

It must be said that the final essay on *The Winter's Tale* is not so severely limited by the classroom method adopted. Here Enright provides an unusual emphasis on the doings of the older generation, and supplies some good commonsense close analysis of Leontes's jealousy. He stresses that the realism in the play far outweighs the much-discussed fairy-tale elements and believes that the reader should experience less compulsion 'to translate the play into abstract symbolism, to supplant the substance by the shadow'.

Another way in which Shakespeare's achievement may be approached is via the control provided by a large central idea which appears under various guises in many plays. Three recent books are concerned on a large scale with that most disputed of topics, namely the Christian content of the works and its critical implications. Robert E. Fitch's *Shakespeare:*

---

[1] Gollancz, 1970.
[2] Chatto and Windus, 1970.

The Perspective of Value[1] is by a professional theologian, who obviously considers himself an amateur lover of the plays. The approach is very schematic and is derived ultimately from Dowden. In part I, after surveying how the plays are saturated with Christian imagery, quotation, Biblical echoes, oaths, prayers, and references to the Homilies, Fitch suggests that a Christian framework of reference can serve as a controling perspective to liberate the meaning of the plays from the prosaic and the literal. The theological progress of the dramatist is seen to be from the confusion of patriotism and piety in the early histories, to the balance of these two qualities in *Henry V*, through *Hamlet* which marks a change in reorientation of religion and in which there is found the weird paradox of the presence of religion as circumstance and the absence of religion as faith, and finally on to the later tragedies and Romances where Shakespeare is seen to be moving within a context of Christian humanism.

The final section is by far the most rewarding, where Shakespeare is presented as a pilgrim, in that he journeyed to a consummation in which all that had gone before is drawn together; and as a *picaro*, because, while he can be engrossed in the here and now, he always raised his eyes to the wider view. Fitch shows that he has thought hard about such things as the function of the critic, the place and weaknesses of rationalism in criticism, the dangers of over-adulation, and the necessary limitations of all critical and theatrical efforts to grasp the 'whole meaning'. Yet, despite this awareness, it is in this part of the volume that we find purely personal responses offered as critical judgments. In sum, the book is one man's unpretentious attempt to record the vision offered by Shakespeare's plays in terms of his own life and beliefs; and while I took exception to many of the critical judgments it contained, I found it pleasant to have known Mr Fitch.

Fitch's conclusion that Shakespeare's final position as a blend of Christianity and Humanism will not satisfy the doctrinaire theist might have been written with the author of a far more confident and assertive work in mind. For, in spite of some modest disclaimers in the preface, Roy W. Battenhouse obviously intends, in his *Shakespearean Tragedy: Its Art and Its Christian Premises*,[2] to set us right once and for all about the real nature of Shakespeare's tragic world. The book is quite obviously the result of many years of study, thought, and hard work on both the plays and the vast body of critical writing surrounding them – a fact reflected in the impeccably scholarly sixty pages of notes and index.

Battenhouse believes that the important dimension of Shakespearian tragedy lies in its moral significance, much of which he thinks can elude our vision or be misconstrued if we bring to the study of the plays intellectual preconceptions such as those of a romantic or Hegelian cast as they are exemplified in the work of A. C. Bradley. In order to correct such one-sided views, he has probed the many-sided implications of Shakespeare's tragic art by 'taking particular care to investigate the pertinence of Christian lore'. The form that this elaborate corrective takes is: an analysis of the profound meaning of *The Rape of Lucrece*, depending on a basically Augustinian perspective in part I; a search for an adequate theory of Shakespearian tragedy in part II, which includes also a brief critical history of important criticism of the plays, a consideration of major medieval ideas, the way Biblical paradigms appear in the works' structures, and a conclusion as to how far the tragedies can be called Christian yet embrace the influence of Aristotle's moral and poetic principles; a part III which amplifies what other critics have said about the Christian structure of *King Lear*, and

[1] The Westminster Press, Philadelphia, 1969.
[2] Indiana University Press, 1969.

analyses *Coriolanus* to show how Shakespeare reorders Plutarch's flawed account by a reliance on a vision stemming from Christian tradition.

There are certain aspects of Battenhouse's book with which no reader can quarrel: for example, the claim that there are both literal and figurative meanings in the plays, or that Shakespeare was brought up as some brand of Christian and initially learned moral principles and values in a Christian context, or that there are in many of the plays direct and indirect references and allusions to the Bible, the Prayer Book, and the Homilies. His working out of the implications of these observations leads Battenhouse to the conclusions that (a) Shakespearian tragedy is rooted in the Christian view of life; (b) it is a process of washing, a lustration which offers us an opportunity for learning to pity and fear what we ought to pity and fear, thereby educating our emotions; and (c) it is a form of tragedy which contains, transforms, and enlarges Aristotle's philosophical concepts and provides us therefore with a far more profound articulation of the tragic experience than the Greek plays, which contain only a grain of this along with embryonic traces of the basic elements of hamartia and catharsis. In fact Battenhouse is convinced that

Tragedy, for the Greeks, ended with a recognition of the Dikê. For Christians [it] ends with a recognition of Divine Providence to which all sons of Adam are subject. The second of these two is but a larger horizon of the first. For if Adam's original sin is the deeper truth behind the hamartia of Oedipus, all tragedies in germ are analogues of Adam's.

In these sentences there may be located the real weakness of the book. Because, for all its attempts at scholarly objectivity and the praiseworthy effort to give the opposition its due, it is the product of what can only be called an obsessive desire of a man, who fervently believes in Christian doctrine, to twist the works of a playwright, in whom generations have found a profound vision of life in all its aspects, into an almost totally orthodox Christianity as it can be derived from a close study of the Bible, St Augustine, and St Thomas Aquinas. There is, of course, no reason why this should not be done and no one can doubt that Battenhouse has done it with complete thoroughness. But one can take exception to his critical methods.

Quite simply the critical approach adopted is to perceive Christian analogy wherever the author wishes it to be. Naturally, Battenhouse notes and discusses the obvious ones; but no section of the text really daunts his ingenuity. If there is no perceptible analogy present, one can be created by the simple expedient of qualifying the word with some appropriate epithet; I noted, for example, the following: inverted, ironic, dark, disjunctive, mock, indirect, upside-down, inverse, travesty, shadow. Once this principle is accepted, then any meal can become some kind of analogy to the Last Supper, any actions taking place on any three days of the week can refer to the Passion, any tomb can become the Holy Sepulchre, any sword Peter's sword, any period of time or number of lines suggestive of forty-two or eleven can be loaded with evil implications, and characters can reflect desired Biblical originals at will (with the forms Christ assumes giving a new meaning so far as Shakespeare's works are concerned to the phrase 'Divine omnipresence').

A far more balanced book is Robert H. West's *Shakespeare and the Outer Mystery*,[1] the purpose of which is to 'inquire reasonably what Shakespeare's tragedies do convey about ultimates in their worlds' by determining 'just how far Shakespeare goes theologically and what sort of evidence (that is dramatic suggestion in speech and events) he gives for outerness'. Like Battenhouse and Fitch, West is willing to allow the presence of given Christian

[1] University of Kentucky Press, 1968.

morality and the original audience's main sympathies; but he asks the question, 'Does this given morality express or deny a cosmic scheme for the play as a whole?'. Taking each of the four major tragedies in turn, he attempts to answer this question by focusing attention on the handling of the obviously 'outer' elements in them. He contends that while the Ghost in *Hamlet* and the Witches in *Macbeth* appeal to a contemporary pneumatology, Shakespeare's handling of them 'is a finely wrought appeal to the contemporary sense of direct experience, but not a verification for the play of any of the rationalisations of such experience'. Thus the pneumatological evidence in *Hamlet* points equally in three directions: to the Catholic apparition, to the paganesque spirit, and to a devil; and West suggests that the playwright deliberately mixed details of all there 'for the sake of dramatic impact and of a kind of philosophical reserve', leaving the audience where all living men must stand in relation to that country from which no traveler returns. Similarly the Witches are presented in terms of Christian demonology, but this does not mean that Shakespeare ratifies to us the full scheme of that demonology; they are deliberately mysterious and inexplicit. Prospero's magic likewise does not ratify any self-contained thaumaturgic system, and the creation of Ariel is deliberately built up from ambiguous spirit-devil evidence.

In dealing with *Othello* and *Lear*, West considers the evidence for the Christianness of these plays. The former's theology is claimed to be general, discursive, and unexplicit, and thus is in marked contrast with the terribly vivid acts of Iago's evil and the particular and immediate passion of the final scene. *Lear*, too, is denied a complete theology: 'To make *King Lear* a stamped and certified exemplum of Christian sin and punishment is to take half of the art out of it and much of the honesty and most of the mystery.' The stress in this play is rather on the biological creativeness of nature and its reciprocal destructiveness, a theme on which West offers one of the most interesting discussions of Lear's sexual nausea and its place in the total scheme of the play. However, both of these plays are seen to express a final faith 'that the universe is God's and evil subordinate in it' and that 'the true tragic compensation is...in the good that resistlessly rises out of agony, or at any rate in the clear vision without wavering or indecision with which Shakespeare's protagonists come to their ends'.

After reading some recent studies in which Shakespeare is seen to take up some well-defined dogmatic position on a particular topic, it is refreshing to read West's emphasis on the magnanimity and comprehensiveness of his tragic vision. Nevertheless, there are points in the book where one cannot help but suspect that there are implications (to such opinions that Iago stands 'in the tragic place of hostile nature, fate, and hell' or that *Lear*'s insistence on Christian virtues brings to it a general sense of a power beyond mankind that sustains the world for purposes that the moral code somehow reflects) that West is either unable or unwilling to perceive. It is hard, too, not to suspect occasionally that Art seems to this critic to be good only when it can be equated with a vague mysteriousness. Still, this is a book well worth reading.

On a rather narrower scale John P. Cutts[1] also approaches Shakespeare's early plays via a single idea and technique. Taking his cue from the mirror scene in *Richard II*, he concentrates on 'mirror-imagery, substance and shadow, seeing and unseeing, fragmentation and synthesis, showing how personae shatter their own brittleness, their own puppetry, into a new and more powerful dramatic life'. It is true that these ideas are to be found in many

[1] *The Shattered Glass: A Dramatic Pattern in Shakespeare's Early Plays* (Wayne State University Press, 1968).

of the plays Cutts deals with, but the book is really a collection of general critical essays. All are interesting to read and most contain ideas which one wishes to think about, but some of the plays need to be forced somewhat to fit into 'the image in the glass idea'. For example, in *The Comedy of Errors* there is very little verbal encouragement for seeing the play in these terms; and one would have thought that if one wishes to consider the question of identity, individual and familial, it is sensible to follow the clear indications given by the metaphorical expression that Shakespeare himself employed. Similarly in *Love's Labour's Lost*, on Cutts's own evidence, there is little mirror imagery save that which he supplies, as he acceptably sums up one aspect of the piece: 'the characters are offered the opportunity to look into the mirror of themselves'. The essays on some of the other plays (e.g. on *King John* or *Romeo and Juliet*) are more successful in conveying the author's critical ingenuity and his very original views (particularly the sections on the role of Sly in *The Taming of the Shrew* and the vigorous assertion of the way in which King John dominates his play), with the most admirable being that on *Richard II*. It should be said, however, that there are moments when the reader of this book does have some misgivings about the critical method adopted. It is praiseworthy that the words of a play should be used extensively in criticism, but Cutts's fertility of imagination occasionally leads him into some dextrous sleight of hand.

Some approaches by means of a single theme lead ultimately to a particular play, and this is the path followed by Jagannath Chakravorty in *The Idea of Revenge in Shakespeare, with Special Reference to 'Hamlet'*.[1] He argues for the presence in Shakespeare's work of a search for a moral handling of the revenge idea: 'What Hamlet wants is to achieve a superior kind of revenge – moral revenge – instead of simple blood-revenge and to act as a regenerator of the time "out of joint".' Prefacing his analysis of this 'search' with a rather shallow appraisal of *Gorboduc* and *The Spanish Tragedy*, Chakravorty sees the young dramatist of *Titus Andronicus* trying to inject certain finer values into the crude materials at his disposal, with the arrow scene serving as Titus's approximation to moral revenge in a conflict that arises from the rival demands of honour, justice, and vengeance.

When Chakravorty turns to *Hamlet*, his work becomes far more interesting. His basic case is that the Prince sees clearly that his task is to transform revenge into redemption and to work out this redemption in the state of Denmark. With this end in view, he examines in detail all parts of the play. He traces the images which make Hamlet's problem clear: the conflict between the Ghost and the hero's ideal self, and the Pyrrhus speech 'composed by Hamlet and recited by the First Player' (*sic*) embodying the parallel between the Greek's pause and the Dane's doubts about blood revenge. All the major scenes are interpreted by Chakravorty to record Hamlet's progress towards his reforming function. For example, the rogue and peasant slave soliloquy is seen in a way that doubts the face value of what Hamlet says is to be the function of 'The Mouse-trap', the 'To be or not to be' speech as a polarization between noble moral revenge and the ignoble physical variety, and the play scene is claimed to have a primarily reforming function for Claudius.

While there are a number of convincing observations in Chakravorty's analysis, it does appear that some of the play's incidents have to be forced to bear rather strained interpretations in order to fit into his scheme. Hamlet's lines beginning ''Tis now the very witching time of night' are glossed over with the assurance that although he says such things,

[1] Jadavpur University Press, Calcutta, 1969.

this does not mean he likes to do them; and the soliloquy behind the King is viewed not as horrible as it is usually taken to be if one assumes (1) that Hamlet does not mean what he says, and (2) that he is not talking about Claudius and himself except as common examples of the offender and the revenger. The final episodes of the play show us, Chakravorty claims, the profound tragedy of spiritual debasement, once Hamlet has given up his higher moral intentions, a point marked by the soliloquy delivered as he watches Fortinbras's army. The remainder of the book looks at elements in other tragedies and comedies that appear to support the belief that Shakespeare's major plays all serve to expose the evil passion of revenge 'from a lofty Christian point of view and provide for its transmutation into mercy and forgiveness'.

Harold Skulsky[1] examines the relationship between conscience and revenge in far more subtle terms. He believes that Hamlet has to choose from the available sanctions for revenge: unlimited retribution and the code of honour. The first of these Skulsky thinks is discredited for the audience in the figure of Pyrrhus, and that the second is set up against the laws of Nature, Christian doctrine, and conscience. Hamlet's progress is thus viewed as being from commitment to unlimited ill-will, through palliation of this by appeals to conscience and charity, until he comes to consider himself as a doomed scourge of God obeying a divine command which he believes supersedes all moral reason. Only Hamlet's final action in the duel rescues him from steady spiritual decline. The functions of the Pyrrhus speech detected in both these studies are but further examples of the way in which this formerly deplored piece of rhetoric is drawing to itself ever-increasing admiration for its subtlety and thematic relevance. Michael Taylor[2] has an interesting note which views it as a representation for Hamlet of a ritualistic epic world

where there is no complexity of motive, no confusion of identity, and which is so far removed from the Prince's own predicament. Starting from an historical point of departure, Clifford Leech takes the same speech to be an admiring pastiche of Marlowe's lines on the death of Priam in *Dido*. He makes a sensitive comparison between the two treatments to show how Shakespeare's changes were made so that the heroic figure may be related to Hamlet's own problems, particularly in the emphasis and place given to the moment of Pyrrhus's pause. The writing of 'The Mousetrap' also is defended by Clare Replogle,[3] who argues that the playlet is neither parody nor burlesque but a successful and serious stylistic experiment, reflecting an amalgam of current dramatic conventions and Shakespeare's own literary habits, and perfectly suited to the situation in which it occurs. One small section of the playlet, the Player King's lines on friendship, is isolated by James I. Wimsatt,[4] who connects them both with the possible origins in medieval and classical texts and the contrasting attitudes represented by Horatio's freedom from Fortune and Rosencrantz and Guildenstern's status as the 'privates' of Fortune, whose vicar is Claudius.

Hamlet has received more respect as a theatre critic than as a dramatist, but too often his advice to the Players has been readily ascribed to Shakespeare himself. One welcomes, therefore, Roy W. Battenhouse's[5] sug-

[1] 'Revenge, Honor, and Conscience in Hamlet', *PMLA*, LXXXV (1970), 78–87.
[2] 'A Note on the "Pyrrhus Episode" in *Hamlet*', *Shakespeare Quarterly*, XXI (1970), 99–103.
[3] 'Not Parody, Not Burlesque: The Play within the Play in *Hamlet*', *Modern Philology*, LXVII (1969), 150–9.
[4] 'The Player King on Friendship', *Modern Language Review*, LXV (1960), 1–6.
[5] 'The Significance of Hamlet's Advice to the Players', *The Drama of the Renaissance: Essays for Leicester Bradner*, ed. Elmer M. Blistein (Brown University Press, 1970), pp. 3–26.

gestion that the advice is characteristic of the Prince's view of drama and life rather than the poet's: 'Shakespeare is dramatizing the inner and real tragedy of Hamlet's self-delusion and thereby engaging our pity and fear, which is the properly Aristotelian purpose of *his* drama'.

Hamlet has been the subject of a second book-length study. Surprised that the style of the play has never been fully treated, Maurice Charney attempts to make good the deficiency in his *Style in 'Hamlet'*.[1] As in his previous work on the Roman plays, he interprets 'style' in its widest sense, which includes all means of expression used by an author to accomplish his purpose, that is, the imaginative embodiment of a theme in an individual and distinctive manner. The plan of the book falls into three main parts: an examination of the major verbal imagery blocks (war, weapons, explosive, poison, secrecy, corruption, acting, etc.); the theatrical physical imagery (gesture, stage action, sound-effects, etc.); and the means of conveying dramatic character. As Charney works at these topics with a remorseless persistence (his own word), the results are very uneven in value. He can, for example, write well on the way in which various imagery chains (e.g. that of disease) have been accepted as central to the play's theme for too long, and can attempt to right the balance by discussing illuminatingly an undernoticed topic like the ideas of limits and confinement and how they help convey in verbal and physical terms the tension between man's finiteness and mortality and his efforts to transcend them. Or he can bring new insights into the enumerative propensities found in Laertes's speeches; the way in which number and money concepts can 'emphasise man's fallible, measurable, material being, that condition of mortality which makes him vulnerable to tragedy'; the opportunities provided by the play's demands for music, stage-effects, and noises. He can also give a

brilliant exposition of just how Claudius effects his control of Laertes; and point out features of the scenic divisions and the way in which the use of a clinching rhymed couplet may be modified or neutralized by a following part-line on exit.

Yet alongside such genuine critical insight, one finds, for example, a very poor chapter on acting, art, and theatre that does little more than draw together all the references in the play to these subjects. Altogether, this is an unsatisfying book, which no one interested in the play can afford to ignore, but which does irritate by its unevenness and inability to offer a coherent critical view of the play while presenting so much that is new, perceptive, and genuinely useful.

One article on the same play that demonstrates in its treatment of a much narrower topic precisely the quality lacking in Charney's book is by S. P. Zitner.[2] Stressing the place of weapons in the metaphorical and dramatic texture of *Hamlet*, he notes that the play 'divides human history into distinct epochs' of an unrecoverable heroic past and the sequestration of violence to the bureaucratic state. In the light of the circumstances of personal violence at the time of the play's writing and Vincentio Saviolo's *Practise* (1595), Zitner shows how Shakespeare used the duelling code to satisfy the genetic demands of tragedy and to characterize his hero. This article is an excellent example of how a specific piece of scholarly research can lead to critical insight into the central values of a major work of art. Another good essay on the play is a product of the recently proliferating approach to Shakespeare via the theatrical life of the plays. In it Stephen Booth views *Hamlet* as a succession of actions upon the understanding of an audience, and demonstrates brilliantly how, in

[1] Princeton University Press, 1969.
[2] 'Hamlet, Duellist', *University of Toronto Quarterly*, XXXIX (1969), 1–18.

arousing expectations and partially fulfilling and partially frustrating them, it causes us to experience a satisfying intellectual triumph based on the realization that 'any two things that pull apart contain qualities that are simultaneously the means of uniting them'.[1]

A number of miscellaneous pieces add to our understanding of some minor aspects of the play. For example, Rebecca E. Pitts[2] claims that in his use of the phrase 'this fell sergeant, Death', Shakespeare is using a well-established Christian tradition instanced by Silvester Du Bartas and *The Lamentation of the Dying Creature*. A good article by Bridget Gellert[3] examines the iconography of the graveyard scene and sets Hamlet against the verbal and pictorial representations of the melancholy man, Saturnine configurations, and combinations of thought and imagination; and R. W. Dent[4] makes us think again about Coghill's suggestion that 'old mole' is a cant term for the Devil, on the basis of evidence provided by *Jack Juggler*. Although one usually thinks of Goethe's interpretation of Hamlet in *Wilhelm Meister* as being original, it is, according to Dennis M. Mueller,[5] similar to that which may be gathered from Wieland's German translation of the play and thus probably of older origin.

D. F. Rauber,[6] by dint of some amusing self-deprecation, encourages us to look at *Macbeth* in the light of the complex interweaving of triadic and diadic patterns. Some of the points made are well worth serious thought, particularly his case for the handling of psychological time in a youth-middle age-old age scheme, and the interrelation of family, sexual, and political elements. Also principally concerned with this play is an intelligent essay by D. W. Harding[7] on women's fantasy of manhood, which contains a notably sensitive analysis of the scene of Lady Macduff's death and its connection with the idea of manliness as it appears in the relationship between the hero and heroine; and a briefer presentation of the idea as it appears in Goneril, Cleopatra, and Volumnia.

King Lear is the subject of a novel kind of contribution to criticism to be found in the 1969 *Jahrbuch* of the Deutsche Shakespeare-Gesellschaft West. This brings together the proceedings of what must have been an exciting Bochum symposium dealing with many aspects of Shakespeare's theatrical craftsmanship as it is found in the play. With his customary subtle response to language, Wolfgang Clemen, together with Fritz Lichtenhahn,[8] discusses how the dramatic impulse shows itself in verse and rhythm; Werner Habicht and Leopold Lindtberg[9] take up the questions of mirror scenes and stage gestures; Horst Oppel and Max Fritzsche[10] deal with stage sets and the verbal depictions of place; and John Russell Brown[11] makes a plea for greater attention to be paid to the lessons that critics can learn from practical theater work. The style of the play is examined in more conventional critical terms

[1] 'On the Value of *Hamlet*', *Reinterpretations of Elizabethan Drama*, ed. Norman Rabkin (Columbia University Press, 1969), pp. 137–76.
[2] 'This Fell Sergeant, Death', *Shakespeare Quarterly*, XX (1969), 486–91.
[3] 'The Iconography of Melancholy in the Graveyard Scene of *Hamlet*', *Studies in Philology*, LXVII (1970), 57–66.
[4] 'Hamlet I, v, 162: "Well said, old mole"', *Notes and Queries*, CCXVII (1970), 128–9.
[5] 'Wieland's *Hamlet* Translation and Wilhelm Meister', *Deutsche Shakespeare-Gesellschaft West Jahrbuch* (1969), pp. 198–212.
[6] 'Macbeth, Macbeth, Macbeth', *Criticism*, XI (1969), 59–67.
[7] 'Women's Fantasy of Manhood', *Shakespeare Quarterly*, XX (1969), 245–53.
[8] 'Die dramatischen Impulse in Vers und Rhythmus', *Deutsche Shakespeare-Gesellschaft West Jahrbuch* (1969), pp. 10–29.
[9] 'Spiegelstellen und Gebärdenführung', *ibid.*, pp. 29–50.
[10] 'Wortkulisse und Buhnenbild', *ibid.*, pp. 50–65.
[11] 'Ein Epilog: Scholars and Actors', *ibid.*, pp. 72–80.

by Emily W. Leider,[1] who sees a movement in *Lear* throughout the work from elaborate language to greater simplicity and on to a kind of renunciation of language itself. This stylistic movement she connects with the idea of the play as a tragedy of reduction in that it turns from superfluity towards necessity and truth. H. W. Donner[2] raises again the difficulty presented by the nature of the ending, and displays a comprehensive knowledge of most that has been written on the subject to arrive at the conclusion that the final scene is as it is because 'Shakespeare has deliberately made us feel that justice has *not* been done...that the crimes committed [are] too terrible to be condoned – too terrible to forget'. This scene is explained in a rather different way by Phyllis Rackin[3] who, emphasizing that many of the positives in the play are created by deluded actions, views Lear's death as his final triumphant assertion of faith, as a creative act – a something that has come out of nothing. An even more positive reading is provided by Roger L. Cox[4] who claims that Shakespeare transcends the narrowly moralistic Aristotelian view of tragedy by infusing the piece with the values to be found in St Paul's Corinthian letters.

In view of so much national and international preoccupation with Race, it is odd that not much recent writing on *Othello* has concerned itself with the hero's colour, which is the starting point of an examination by Robert F. Fleissner[5] of the metaphysical question: *how* is Othello black? He suggests that there is sufficient evidence to indicate that Shakespeare was aware of 'pre-Mesmeric forces at work', and positing a connection between the play and both Gilbertus's *De Magnete* and Jonson's *The Magnetick Lady*, opines that the point of the play is that Othello 'through magnetic coition' joins harmoniously with Desdemona so that 'neither blackness nor whiteness prevails'. In an essay that well exemplifies her ability to

work subtly from small to large issues, Madeleine Doran[6] examines the syntax of the same play, stressing the importance of Iago's use of the conditional sentence and demonstrating how 'in the interplay of assertion and negation...the bare bones of a fable are given dramatic life and sensibility'. Almost every passage she deals with displays how syntax can show intimately the movement of a character's mind, perhaps the most provocative being her reading of Othello's final speech about which she concludes 'the relation of the condition to its conclusion is necessary. The truth is this and no other. To read the speech otherwise, with reservations about Othello's motives or the psychology of jealousy, is not to have attended to the syntax of the play in its dramatic functioning'. In a somewhat unconditional piece, Stewart A. Baker[7] uses the punctuation of the Quartos rather than the Folio to support his belief that the 'cause' for Othello is Desdemona's 'blood' (= sexual appetite).

Among the Roman plays, *Coriolanus* and *Julius Caesar* seem to have settled down in criticism within some fairly well-defined limits of excellence in which there may nevertheless be disagreement about details and focus. But the nature of *Antony and Cleopatra* somehow continues to elude definition. Some critics find it to be one of Shakespeare's greatest plays (without ever persuading us why exactly) while

[1] 'Plainness of Style in *King Lear*', *Shakespeare Quarterly*, XXI (1970), 45–53.

[2] '"Is this the Promised End?" Reflections on the Tragic Ending of *King Lear*', *English Studies*, L (1969), 503–10.

[3] 'Delusion as Resolution in *King Lear*', *Shakespeare Quarterly*, XXI (1970), 29–34.

[4] '*King Lear* and the Corinthian Letters', *Thought*, XLIV (1969), 5–28.

[5] 'The Magnetic Moor: An Anti-Racist View', *Journal of Human Relations*, XVII (1969), 546–57.

[6] 'Iago's "if": An Essay on the Syntax of *Othello*', *Drama of the Renaissance*, pp. 69–99.

[7] 'Othello's "Cause": A New Reading', *English Language Notes*, VII (1969), 96–8.

others appear to regard it as the hideous dramatic mistake of a master poet. In a book devoted to this play and its relationship to the rest of the canon, Julian Markels[1] sets out to demonstrate how it is a totally balanced work of art. He sees the play as forcing us to hold 'poised in our minds two morally contradictory actions' so that 'we transform all moral actions into postures, which become not false poses but the protean forms of life. Step by step... Shakespeare has made us amoral, in order to produce at last an imaginative experience of omniscience to accompany the experience of timelessness'. He contends that the conventional view of Antony torn by the conflicting worlds of Egypt and Rome is a wrong one; rather Markels's Antony devotes himself wholly to each world in turn so that in his life he rhythmically makes each one a measure and condition of the other so that the values of both are affirmed and fulfilled.

By emphasizing the techniques of inconsistency and discontinuity that shape the action, Markels argues that this is appropriate in that evil and good are seen not to reside in specific characters but to exist as aspects of Antony's divided being which are in endlessly renewed conflict. The ends of the lovers thus become transfigurations of death and mystically fuse values which have formerly been in opposition: for Antony, personal and public virtue, honor and love; for Cleopatra, safety and honor, private and public values, with the right to patronize her aspirations and to turn from whore into wife. The stylistic variety in the play is also taken by Markels to reflect this early division and final blending, and there is some fine analysis of the two opposing syntactical rhythms, the vastness and abstraction of the diction, the cosmic imagery, and the worldly moral judgments of the other characters on the lovers.

Markels sees *Antony and Cleopatra* as being 'beyond *Lear*' in that the later play presents us with a world in which good, by endlessly renewed beginnings, can dominate while evil simply endures. This is an intelligent, articulate, and perceptive piece of criticism. It is perhaps rather longwinded and repetitive in making some of its points, and one is sometimes inclined to take exception to the idea of Shakespeare as 'developing' in so many ways. One would have thought an equally good case might be made for a Shakespeare who examined certain basic human problems with continually changing focus in the light of increasing experience and expertise.

Another critic who would agree with Markels's claim that death in this play is apotheosis instead of tragically catastrophic is J. L. Simmons[2] who has written a fine essay on the comedy in the drama. He notes the familiar comic pattern and thematic concerns as they are related to the workaday and holiday worlds of Rome and Egypt; and after some illuminating comment on Enobarbus as a sort of tragic clown, gives a close reading of the final scene from which Cleopatra emerges as the queen of comedy arranging the happy ending of a marriage in death and finding within tragedy the comic wholeness of life. In a less ambitious article, Paul L. Rose[3] attempts to define the play's political impact on its original audience and how this might have reacted with the more obvious emotional response.

In a general perceptive essay on *Julius Caesar*, A. W. Bellringer[4] charts the way in which it celebrates a point in history where an irrelevant past of the politics of the City (in

---

[1] *The Pillar of the World: 'Antony and Cleopatra' in Shakespeare's Development* (Ohio State University Press, 1968).

[2] 'The Comic Pattern and Vision in *Antony and Cleopatra*', *ELH*, XXXVI (1969), 493–510.

[3] 'The Politics of *Antony and Cleopatra*', *Shakespeare Quarterly*, XX (1969), 379–90.

[4] '*Julius Caesar*: Room Enough', *Critical Quarterly*, XII (1970), 31–50.

all its nobility, capacity for sacrifice, firm sentiment, and idealism) is giving way to a newer politics which sound the prelude to empire. More specialized aspects of the play are handled by Harold Fisch,[1] who shows how the imagery pattern of stone statues–blood–stony hearts–weapons–human emotions can suggest that paganism carries within itself 'the question of its basic inadequacy as a way of life for treating men and women'; and by Joseph S. M. J. Chang,[2] who views the play against the development of Renaissance historiography and concludes that it is a dramatic representation of the ironic discrepancy between man's desired and created realities, with Brutus as Shakespeare's paradox of good performing evil and a personification of the irreconcilable gap between intention and act.[3]

Katherine Stockholder[4] resurrects the problem of the divided image we get of Coriolanus as warrior and boy, and argues that the compulsion he feels to maintain his public persona arises ultimately from his denial of human tenderness in himself, and that this weakness, in forcing him to measure up to external expectations, makes him susceptible to the manipulations of others.

The two other classical plays have also been the object of some good research. In a very thorough piece, which possibly claims too much for its evidence, Anne Lancashire[5] makes a close comparison between *Timon of Athens* and the morality play to prove it Shakespeare's 'own secularized anti-traditional morality play' and a moral exemplum based on debate that shows the destruction rather than the salvation of the Everyman figure. Similarly systematic but more acceptable in its conclusions is J. E. Reese's[6] demonstration of the structural, dramatic and verbal techniques of stylization by which Shakespeare managed to de-emphasize the physical horror of the materials he employed in *Titus Andronicus*. And for the same play Nancy L. Harvey[7] claims another

possible source, arguing persuasively and unpretentiously for the influence of the scene dealing with the 'Slaughter of the Innocents' in *The Shearmen and Taylors' Play* of the Coventry Mystery Cycle on the shaping of the slaying of Alarbus.

There are three good but very different general articles on Shakespeare's comedy. Northrop Frye[8] delivers a typically witty and civilized essay, packed with fertile connections which provoke the reader to a re-consideration of his own ideas. Taking the definitions of the Old and the New Comedy as his starting point, he ranges through ancient and modern drama suggesting that Shakespeare's employment of the new form in all his comedies save *Troilus and Cressida* removes him from direct structural influence on modern dramatists who write for a stage where Old Comedy is established and where 'as we enter the age of anarchism it is likely to remain'. More specifically geared to Shakespeare's work is V. Y. Kantak's[9] able summary of the way in which the comedies have proved resistant to most critical approaches. This leads him to a plea for a more inclusive appreciation which would stress the playing

[1] '*Julius Caesar* and the Bleeding Statue', *Bar Ilan* (Volume in Humanities and Social Sciences, Jerusalem, 1969), pp. 1–6.

[2] '*Julius Caesar* in the Light of Renaissance Historiography', *JEGP*, LXIX (1970), 63–71.

[3] J. C. Maxwell reminds us that Brutus's philosophy which caused him to blame Cato for his suicide is from Plato's *Phaedo* and not from the Stoics as many editors of the play claim; see 'Brutus's Philosophy', *Notes and Queries*, CCXVII (1970), 128.

[4] 'The Other Coriolanus', *PMLA*, LXXXV (1970), 228–36.

[5] '*Timon of Athens*: Shakespeare's *Dr Faustus*', *Shakespeare Quarterly*, XXI (1970), 35–44.

[6] 'The Formalization of Horror in *Titus Andronicus*', *ibid.*, 77–84.

[7] '*Titus Andronicus* and *The Shearmen and Taylors' Play*', *Renaissance Quarterly*, XII (1969), 27–31.

[8] 'Old and New Comedy', *Shakespeare Survey 22* (Cambridge, 1969), 1–5.

[9] 'An Approach to Shakespearian Comedy', *ibid.*, 7–14.

and festive elements, the doubleness of view, ambiguity and montage-like structures. M. A. Shaaber[1] also notes the limitations of some recent criticism which tends to seek out the common denominators of the plays rather than the nature of their variety. He has the courage to tackle the huge subject of Shakespeare's comic view of love, and does so with great common sense and some memorable phrasing. He emphasizes the fact that the comic vision of life and love they embody is to be located in the simultaneous acceptance of folly and glory. Two other good general essays compare Shakespeare's comedy with that of other writers. In a superb example of what comparative literary study can be, Michel Grivelet[2] winds himself into the topic of the comic ambiguity in man's 'doubtfulness of being one or two, identical with himself or not' as it makes its appearance in *The Comedy of Errors* and *Amphitryon*. His conclusion is: 'In the mystic experience of love, Shakespeare seems to say, man newly made overcomes his contradictions. While, for Molière, perplexity can only be eased by letting protean life overwhelm all care for consistency.' In the light of the deliberate comic confusion found in some modern plays, Herbert S. Weil[3] notes the way in which Shakespeare's comic structures offer a variety of possible responses to the audience, co-existent with the predominant air of festivity, and allow us to relate the part of the truth we see to whatever whole we can imagine and understand.

The two more difficult of the early comedies, *The Two Gentlemen of Verona* and *Love's Labour's Lost*, are approached theatrically and verbally by Ralph Berry[4] and Robert Weimann[5] respectively. Weimann gives an unusually high estimate of the former play's dramatic coherence and artistic integrity, by employing some subtle perception into the relationship between actor and character, illusion and reality, and the imaginative flexibility of audience and player, chiefly in connection with the character of Launce. Berry examines the latter play as an evolving analysis of humanity's primary symbol for reality – words; and provides an illuminating but over-neat presentation of the verbal attitudes manifested by the contrasting character groups.

Working from the part played by hearsay in *Much Ado About Nothing*, Steven Rose[6] sees Shakespeare as undermining our notions of romantic love and the integrity of human personality only to re-establish in Beatrice and Benedick how need rather than false image produces a true relationship. D. J. Palmer[7] also examines the nature of the curative properties of comedy in an intelligent essay on *As You Like It*. He denies that the structure is intended to illustrate a series of contrasting attitudes to love, and argues by skillful analysis of the principal character encounters that the Forest of Arden forces people into confrontations with themselves by constituting a realm where Art and Nature meet. A fresh look at some of the disputed words and meanings in the same play is taken by Ernst Leisi and Christine Trautvetter[8] in an important article.

I think it could be claimed that *Measure for Measure* has emerged theatrically as the Shakespearian comedy for our time. Describing

[1] 'The Comic View of Life in Shakespeare's Comedies', *Drama of the Renaissance*, pp. 165–80.

[2] 'Shakespeare, Molière, and the Comedy of Ambiguity', *Shakespeare Survey 22* (Cambridge, 1969), 15–26.

[3] 'Comic Structure and Tonal Manipulation in Shakespeare and Some Modern Plays', *ibid.*, 27–34.

[4] 'The Words of Mercury', *ibid.*, 69–77.

[5] 'Laughing with the Audience: *The Two Gentlemen of Verona* and the Popular Tradition of Comedy', *ibid.*, 35–42.

[6] 'Love and Self-Love in *Much Ado About Nothing*', *Essays in Criticism*, XX (1970), 143–50.

[7] 'Art and Nature in *As You Like It*', *Philological Quarterly*, XLIX (1970), 30–40.

[8] 'Some New Readings in *As You Like It*', *Deutsche Shakespeare-Gesellschaft West Jahrbuch* (1969), pp. 143–51.

one moment in a recent Ontario production, Clifford Leech[1] suggests that one of the functions of the Duke's persuading Isabella to confess publicly to her lie about Angelo's crime is not only to teach her mercy but also to stretch her mind to encompass the range of what is thinkable. Herbert Weil[2] makes high claims for the same play in a laudable attempt to perceive a unity in the varied materials. Although concerned principally with the nature of the copy that lies behind the Folio text of this play, John Wasson's[3] argument that what we have are foul papers specially revised for performance at court has a number of critical implications.

The two other problem comedies have also received some attention. Rolf Soellner[4] gives a close reading of the Trojan debate in *Troilus and Cressida*, often going over some very familiar ground but convincingly documenting its indebtedness to Cicero's *De officiis*; and Roger Warren,[5] noting some strong parallels between Helena's idiom in *All's Well That Ends Well* and those sonnets addressed to the friend, finds the play to be a personal statement about the nature of love rather than a reflection of indifference and cynicism towards value.[6]

Jonson himself forced upon us the contrast between his own comic world and that of Shakespeare's Romances, and two distinguished critics have taken up his challenge. In his urbane and informed way, Harry Levin[7] weaves an elegant commentary on the nature of Jonson's famous attack in *Bartholomew Fair*, and then proceeds to an allusive discussion of the two dramatists' treatment of magic in *The Tempest* and *The Alchemist*. Robert Ornstein[8] views the two writers as being at opposite comic poles: Jonson's comedies present life that is irredeemable not because of its depravity but because it exists outside of time and the possibilities of change and redemption which the Shakespearian life within time offers. The art of the playwrights is connected in a

different way by D. C. Boughner,[9] who suggests that the neo-classical art of *The Tempest* is not limited to an observance of the three unities, but is also to be found in its manipulation of the four-part structure of prologue, protasis, epitasis, and catastrophe, invented by Terence and naturalized on the English stage by Jonson. Beginning with the masque and the subsequent famous speech in act IV of the same play, A. Duţu[10] suggests that because Prospero realizes he cannot bring Caliban into the united world his patience and wisdom have created, he abandons the theme of reconciliation for the theme of harmony and seeks to oppose to the inexorable flow of devastating time the ritual of love which alone can confer on man the possibility of perpetual renewal and authentic existence.

C. L. Barber[11] focusses on the special sort of dramatic action in *Pericles* and *The Winter's Tale* which transforms characters into sacred figures who yet remain human. He contrasts

[1] '"More than our brother is our chastity"', *Critical Quarterly*, XII (1970), 73–4.

[2] 'Form and Contexts in *Measure for Measure*', *ibid.*, 55–71.

[3] '*Measure for Measure*: A Text for Court Performance?', *Shakespeare Quarterly*, XXI (1970), 17–24.

[4] 'Prudence and the Price of Helen: The Debate of the Trojans in *Troilus and Cressida*', *ibid.*, XX (1969), 255–63.

[5] 'Why does It End Well? Helena, Bertram, and The Sonnets', *Shakespeare Survey 22* (Cambridge, 1969), 79–92.

[6] In this connection see also Warren's article '*A Lover's Complaint, All's Well*, and the Sonnets', *Notes and Queries*, CCXVII (1970), 130–2.

[7] 'Two Magian Comedies: *The Tempest* and *The Alchemist*', *Shakespeare Survey 22* (Cambridge, 1969), 47–58.

[8] 'Shakespearian and Jonsonian Comedy', *ibid.*, 43–6.

[9] 'Jonsonian Structure in *The Tempest*', *Shakespeare Quarterly*, XXI (1970), 3–10.

[10] 'Le Réveil de Prospero', *Études Anglaises*, XXII (1969), 225–30.

[11] '"Thou that beget'st him that did thee beget"': Transformation in *Pericles* and *The Winter's Tale*' *Shakespeare Survey 22* (Cambridge, 1969), 59–67.

the Romances, which deal with the freeing of family ties from the threat of sexual degradation, with the festive comedies, where sexuality is freed from the ties of family. He subtly demonstrates how the final reconciliations effect not only restoration and recovery but also the transformation of some quality that was formerly destructive into its full positive potential. Shakespeare's powers of audience control in the latter play are illustrated by William H. Matchett[1] in his analysis of the verbal ambiguities in the presentation of Leontes's jealousy, the mixed tragic and comic responses demanded by the death of Antigonus, and the way the limits of language are transcended by stage action in the statue scene. The poisoned cup image in Leontes's speech is connected with Sonnet 114 by Roger Warren[2] in a nice exercise in metaphor study. The part played by music in all the last plays is the subject of a good paper by Catharine M. Dunn.[3] She deals first with the cosmological view of music and the tripartite division of *musica mundana*, *musica humana*, and *musica instrumentalis* formulated by Boethius, and discusses the specific and wide use of the philosophical concepts of music found in *Pericles*, the musical symbolism for recognition in *Cymbeline*, the organically used but predominantly practical music of *The Winter's Tale*, and the music of *The Tempest* that shapes chaos into love and harmony.

The second historical tetralogy has been the subject of some good criticism and research. Alvin Kernan[4] deals with the whole sequence with a view to defining its claims to being considered an English Epic. In a discussion of quite exceptional clarity, he illustrates its historical, political, social, psychological, spatial, temporal, mythic, ceremonial, and ritual movements, and the way in which these various levels of meaning are interwoven at every point – scene parallels, character interrelationships, and complex poetic statement.

In an equally well-digested piece, Fredson Bowers[5] articulates the themes and art of *1 Henry IV*, dealing with the problems of structure that Shakespeare faced, the testing of Hal, and the roles of Falstaff and Hotspur to display how Hal becomes an association of 'personal and of national honor...transcending Falstaff's materialism, Henry's expediency, and Hotspur's fatal distortion' so that 'the education of the future hero king, Henry V, is complete'. The scene of Hal's second reformation in the second part of the play is ably defended by E. T. Schell[6] as Shakespeare's solving of a structural problem by using the folkloric image of Hal, adjusting and sharpening the picture of the Prince so far presented, and then turning it towards the needs of the play at this point. In a piece of immaculately thorough historical research of a kind now unfashionable with regard to Shakespeare, Alice L. Scoufos[7] presents the evidence for her contention that the appearance of the name 'Harvey' among Falstaff's crew at Gadshill can be seen as a satiric allusion to Sir William Harvey, his political alignment with the Cobham–Cecil faction, and his antagonizing of the Earl of Southampton (and hence Shakespeare) by his marriage with Wriothesley's mother. The article takes its place in this section of the review by virtue of Scoufos's strong though undisplayed claims

[1] 'Some Dramatic Techniques in *The Winter's Tale*', ibid., 93–108.
[2] '"Gust" and Poisoned Cups in *The Winter's Tale* and Sonnet 114', *Notes and Queries*, CXVII (1970), 134.
[3] 'The Function of Music in Shakespeare's Romances', *Shakespeare Quarterly*, XX (1969), 391–408.
[4] '*The Henriad*: Shakespeare's Major History Plays', *Yale Review*, LIX (1969), 3–32.
[5] 'Theme and Structure in *King Henry IV*, Part I', *Drama of the Renaissance*, pp. 42–68.
[6] 'Prince Hal's Second "Reformation"', *Shakespeare Quarterly*, XXI (1970), 11–16.
[7] 'Harvey: A Name-Change in *Henry IV*', *ELH*, XXXVI (1969), 297–318.

for the critical importance of the kind of scholarship she so perfectly exemplifies.

A monograph of mixed quality takes the *Henry VI* plays as its subject. In it Don M. Ricks[1] unfortunately feels obliged to preface his study of the plays' structure with a shallow run-through of the published material on Shakespeare's history plays. Then in well-planned essays, which no reader of the plays should miss, he isolates the three basic types of scene in part 1, and subtly detects from whence is derived the impression of rapid forward movement of the action. Part 2 is seen to concentrate long complex scenes, which carry the theme of factional intrigue, in the earlier part, and shorter scenes later in the play showing the dissolution of law and its effect on the nation. Part 3 is 'not so much a play as an experience, not so much a dramatic structure as a surrealistic montage of the faces of humanity twisted into expressions which reflect the substratum of violence'. In an article which seeks to put an end to the Tillyardian view of the same trilogy as a dramatic exploration of England's guilt, A. L. French[2] examines all the passages that allude to Richard II and finds no real dramatic emphasis on the fact of the deposition in any of them.

King John has received two quite opposed readings in essays by J. R. Price[3] and J. L. Simmons.[4] Price views the plays as theatrical rather than propagandist, with Shakespeare creating each scene to achieve provocative ambiguity; whereas Simmons makes a detailed comparison of the play with the *Troublesome Raigne* and concludes that it is a carefully structured and dramatically coherent testing and confirmation of the orthodox ideas of the necessity for obedience and of the evils of usurpation and rebellion.

Some of the most rewarding insights into Shakespeare's plays can often come from studies not of individual works, but of techniques and devices that are common to many.

Most such studies make modest claims, despite their obvious value. One of these is S. Viswanthan's[5] excellent look at what he calls 'illeism with a difference', by which he means the form used by Shakespeare to make a character refer to himself not in the first person but by his own name. He detects its most frequent occurrence in *Julius Caesar, Troilus and Cressida, Hamlet* and *Othello* and, after analyzing the technical uses, offers some fascinating speculations on the theatrical, thematic, and contemporary implications of them. Another is Manfred Weidhorn's[6] examination of how characters, sure of their selfhood, postulate an hypothetical exchange of identity by temporarily adopting another name to see themselves and their motives from a different perspective.

Some examples of one of Shakespeare's favourite dramaturgical practices are examined by Ernest Schanzer,[7] who sets out the various effects produced by 'plot echoes'. Adding to the many functions of the 'mirror scene', detailed by Hereward T. Price[8] some years ago,

---

[1] *Shakespeare's Emergent Form: A Study of the Structure of the Henry VI Plays* (Utah State University Monograph Series xv.1 (1968)).

[2] '*Henry VI* and the Ghost of Richard II', *English Studies*, L, Anglo-American Supplement (1969), xxxvii–xliii.

[3] 'King John and Problematic Art', *Shakespeare Quarterly*, XXI (1969), 25–8.

[4] 'Shakespeare's *King John* and its Source: Coherence, Pattern, and Vision', *Tulane Studies in English*, XVII (1969), 53–72.

[5] '"Illeism With a Difference" in Certain Middle Plays of Shakespeare', *Shakespeare Quarterly*, XX (1969), 407–16.

[6] 'The Rose and its Name: On Denomination in *Othello, Romeo and Juliet, Julius Caesar*', *Texas Studies in Literature and Language*, XI (1969), 671–86.

[7] 'Plot-Echoes in Shakespeare's Plays', *Deutsche Shakespeare-Gesellschaft West Jahrbuch* (1969), pp. 103–21.

[8] 'Mirror Scenes in Shakespeare' in *Joseph Quincy Adams Memorial Studies*, ed. James G. McManaway (Washington, 1948).

Mildred E. Hartsock[1] re-examines the Garden Scene in *Richard II*, the Mad Scene in *Hamlet*, and the music underground in *Antony and Cleopatra* to illustrate how such incidents change the direction of the audience's sympathy. Two character types have also received some attention in Gisela Lord's[2] detailed discussion of Shakespeare's presentation of the Pedant; and in Hugh C. Evans's[3] expert use of contemporary documents to show the relationship between the comic constables in the plays and their historical counterparts. A whole world, Sidney's Golden one, is examined by Inge Leimberg[4] as it makes its appearance in the comedies in poetry, characters, methods of depiction, and most interestingly in the 'happy catharsis'.

A number of scholars take technical linguistic approaches to various sections of the canon. Arguing that most of the best English lyric poetry strives toward dramatic life, David Parker[5] claims that many of the *Sonnets* can be viewed as elaborate disguises of the imperative mood. Among the other poems, *The Phoenix and the Turtle* is connected with the destruction of love and the period of *Othello* and *Troilus and Cressida* rather than the triumph of love and *Antony and Cleopatra* and the Romances. Various aspects of Shakespeare's vocabulary have also received some research. Compound words and neologisms are analyzed by Herbert Voitl;[6] and Paul Jorgensen[7] examines the words connected with torment, death, opprobrium, and dread atmosphere in *Titus Andronicus*, *Hamlet*, and *Macbeth* and the contribution they make to the tragic effect. Werner Sedlak[8] brings out the variety possible in the blank verse line; and Ludwig Borinski[9] focusses on the forms of utterance which are persistently present in Shakespeare's prose.

As the history of Shakespearian criticism almost constitutes a history of English literary taste, it has become increasingly necessary that some scholars attempt to digest for us the most influential and representative writings on the plays at various periods. One feels inclined to welcome, therefore, even before opening it a book entitled *Shakespeare and the Victorians: The Roots of Modern Criticism*[10] by Aron Y. Staviski. The plan of the book is sound and the approach to the subject well thought out. In his introduction Staviski places Victorian criticism, first, by noting that good modern criticism has absorbed the historical perspective created by the Victorians and coupled it with the romantic imaginative insight as principally articulated by Coleridge; and, second, by contending that the centre of Victorian criticism derives from an earlier generation and has a good deal more in common with Johnson than is generally recognized. Dowden is strongly defended against charges of his insensitivity to poetry, and the convenience of his 'four periods' handled with refreshing good sense. But the material appears to escape from the author's control as he charts the Bacon–Shakespeare feuding, and inadequately deals with the row between Swin-

[1] 'Major Scenes in Minor Key', *Shakespeare Quarterly*, XXI (1970), 55–62.
[2] 'Die Figur des Pedanten bei Shakespeare', *Deutsche Shakespeare-Gesellschaft West Jahrbuch* (1969), pp. 213–44.
[3] 'Comic Constables – Fictional and Historical', *Shakespeare Quarterly*, XX (1969), 427–34.
[4] 'Shakespeares Komödein und Sidney's "Goldene Welt"', *Deutsche Shakespeare-Gesellschaft West Jahrbuch* (1969), pp. 174–97.
[5] 'Verbal Moods in Shakespeare's Sonnets', *Modern Language Quarterly*, XXX (1969), 331–9.
[6] 'Shakespeares Komposita. Ein Beitrag zur Stilistik seiner Wortneuprägungen', *Deutsche Shakespeare-Gesellschaft West Jahrbuch* (1969), pp. 152–73.
[7] 'Shakespeare's Dark Vocabulary', *Drama of the Renaissance*, pp. 108–22.
[8] 'Typen des Blankverses bei Shakespeare', *Deutsche Shakespeare-Gesellschaft West Jahrbuch* (1969), pp. 122–42.
[9] 'Konstante Stilformen in Shakespeares Prosa', *ibid.*, pp. 81–102.
[10] University of Oklahoma Press, 1969.

burne and Furnivall. The virtues of more modern criticism are also dealt with in a pleasantly written essay by Charles Haywood,[1] who considers Bernard Shaw's stress in his theater notices on the 'Shakespearian music' he so valued.

Three articles are examples of the newly emerging theatrical school of Shakespeare criticism. John Russell Brown[2] defends the whole approach emphasizing the value in perceiving the variety, instability, and theatrical potentialities of a play text. As demonstrations of just what is possible by working roughly along the lines Brown suggests, there are Daniel Seltzer's[3] discussion of the modern theater's attempts to reconstitute Shakespeare for our own age, and Robert Hapgood's[4] survey-commentary of productions which have offered him very different experiences of the plays. However, against every critical enthusiasm there is always a cooling card to be played; and this is what Patrick Cruttwell[5] does as he warns us against the dangers of Jan Kott and the limitations of our contemporaneity: 'See Shakespeare as "our contemporary" – which always means, in practice, "my view of what our contemporary should be" – and you are narrowing and impoverishing your mind and imagination. You are denying the possibility of ever, even in imagination, escaping from the trap of time.'

[1] 'George Bernard Shaw on Shakespearian Music and the Actor', *Shakespeare Quarterly*, XX (1969), 417–26.
[2] 'The Theatrical Element of Shakespeare Criticism', *Reinterpretations of Elizabethan Drama*, pp. 177–95.
[3] 'Shakespeare's Texts and Modern Productions', *ibid.*, pp. 89–115.
[4] 'Shakespeare and the Included Spectator', *ibid.*, pp. 117–36.
[5] 'Shakespeare is Not Our Contemporary', *Yale Review*, LIX (1969), 33–49.

2. SHAKESPEARE'S LIFE, TIMES, AND STAGE

reviewed by LEAH SCRAGG

Innumerable insights into the personality and private life of the world's foremost playwright have, it seems, long lain readily available to us had we but viewed that riddling perspective, his sonnets, aright, perceiving there not one face but two – the authentic features of the dramatist side by side with those of 'his patron, his companion in a turbulent love affair, his correspondent in the sonnets, and the woman who influenced him throughout his creative life',[1] the Countess of Southampton. Seen, as Elizabeth Beach would have us see them, as a kind of verse dialogue between Shakespeare and his equally gifted patroness, the *Sonnets* cease to be problematic, Shakespeare's sexual reputation is vindicated, and we are presented with a treasure-house of knowledge about the bard and his beloved. Unfortunately the reviewer lacked the necessary faith in Lady Mary's creative ability to pass into this biographical wonderland. More conventional means of plucking out the heart of the mystery have been employed in Donald Neil Friesner's 'William Shakespeare, Conservative'.[2] Friesner ponders the dramatist's social background, his firm links with Stratford, and the political philosophy of the plays, and postulates a Shakespeare conservative by temperament and conviction. The limitations of this particular deductive method are self-

[1] Elizabeth Beach, *Shakespeare And The Tenth Muse* (Willoughby Books, Hamburg, New Jersey, 1969), p. 19.
[2] *Shakespeare Quarterly*, XX (1969), 165–78.

evident – attitudes are not necessarily determined by social origin nor do the plays lend themselves to easy categorisation. The detective endeavours of both Beach and Friesner pale however beside the dazzling ingenuity of B. N. De Luna's *The Queen Declined*,[1] an interpretation of *Willobie His Avisa* together with a text of the original edition. Since the poem contains both the earliest known allusion to Shakespeare and a character which has been thought to represent him, expectation runs high through a Holmesian investigation in the course of which Avisa is identified as Elizabeth and her successive suitors as Thomas Seymour, Philip II, Alençon, Hatton-Hapsburg, and Dudley-Devereux, only to be dashed by the discovery that the identity of W. S., his sudden appearance in the poem, and his relationship with the Dudley-Devereux figure are to remain unexplored.[2] More information emerges as one turns from studies centring on the personality of the dramatist to those concerned with the life and works. Douglas Hamer[3] has amassed a telling weight of evidence against the view that Shakespeare was the William Shakeshafte numbered among the household of Alexander Houghton of Lea Hall, near Preston; Thomas Clayton[4] has provided scholars with some 'aids' to the study of the 'Shakespearian' addition to *The Booke of Sir Thomas Moore* in the form of a modern spelling text, concordance, orthographical indexes, etc.; and John Wasson,[5] concerned with both the nature of court productions and the circumstances in which *Measure for Measure* was performed, has suggested that Shakespeare had a command performance in view during the composition of the play. Collaborative works have also been the subjects of scholarly deliberations. D. J. Lake has devoted two articles[6] to the claims of various dramatists for the role of Shakespeare's partner in *Pericles*, advancing Wilkins as the most likely candidate, and John Freehafer,[7] stepping tentatively across

ground yet more infirm, has argued that *The Double Falsehood* is an adaptation of *Cardenio*, that 'Theobald did indeed possess three manuscripts of *Cardenio*; that *Cardenio* was written by Shakespeare and Fletcher; that it was based on the 1612 Shelton translation of *Don Quixote*; [and] that *Cardenio* was cut and perhaps altered during the Restoration period, then altered by Theobald'. Having noted this attempt to augment the canon one should perhaps mention that the anti-Shakespearians have not been idle, and that *A Digest Of Comment In Recently Published Books On Stratford And The Shakespeare Controversy*[8] has appeared. Entries, culled from a variety of scholarly and not-so-scholarly sources, range from verbatim quotations with significant omission (cf. the extract from Sampson's *Concise Cambridge History of English Literature*) to passages compiled from words and phrases unrelated in the original (cf. the extract from Danby's *Shakespeare's Doctrine of Nature*). Altogether a dishonest publication not to be taken very seriously.

Sources major and minor have been advanced

[1] Clarendon Press, Oxford, 1970.
[2] The introduction seems oddly incomplete in other respects. Discussion of textual corruption, for example, is limited to a table on the use of the ampersand.
[3] 'Was William Shakespeare William Shakeshafte?' *The Review of English Studies*, XXI (1970), 41–8.
[4] 'The "Shakespearean" Addition In The Booke Of Sir Thomas Moore: Some Aids To Scholarly And Critical Shakespearean Studies', *Shakespeare Studies Monograph Series*, I (Wm. C. Brown Co., Dubuque Iowa, 1969).
[5] '*Measure for Measure*: A Text for Court Performance?', *Shakespeare Quarterly*, XXI (1970), 17–24.
[6] 'Wilkins and *Pericles* – Vocabulary (1)', *Notes and Queries*, CCXIV (1969), 288–91, and 'The *Pericles* Candidates – Heywood, Rowley, Wilkins', *ibid.*, CCXV (1970), 135–41.
[7] '*Cardenio*, by Shakespeare and Fletcher', *Publications of the Modern Language Association of America*, LXXXIV (1969), 501–13.
[8] *The Shakespeare Controversy* (Francis Carr Publications, 1967).

for a large proportion of the canon. Two writers have contributed to the *Ur-Shrew/A Shrew/The Shrew* issue, W. Braekman[1] examining the German 'Titus' play of 1620 and Jan Vos's *Aran En Titus* in an attempt to establish the existence of the *Ur-Shrew* and to determine the nature of Shakespeare's modification of it, Peter Alexander[2] arguing that *A Shrew* is a pirated version of *The Shrew* in which the final scene of Shakespeare's play is preserved. Standish Henning[3] has pointed to Scot's *Discovery of Witchcraft* (1584) as a source for Shakespeare's diminutive fairies in *A Midsummer Night's Dream*; Robert F. Willson[4] has challenged the view that the Mechanicals' interpretation of the story of Pyramus and Thisby is a parody of Mouffet's 'Of the Silkwormes and their Flies' and suggested Golding's *Metamorphoses* in its place; D. S. Bland[5] has brought information to light supporting the identification of Broke of the Inner Temple with the author of *Romeus and Juliet*; Frederick W. Sternfeld and Mary Joiner Chan[6] have tried to establish a musical text for Evans's garbled version of 'Come Live With Me' in *The Merry Wives*; Lord McNair, Q.C.,[7] having duly weighed the evidence, has acquitted Shakespeare of caricaturing the Master of Gonville in his Dr Caius; Barbara K. Lewalski,[8] also concerned with nomenclature, has advanced Chapman's *Hero and Leander* as a source for *Much Ado*; John W. Velz[9] has discerned in *Julius Caesar* 'a Senecan antithesis between the clement king who is motivated by just cause and the tyrant with his "intollerable vice of selfe-will"', and suggested that Seneca's *De Clementia* may be the source for the Jonsonian version of lines spoken by Julius Caesar; M. D. Faber[10] has detected Paul's Epistle to the Philippians behind Hamlet's 'canon 'gainst self-slaughter' (I, ii, 32); Yngve B. Olsson[11] has studied various redactions of the Hamlet story and considered the possibility that Albert Kranz's *Chronica Regnorum Aqui-*

lonarium Daniae Svetiae Norvagiae may have provided the skeleton of Shakespeare's play; Sir James Fergusson of Kilkerran, in a collection of studies throwing light on a variety of aspects of Scottish history,[12] has traced the career of James Stewart of Bothwellhaugh and his wife Elizabeth, possible antecedents of Macbeth and his Queen; S. R. Swaminathan[13] has proposed that Macbeth's image of Pity as a naked new-born babe striding the blast may derive from medieval art; Helen Morris[14] has suggested that Dürer's Apocalypse woodcuts

[1] *Shakespeare's Titus Andronicus, Its Relationship To The German Play Of 1620 And To Jan Vos's Aran En Titus* (Seminar of English and American Literature of the University of Ghent, Ghent, 1969).

[2] 'The Original Ending of *The Taming of the Shrew*', *Shakespeare Quarterly*, XX (1969), 111–16.

[3] 'The Fairies of *A Midsummer Night's Dream*', *ibid.*, 484–6.

[4] 'Golding's *Metamorphoses* and Shakespeare's Burlesque Method in *A Midsummer Night's Dream*', *English Language Notes*, VII (1969–70), 18–25.

[5] 'Arthur Broke, Gerard Legh and the Inner Temple', *Notes and Queries*, CCXIV (1969), 453–5.

[6] '"Come live with me And be my love"', *Comparative Literature*, XXII (1970), 173–87.

[7] 'Why is the Doctor in *The Merry Wives of Windsor* called Caius?', *Medical History*, XIII (1969), 311–39.

[8] 'Hero's Name – and Namesake – in *Much Ado About Nothing*', *English Language Notes*, VII (1969–70), 175–9.

[9] 'Clemency, Will, and Just Cause in *Julius Caesar*', *Shakespeare Survey 22* (Cambridge, 1969), 109–18.

[10] 'Hamlet's "Canon" Revisited', *Shakespeare Quarterly*, XXI (1970), 97–9.

[11] 'In Search of Yorick's Skull: Notes on the Background of Hamlet', *Shakespeare Studies*, IV (1968), 183–220.

[12] *The Man Behind Macbeth and other studies* (Faber and Faber, 1969). Also of interest to Shakespearian scholars is the first item in the collection tracing the history of Laurence Fletcher's visit to Scotland in 1599 with a company of players, James's patronage of him, and the repercussions of this visit after James's accession.

[13] 'The Image of Pity in *Macbeth*', *Notes and Queries*, CCXV (1970), 132.

[14] 'Shakespeare and Dürer's Apocalypse', *Shakespeare Studies*, IV (1968), 252–62.

may have influenced the imagery of *Antony and Cleopatra*; both the same writer[1] and Kenneth Muir[2] have pointed to similarities between the conduct of Cleopatra and Queen Elizabeth, the latter also drawing attention to resemblances between Shakespeare's play and Jodelle's *Cléopâtre Captive*; Naseeb Shaheen[3] has commented upon the large number of Biblical allusions in *Cymbeline* and discussed the 'patterns' that emerge from their use; and James U. Rundle[4] has argued that Shakespeare had Thomas Sackville's Induction to *A Mirror for Magistrates* 'not only in mind but probably in hand' when composing Sonnet 30. Finally, in two rather more general studies, Hugh C. Evans[5] has placed Shakespeare's comic constables in their historical context, and John J. O'Connor[6] has traced the influence of *Amadis de Gaule* on Elizabethan literature, devoting a section to its impact on the Elizabethan stage.

Two very elementary publications provide a convenient link between Shakespeare's life and his times – *The Shakespeare Book* by Levi Fox[7] and *Aspects of Shakespeare* by Erik Frykman and Göran Kjellmer.[8] The former, as one would expect from its association with the Shakespeare Birthplace Trust, illustrates all that is illustratable in the life of the dramatist while emphasizing the strength of the association with Stratford; the latter, directed towards Swedish university students, is concerned to explain the social, historical and literary context to non-English students and to provide elementary bibliographical and linguistic information. More suitable for English students, though still directed towards the general reader rather than the scholar, are John F. H. New's *The Renaissance and Reformation. A Short History*,[9] a very readable account of the political, cultural and religious movements of the fourteenth, fifteenth and sixteenth centuries, and *The Making of Britain 2: Life and Work from the Renaissance to the Industrial Revolution*,

by T. K. Derry and M. G. Blakeway[10] which includes a section on Shakespeare's England.

A variety of aspects of Renaissance social, political and religious life and thought have been the subjects of scholarly articles. Most wide-ranging is a discussion by Ludwig Borinski[11] of English and German humanistic and reform movements, while more limited in scope are Roger B. Manning's[12] study of the enforcement of the religious settlement in Sussex 1558–1603, Joel J. Epstein's[13] account of Francis Bacon's involvement in the Union issue 1603–8, and R. W. Kenny's[14] investigation into the 'Catholicism' of the commander of Elizabeth's anti-Spanish fleet.[15] Turning from

[1] 'Queen Elizabeth I "Shadowed" in Cleopatra', *The Huntington Library Quarterly*, XXXII (1968–9), 271–8.
[2] 'Elizabeth I, Jodelle, and Cleopatra', *Renaissance Drama*, New Series II (1969), 197–206.
[3] 'The Use of Scripture in *Cymbeline*', *Shakespeare Studies*, IV (1968), 294–315.
[4] 'The "Source" of Shakespeare's Sonnet 30', *Notes and Queries*, CCXV (1970), 132–3.
[5] 'Comic Constables – Fictional and Historical', *Shakespeare Quarterly*, XX (1969), 425–33.
[6] '*Amadis de Gaule' and Its Influence on Elizabethan Literature* (Rutgers University Press, New Brunswick, New Jersey, 1970).
[7] Jarrold and Sons, Norwich, n.d.
[8] Almqvist & Wiksell, Stockholm, 1969.
[9] John Wiley and Sons, 1969.
[10] John Murray, 1969.
[11] *Englischer Humanismus und deutsche Reformation*, Veröffentlichung der Joachim-Jungius-Gesellschaft der Wissenschaften, Hamburg (Vandenhoeck & Ruprecht, Göttingen, 1969).
[12] *Religion and Society in Elizabethan Sussex* (Leicester University Press, 1969).
[13] 'Francis Bacon and the Issue of Union, 1603–1608', *The Huntington Library Quarterly*, XXXIII (1970), 121–32.
[14] 'Notes on the "Catholicism" of Charles Earl of Nottingham', *Notes and Queries*, CCXIV (1969), 461–4.
[15] A sidelight on the social history of the period is provided by S. E. Sprott's investigation into the 'damned crew', a group of roisterers active in London between 1590 and 1620, headed at one stage of their history by Sir Edmund Baynham ('The Damned Crew', *Publications of the Modern Language Association of America*, LXXXIV (1969), 492–500).

history to historiography one must note Peter Burke's book, *The Renaissance Sense of the Past*,[1] an analysis of the key characteristics of Renaissance historical thought and of the historical conditions from which that thought emerged. Also concerned with the history of ideas are articles by N. W. Bawcutt,[2] contributing to our understanding of the Elizabethan response to Machiavelli, Robert J. Bauer,[3] tracing the history of the concept that the propagation of ideas and the procreation of children are analogous, and S. K. Heninger, Jr,[4] furnishing us with the second part of an invaluable survey of Tudor literature on the physical sciences. Our knowledge of the educational system at the Inns of Court in the Elizabethan period had been advanced by a study[5] of the twenty-four printed law-books belonging to Sir Thomas Egerton that are now in the Huntington Library. Egerton's annotations throw light not only on his own thought but on the Inns of Court curriculum, providing evidence that invalidates the view that the Inns of Court were in decay during the period.[6] Renaissance art has been the subject of two magnificently illustrated books by André Chastel, *The Myth of the Renaissance 1420–1520*,[7] and *The Crisis of the Renaissance 1520–1600*.[8] The former attempts to establish a more balanced view of the rise of Italian humanism and the decline of Gothic art in the north, emphasising the interaction between the two movements, the high degree of contact between north and south, and the complexity of response by which 'the aspirations expressed by Renaissance man assume the haunting, compelling character one associates with a dream or a myth'. The second book by contrast depicts an age of conflict and the explosive works of men 'divided' within themselves. More modest in scope, but possibly of more immediate interest to Shakespearian scholars, is *The Elizabethan Image*,[9] a lavishly illustrated, highly informative catalogue to the exhibition

organised by the Tate Gallery from November 1969 to February 1970 reconstituting seventy-five years of English painting from the death of Holbein to the advent of Van Dyck. Renaissance concepts of the relationship between art and nature have been the subject of an article by A. J. Close,[10] which distinguishes between a variety of theories, traces them back to their classical origins, and examines the context in which each is found. Our knowledge of Renaissance music has been furthered by two articles of interest to the student of Shakespeare's times. John Caldwell has discussed 'The Pitch of Early Tudor Organ Music'[11] and Paul Doe[12] has thrown considerable light on the history of Renaissance church music in the course of an attempt to date Tallis's 'Spem in alium'. Lastly a detailed analysis[13] of the Somersetshire speech of Thomas Whythorne, Elizabethan musician and composer, as ren-

[1] Edward Arnold, 1969.
[2] 'Some Elizabethan Allusions to Machiavelli', *English Miscellany*, XX (1969), 53–74.
[3] 'A Phenomenon of Epistemology in the Renaissance', *Journal of the History of Ideas*, XXXI (1970), 281–8.
[4] 'Tudor Literature of the Physical Sciences', *The Huntington Library Quarterly*, XXXII (1968–9), 249–70.
[5] Louis A. Knafla, 'The Law Studies of an Elizabethan Student', *ibid.*, 221–40.
[6] Also on educational matters in part is Norman Farmer, Jr's article 'Fulke Greville and Sir John Coke: An Exchange of Letters on a History Lecture and Certain Latin Verses on Sir Philip Sidney', *ibid.*, XXXIII (1969–70), 217–36, throwing light on the motivation behind the establishment of the first History lectureship at Cambridge.
[7] Trans. Stuart Gilbert (Skira, Geneva, 1969).
[8] Trans. Peter Price (Skira, Geneva, 1968).
[9] By Roy Strong (Arno Press, New York, 1969).
[10] 'Commonplace Theories of Art and Nature in Classical Antiquity and in the Renaissance', *Journal of the History of Ideas*, XXX (1969), 467–86.
[11] *Music and Letters*, LI (1970), 156–63.
[12] 'Tallis's "Spem in alium" and the Elizabethan Respond-Motet', *ibid.*, 1–14.
[13] Rupert E. Palmer, Jr, *Thomas Whythorne's Speech* (Anglistica XVI, Copenhagen, 1969).

dered in the 'newe Orthografie' of his manuscript autobiography must be noted before turning to the literary arts.

Many aspects of the non-dramatic literary scene and of the biographies of its principal figures have been illuminated in the past year. Julia G. Ebel[1] has considered Elizabethan translation literature 1557–88 and maintained that the translators 'gave form to a cultural nationalism without which the achievements of the subsequent period would be unimaginable'; Forrest G. Robinson,[2] also concerned with translation literature, has reconsidered the question of the authorship of the Sidney–Golding version of *De La Verité De La Religion Chrestienne*; Leland Ryken[3] has set Sidney's *Astrophel and Stella* in the 'mainstream' of Renaissance literature (*Faerie Queene*, Elizabethan–Jacobean drama, Milton) by seeing the sequence as centring upon a choice situation, and Astrophel not as a divided man but one who has 'actively chosen' a particular set of values and is 'emphatic' in his commitment to them; Charles S. Levy[4] has recorded letters by Sidney not noted in the Feuillerat edition (summarising the contents of unpublished items) and listed manuscript letters to Sidney not included in major collections; John Buxton and Bent Juel-Jensen[5] have announced the discovery of Sir Philip Sidney's first passport, a document which they claim is of major interest since it 'enabled him to go... on the travels which were to be of crucial importance, not only for his own development, but for the whole of the English Renaissance'; C. G. Harlow[6] has brought forward further evidence on the Nashe–Harvey controversy; Charles Kendrick Cannon[7] has considered the critical theory lying behind Chapman's notorious obscurity; Philip J. Finkelpearl[8] has supported the attribution of *Salmacis and Hermaphroditus* to Francis Beaumont; H. C. Schulz[9] has recorded the discovery of the autograph of Sir John Beaumont; Roger D. Sell[10] has dis-

cussed the significance of the discovery for the editor of Beaumont's poems; and W. R. Gair,[11] in a consideration of the work of Sir Thomas Salusbury, has suggested that there may have been 'a great deal more literary, philosophical and dramatic activity in local provincial circles in the period immediately preceding the Civil War than has previously been suspected'.

Among the year's many important contributions to the study of the pre-Shakespearian stage, pride of place must undoubtedly go to two Early English Text Society publications: *Non-Cycle Plays and Fragments* edited by Norman Davis and *The Macro Plays* edited by Mark Eccles.[12] The former, though based on the 1909 *The Non-Cycle Mystery Plays* of Osborn Waterhouse, now includes additional material hitherto available only in periodicals, together with a transcript and discussion of the

[1] 'Translation and Cultural Nationalism in the Reign of Elizabeth', *Journal of the History of Ideas*, XXX (1969), 593–602.

[2] 'A Note on the Sidney-Golding Translation of Philippe de Mornay's *De La Verité De La Religion Chrestienne*', *Harvard Library Bulletin*, XVII (1969), 98–102.

[3] 'The Drama of Choice in Sidney's *Astrophel and Stella*', *Journal of English and Germanic Philology*, LXVIII (1969), 648–54.

[4] 'A Supplementary Inventory of Sir Philip Sidney's Correspondence', *Modern Philology*, LXVII (1969), 177–81.

[5] 'Sir Philip Sidney's First Passport Rediscovered', *The Library*, XXV (1970), 42–6.

[6] 'Did Gabriel Harvey Read Nashe's *Christ's Tears*?', *Notes and Queries*, CCXIV (1969), 459–61.

[7] 'Chapman on the Unity of Style and Meaning', *Journal of English and Germanic Philology*, LXVIII (1969), 245–64.

[8] 'The Authorship of *Salmacis and Hermaphroditus*', *Notes and Queries*, CCXIV (1969), 367–8.

[9] 'A Hitherto Unrecorded Autograph', *The Huntington Library Quarterly*, XXXIII (1969–70), 283.

[10] 'The Handwriting of Sir John Beaumont and the Editing of His Poems', *ibid.*, 284–91.

[11] 'The Salusbury Circle at Llewenni', *Research Opportunities in Renaissance Drama*, XI (1968), 73–9.

[12] Oxford University Press, 1970 and 1969 respectively.

Shrewsbury music, a new introduction and freshly compiled glossary. The appearance of a reliable modern edition of *The Macro Plays* is equally welcome. Introductory material goes somewhat beyond that of the *Non-Cycle Plays and Fragments* (deliberately limited to 'some notes on verse technique and linguistic indications of date and place of composition') to include information on sources and staging, and a brief critical commentary on each play. Undoubtedly both volumes will prove invaluable to the student of the medieval stage. The publication of primary material has also been forwarded by Oxford University Press and Mouton Press. The former have re-issued their World's Classics volume of 1934, *Five Pre-Shakespearean Comedies* (edited by Frederick S. Boas), as a paperback (1970), while the latter have published a full critical edition of *Clyomon and Clamydes*,[1] a play which, the editor suggests, 'reflects a fairly typical use of a popular idiom that was to flower later in the hands of genius'. The debate surrounding the staging of late medieval drama has occasioned a number of very interesting articles in recent months. Chief among these is a two-part study by Natalie Crohn Schmitt[2] questioning the existence of a medieval theatre in the round. Part one takes issue with Southern's interpretation of the *Castle of Perseverance* drawing, arguing that the sketch presents not a playing area but a set design (thus the 'moat', for example, relates to actors rather than audience – with action taking place both within and without it), while part two examines the ancillary evidence for a theatre in the round advanced by Southern, Arthur Freeman and Merle Fifield and finds it to be insubstantial. Less convincingly, Martin Stevens,[3] also concerned with a reconsideration of traditional assumptions (and, in some instances, with the same evidence) has discussed the staging of the Wakefield Plays, concluding, with Marvin Rose, that the cycle was performed 'in one fixed location, on a multiple stage, and in the round'. A delightful item on medieval stage decoration has appeared by Anna J. Mill[4] demonstrating the scholarly confusion that has arisen over stage properties for the Corpus Christi plays consequent upon the failure to distinguish between 'p' and 'x' in sixteenth-century manuscripts, while information regarding the legal sanctions surrounding the performance of plays has been advanced by Peter Goodstein,[5] who has shown that a proclamation of Henry VIII provides evidence of an early attempt by the crown to control the places where actors performed. The intimacy of the relationship between actor and audience on the Tudor stage has been demonstrated by Robert Carl Johnson[6] ('the physical presence of the spectators is not. . .ignored but utilized'), experienced by Joel H. Kaplan and George Shand[7] ('theatrically sound and intellectually honest interpretations of medieval and Tudor plays have generally shown them to be more complex and formidable achievements than one might guess from a merely literary acquaintance'), and discussed (in terms of its impact on the later stage) by Robert Weimann.[8] On the strictly literary front,

[1] Ed. Betty J. Littleton (The Hague, 1968).

[2] 'Was There A Medieval Theatre In The Round?: A Re-Examination Of The Evidence (Part I)', *Theatre Notebook*, XXIII (1968–9), 130–42, and 'Was There A Medieval Theatre In The Round?: Part II', *ibid.*, XXIV (1969–70), 18–25.

[3] 'The Staging of the Wakefield Plays', *Research Opportunities in Renaissance Drama*, XI (1968), 115–28.

[4] 'Medieval Stage Decoration: That Apple Tree Again', *Theatre Notebook*, XXIV (1969–70), 122–4.

[5] 'New Light on an Old Proclamation', *Notes and Queries*, CCXV (1970), 212.

[6] 'Audience Involvement In The Tudor Interlude', *Theatre Notebook*, XXIV (1969–70), 101–11.

[7] 'The *Poculi Ludique Societas*: Medieval Drama at the University of Toronto', *Research Opportunities in Renaissance Drama*, XI (1968), 141–61.

[8] 'Laughing with the Audience: *The Two Gentlemen of Verona* and the Popular Tradition of Comedy', *Shakespeare Survey 22* (Cambridge, 1969), 35–42.

William F. Munson[1] has argued against the presence of traditional liturgical typology in the Towneley *Isaac*; Helen Thomas[2] has disputed the proposition that *Jacob and Esau* is 'rigidly Calvinistic'; and John R. Elliott, Jr[3] has described the evolution of Mystery into History. Two textual studies are of particular interest. Anna Jean Mill[4] has disputed Professor MacQueen's proposition that Lindsay's *Satyre of the Thrie Estaitis* was first performed 'some time during the earlier fifteen-thirties', arguing that the maturity of the work, the possible impact of French models, and the dangers of presenting too topical a play all point to the Linlithgow version of 1540 as the earliest text, while Robert Carl Johnson,[5] on a narrower issue, has compared *Johan Johan* with the French farce from which it was translated to arrive at a very convincing reassignment of lines 242–60. One final item remains to be mentioned before turning to Shakespeare's contemporaries – Beatrice Corrigan's illustrated account of the 'Commedia dell'Arte Portraits in the McGill Feather Book',[6] in which a number of the remarkable feather portraits are illustrated and the actors depicted in them identified.

Bibliographical aids to scholarly researches have appeared in unusual profusion this year. Checklists of holdings of Renaissance plays in the Newberry Library,[7] the University of London Library,[8] and the Library of the University of Illinois[9] have been published, and George W. Ray[10] has produced a list of additions to Professor Yamada's Chapman bibliography. Of the year's general studies on aspects of the Renaissance stage, probably that with the largest claims is *Reinterpretations of Elizabethan Drama*,[11] a collection of papers which the editor (Norman Rabkin) would have us believe reflects 'the emergence of a new paradigm for the study of Renaissance drama if not of all theatrical art'. The papers exemplifying the 'new paradigm' ('the play as it impinges on its audience, as it is experienced') are of a much more varied kind than the introduction would lead one to expect. Some are wholly conventional critical studies (cf. Max Bluestone's '*Libido Speculandi*: Doctrine and Dramaturgy in Contemporary Interpretations of Marlowe's *Doctor Faustus*'), some consist of random observations on particular productions (cf. Robert Hapgood's 'Shakespeare and the Included Spectator'), others substitute 'the audience' for the old 'I' or authorial voice of conventional criticism (cf. Stephen Booth's 'On the Value of *Hamlet*'). If these essays do represent a new paradigm (and no one can be unaware of the increasing emphasis on theatrical criticism), they fail to furnish the 'new approach' with either a terminology or a convincing exponent. (John Russell Brown's denial of our ability 'to know for sure what is *in* any *play*' reads like a counsel of despair, not a clarion call to a new approach.)

Still concerned with the period as a whole are three essays on the structure, material and

[1] 'Typology and the Towneley Isaac', *Research Opportunities in Renaissance Drama*, XI (1968), 129–39.

[2] '*Jacob and Esau* – "rigidly Calvinistic"?', *Studies in English Literature 1500–1900*, IX (1969), 199–213.

[3] 'The History Play as Drama', *Research Opportunities in Renaissance Drama*, XI (1968), 21–8.

[4] 'The Original Version of Lindsay's *Satyre of the Thrie Estaitis*', *Studies in Scottish Literature*, VI (1968–), 67–75.

[5] 'A Textual Problem in *Johan Johan*', *Notes and Queries*, CCXV (1970), 210–11.

[6] *Renaissance Drama*, New Series II (1969), 167–88.

[7] Stuart Omans, 'Newberry Library: English Renaissance Drama from the Silver Collection', *Research Opportunities in Renaissance Drama*, XI (1968), 59–63.

[8] 'English Renaissance Plays in the University of London Library' (Author unspecified), *ibid.*, 65–72.

[9] Akihiro Yamada, 'A Checklist of English Printed Drama Before 1641 at the Library of the University of Illinois', *ibid.*, 31–53.

[10] 'George Chapman: A Checklist of Editions, Biography, and Criticism 1946–65 – Addenda', *ibid.*, 55–8.

[11] Columbia University Press, 1969.

impact of Renaissance productions. 'The Elizabethan "Three-Level" Play' by Richard Levin[1] points out that in many Renaissance dramas we have not two but three levels of action, each involving a distinct social group; 'The Pervasiveness of Violence in Elizabethan Plays' by Maurice Charney[2] suggests that the un-Senecan use of onstage violence was designed to produce 'an emotional impact that could not be achieved in any other way'; and 'Three Types of Renaissance Catharsis' by O. B. Hardison[3] distinguishes between three Renaissance critical theories and argues that Shakespeare self-consciously employs them all. Two of the recurrent character types of the Renaissance stage have also been the subject of general surveys. Edgar Rosenberg[4] has discussed the stage history of the Jew in a study interesting in the consistency of characterisation it reveals but unfortunate in its failure to distinguish between the Jew as a national type and the Jew as a conventional stage villain,[5] while Vanna Gentili[6] has considered the roles of fool, madman and melancholic in a wide-ranging review of the function of madness (taken in the widest sense) on the Elizabethan–Jacobean stage.[7]

Shakespeare's fellow dramatists have, as always, furnished material for numerous scholarly disquisitions. A. B. Taylor has argued that Peele's *The Arraignment of Paris* is indebted to Golding's *Metamorphoses*.[8] Writers on Lyly have analysed his 'court comedies' (distinguishing three distinct methods by which Renaissance ideas are given allegorical form),[9] translated and commented upon his commendatory verses to Case's *Sphaera Civitatis* (1588),[10] and ingeniously explained the bawdy implications of his (and Shakespeare's) use of such words as 'rope' and 'hanging'.[11] Arthur Freeman on the printing of *The Spanish Tragedy*[12] and Barry B. Adams[13] on the 'formalistic or aesthetic' interpretation imposed on the audience by the structure of the play have

provided two of the year's more important contributions to the study of the most popular product of the Elizabethan stage, though one must also note that there has been an account of the 'Empedoclean dualism' of its action.[14] Marlovian essayists have been unwontedly disputatious.[15] Timothy G. A. Nelson,[16] in defiance of conventional views (and with very little evidence to support his case), has urged that Tamburlaine's final challenge ('to Death itself')

[1] *Renaissance Drama*, New Series II (1969), 23–37.

[2] *Ibid.*, 59–70.

[3] *Ibid.*, 3–22.

[4] 'The Jew in Western Drama', *Bulletin Of The New York Public Library*, LXXII (1968), 442–91.

[5] Perhaps one should note here Björn Collinder's article on the most famous Jew of Western Drama, 'Shylock und das Zwölftafelgetz', Särtryck ur kungl. Humanisticka Vetenskaps-Samfundet i Uppsala, *Årsbok 1967–1968*, 1–20.

[6] *Le Figure Della Pazzia Nel Teatro Elisabettiano*, Collezione di studi e testi diretta da M. Marti e A. Vallone, No. 11 (Edizioni Milella, Lecce, 1969).

[7] Also concerned with the figure of the fool is William Willeford, whose sweeping survey, *The Fool and His Scepter* (Northwestern University Press, 1969), covers the multiple images of the clown from court jester to silent film.

[8] 'George Peele and Golding's *Metamorphoses*', *Notes and Queries*, CCXIV (1969), 286–7.

[9] Peter Saccio, *The Court Comedies of John Lyly* (Princeton University Press, Princeton, New Jersey, 1969).

[10] R. W. Dent, 'John Lyly in 1588', *English Language Notes*, VII (1969–70), 9–11.

[11] Anne Lancashire, 'Lyly and Shakespeare on the Ropes', *Journal of English and Germanic Philology*, LXVIII (1969), 237–44.

[12] 'The Printing of *The Spanish Tragedy*', *The Library*, XXIV (1969), 187–99.

[13] 'The Audiences of *The Spanish Tragedy*', *Journal of English and Germanic Philology*, LXVIII (1969), 221–36.

[14] Sacvan Bercovitch, 'Love and Strife in Kyd's *Spanish Tragedy*', *Studies in English Literature 1500–1900*, IX (1969), 215–29.

[15] With the exception of H. J. Oliver who has given a mild account of William Oxberry's rare early nineteenth-century edition of the works ('Oxberry's "Marlowe"', *Notes and Queries*, CCXIV (1969), 287–8).

[16] 'Marlowe and His Audience: A Study of *Tamburlaine*', *Southern Review*, III (1968–), 249–63.

is accepted and his final claim (that 'he is being translated to heaven to a throne among the gods') 'upheld'; A. L. French[1] has sought (with disturbing effectiveness) to explode the 'intellectualism' of both Dr Faustus and his creator by close analysis of the text of the play; T. W. Craik[2] has taken issue with Greg and post-Greg contenders that Faustus's damnation is sealed by intercourse with Helen; and Clifford Davidson[3] has defended the thematic relevance of the activities of Faustus at Rome (1616 version). Two comparative studies have attempted to set Marlowe's work in a tradition of thought or stagecraft. K. Smidt's 'Two Aspects of Ambition in Elizabethan Tragedy: *Doctor Faustus* and *Macbeth*'[4] provides us with a brief survey of Elizabethan attitudes to ambition, together with a superficial account of *Faustus* and *Macbeth*, adding little to our understanding of either, while Sidney R. Homan's 'Chapman and Marlowe: The Paradoxical Hero and the Divided Response',[5] linking Tamburlaine, Faustus, Bussy and Byron as 'paradoxical heroes' leaves the reader wondering how many Elizabethan–Jacobean heroes escape the definition. A number of those miscellaneous entries clustering around 1599 in Harbage's *Annals* have enjoyed an unaccustomed share of literary limelight. *Look About You*, classed as a 'comedy' by Harbage and normally regarded, according to Anne Lancashire, as a 'historical romance', has been reclassified as a 'history play'[6] by virtue of its firm basis in Holinshed, and its concern with history 'for purposes of political didacticism and the stimulation of patriotism, in relation to contemporary problems'; attention has been drawn to the popularity of the lost Mandeville play,[7] and the theory has been advanced that *Lust's Dominion* is a collaborative piece first produced in 1600 (revised post-Gunpowder Plot) rather than a Marlovian play new vamped[8]. Two books and two articles have appeared emphasising the achievement of Thomas Dekker.

George R. Price[9] has made a full study of the life, the independent and collaborative works, and the social and religious thought of the dramatist in an attempt 'to discover as fully as possible how Dekker utilized early Elizabethan dramatic traditions', while James H. Conover, in *Thomas Dekker: An Analysis of Dramatic Structure*,[10] has taken the six plays most likely to be of sole authorship and examined their various lines of action in order to 're-evaluate Thomas Dekker as a play-craftsman'. Price's view that Dekker's notorious indifference to structure is more apparent than real is supported by Conover's conclusion that of the six structures considered only two are 'seriously marred'. Joel H. Kaplan[11] has shown the failure of the 'translation of virtue into festival' in *Old Fortunatus* and its success in *The Shoemakers' Holiday*, and David M. Bergeron,[12] in an interesting discussion of Dekker's Lord Mayor's shows, has suggested that the 'quasi-morality play structure of the 1612 show' (Dekker's best) is probably his unique contribution to

[1] 'The Philosophy of *Dr. Faustus*', *Essays in Criticism*, XX (1970), 123–42.

[2] 'Faustus' Damnation Reconsidered', *Renaissance Drama*, New Series II (1969), 189–96.

[3] 'Doctor Faustus at Rome', *Studies in English Literature 1500–1900*, IX (1969), 231–9.

[4] *English Studies*, L (1969), 235–48.

[5] *Journal of English and Germanic Philology*, LXVIII (1969), 391–406.

[6] Anne Lancashire, '*Look About You* as a History Play', *Studies in English Literature 1500–1900*, IX (1969), 321–34.

[7] C. W. R. D. Moseley, 'The Lost Play of Mandeville', *The Library*, XXV (1970), 46–9.

[8] Philip J. Ayres, 'The Revision of *Lust's Dominion*', *Notes and Queries*, CCXV (1970), 212–13.

[9] *Thomas Dekker* (Twayne's English Authors Series, Twayne Publishers, New York, 1969).

[10] *Studies in English Literature*, XXXVIII (Mouton, The Hague, 1969).

[11] 'Virtue's Holiday: Thomas Dekker and Simon Eyre', *Renaissance Drama*, New Series II (1969), 103–22.

[12] 'Thomas Dekker's Lord Mayor's Shows', *English Studies*, LI (1970), 2–15.

the genre. Two articles on the plays of the early 1600s are worthy of note before turning to scholarly lucubrations on the major dramatist of the Jacobean period. Joel Kaplan's discussion of the festival nature of *The Shoemakers' Holiday* has a companion piece in an essay by the same writer on the mood of *The Fawn*,[1] which, he argues, combines the satiric tone of *The Malcontent* with the saturnalian exuberance of *The Dutch Courtesan*. Current interest in dramatic structures is reflected in John Canuteson's[2] analysis of the parallel plotting in *A Woman Killed with Kindness*, an awareness of which, Canuteson believes, confirms 'our suspicions that Frankford is not a tragic figure but a despicable one'.

Critical commentary on the predictable Jonsonian plays continues to proliferate, though, with the exception of a sound piece of scholarship from T. W. Craik[3] (demonstrating the appropriateness of Volpone's reference to 'young Antinous' during the attempted seduction of Celia), minimal illumination is to be derived from the year's vulpine research. Charles A. Hallett,[4] in an attempt to interpret *The Fox* in the light of the Christian application of the beast fable on which the play is based, has raised more questions than he has answered; while Alexander Leggatt[5] has presented us with an 'actor-playwright' Volpone who destroys himself 'for the sake of his art' (exit the bond between the predators and their prey). The year's most valuable contribution to Jonsonian studies, however, is undoubtedly volume IV of The Yale Ben Jonson, *Ben Jonson: The Complete Masques*, edited by Stephen Orgel.[6] Complete with a full introduction and Jonson's own notes and glosses, the volume ('the most carefully edited and annotated text available') should prove invaluable to the student of the Stuart masque. Another 'standard' edition, that of *The Atheist's Tragedy* by Irving Ribner, has been criticised by J. C. Maxwell,[7] who points out that Ribner

has ignored Wilkins's 1792 and 1794 reprints of the play which anticipate a number of later emendations, and in one case offer a better reading than later editions. Webster has, as always, stimulated a large body of learned commentary. Chief among the critical studies is *John Webster*, a collection of papers given at the York conference on Webster and edited by Brian Morris for the Mermaid Critical Commentaries series.[8] Contributions are disparate in kind, ranging in subject from Webster's relationship with his audience and contemporaries, through the staging of the plays, to critical and comparative essays on form and meaning. Though individual articles are undoubtedly of interest (notably '*The Devil's Law-Case* – An End or a Beginning?' by Gunnar Boklund, 'The Power of *The White Devil*' by A. J. Smith, and 'Webster's Realism, or, "A Cunning Piece Wrought Perspective"' by Inga-Stina Ewbank), one cannot but wonder what justification there can be for producing these particular items, representing neither the most valuable essays on Webster nor a single approach to the study of his work, in book form. In the main, this is a collection of literary ephemera, and its contents belong, if anywhere, in the periodicals. Moreover, though one can accept Brian Morris's decision not 'to impose any editorial uniformity on con-

---

[1] 'John Marston's *Fawn*: A Saturnalian Satire', *Studies in English Literature 1500–1900*, IX (1969), 335–50.

[2] 'The Theme of Forgiveness in the Plot and Sub-plot of *A Woman Killed with Kindness*', *Renaissance Drama*, New Series II (1969), 123–41.

[3] 'Volpone's "Young Antinous"', *Notes and Queries*, CCXV (1970), 213–14.

[4] 'The Satanic Nature of Volpone', *Philological Quarterly*, XLIX (1970), 41–55.

[5] 'The Suicide Of Volpone', *University Of Toronto Quarterly*, XXXIX (1969–70), 19–32.

[6] Yale University Press, 1969.

[7] '*The Atheist's Tragedy*: 1792 and 1794', *Notes and Queries*, CCXV (1970), 214–15.

[8] Ernest Benn, 1970.

tributors', one must insist that such aids to reading as the justification of type (p. 178), the *regular* use of a blank line between quotations (p. 217) and consistency in the use of the full stop (p. 219) all fall within the editorial sphere. *John Webster*, a recent volume in the 'Penguin Critical Anthologies', edited by G. K. and S. Hunter, gives a useful historical survey of Webster criticism[1] while factual and valuable contributions to the study of Webster's work have appeared in the periodicals. R. K. R. Thornton[2] has argued, very convincingly, that the 'thing armed with a rake' that haunts the Cardinal's fishpond derives from allegorical representations of the simoniacal churchman and thus presents us with an emblem of his adherence to worldly values; Clive Hart[3] has produced a supplementary list of press variants in the first quarto of *The Duchess of Malfi* and collated a number of quartos of *The White Devil*; D. C. Gunby[4] has suggested that Ferdinand's insistence in the opening moments of *The Duchess of Malfi* that his court should laugh only when he laughs derives from a speech by Silius in the first scene of *Sejanus*; and Charles R. Forker,[5] in a discussion of Webster's contribution to Overbury's *Characters*, has argued that the dramatist was associated with the work from the outset and was 'personally responsible for collecting the original group of characters...and seeing them through the press'. Two writers have been concerned with Massinger's relationship to contemporary literary modes. Peter Mullany,[6] in a consideration of *The Maid of Honour*, has maintained that far from showing a concern for serious moral issues, Massinger merely exploits moral dilemmas 'for the same theatrical ends that characterize Fletcherian tragicomedy', while C. A. Gibson[7] has examined the growth of the 'composite mistress cliché' and argued that Massinger gives 'fresh life to [this] commonplace idea by adapting it to a variety of dramatic contexts'. The serious moral concern

that Peter Mullany denies to *The Maid of Honour* C. A. Gibson would presumably attribute to act II, scene vi at least of *The Renegado*, which he sees[8] as conveying covert criticism of court immorality. Some interesting articles have appeared on Ford. S. Gorley Putt[9] has taken issue with Stavig on the complexity of Ford's characters, emphasising the dramatist's modernity in 'accepting the existence of a golden human value in a protagonist quite severely judged'; Juliet McMaster[10] has pointed to a three-level plot structure running throughout Ford's work; Jonas A. Barish,[11] in possibly the year's most persuasive contribution to Ford scholarship, has suggested that critics have distorted *Perkin Warbeck* by viewing it as Tudor myth rather than drama, and argued that the play has Shakespearian analogies in its presentation of a conflict between an efficient man and one who captures our imaginative sympathy; Peter Ure[12] has advanced fresh evidence to support a date early in the 1630s for the same

[1] Penguin Books, Harmondsworth, 1970.
[2] 'The Cardinal's Rake in *The Duchess of Malfi*', *Notes and Queries*, CCXIV (1969), 295–6.
[3] 'Press Variants in *The Duchess of Malfi* and *The White Devil*', *ibid.*, 292–3.
[4] 'Webster: Another Borrowing from Jonson's *Sejanus*', *ibid.*, CCXV (1970), 214.
[5] '"Wit's descant on any plain song": The Prose Characters of John Webster', *Modern Language Quarterly*, XXX (1969), 33–52.
[6] 'Religion in Massinger's *The Maid of Honour*', *Renaissance Drama*, New Series II (1969), 143–56.
[7] 'Massinger's "Composite Mistresses"', *Journal Of The Australian Universities Language And Literature Association*, XXIX (1968), 44–51.
[8] '"Behind the Arras" in Massinger's *The Renegado*', *Notes and Queries*, CCXIV (1969), 296–7.
[9] 'The Modernity of John Ford', *English*, XVIII (1969), 47–52.
[10] 'Love, Lust, and Sham: Structural Pattern in the Plays of John Ford', *Renaissance Drama*, New Series II (1969), 157–66.
[11] '*Perkin Warbeck* as Anti-History', *Essays In Criticism*, XX (1970), 151–71.
[12] 'A Pointer to the Date of Ford's *Perkin Warbeck*', *Notes and Queries*, CCXV (1970), 215–17.

play; and R. Jordan[1] has argued that Plutarch's account of the Spartans' reception of the news of their defeat at Leuctra lies behind Calantha's dance in *The Broken Heart*. Finally, works by two dramatists who receive scant scholarly notice have been the subject of brief articles. J. C. Maxwell[2] has drawn attention to an echo of *The White Devil* in Ludowick Carlell's *Osmond the Great Turk*, and Edwin F. Ochester[3] has suggested that Shirley drew on Heywood's *The Iron Age* in addition to Ovid's *Metamorphoses* XIII for *The Contention of Ajax and Ulysses*.

Outstanding among contributions to the study of Shakespeare's stage (not least in the controversy it is likely to arouse) is Frances A. Yates's latest broadside in the debate over the Fludd engravings, *Theatre of the World*.[4] Step by step the author demonstrates that Vitruvius's work was known in England, that his thought was promulgated to the artisan class by Dee, that the artisan class (in the person of James Burbage) built the Theatre, that Robert Fludd was also in the Dee–Vitruvius tradition, and that between the Vitruvian ground plan and Fludd's memory system we may reconstruct the ground plan and *frons scenae* of the Globe – 'a religious theatre' close in 'spirit' to the theatres of the ancient world. Unfortunately, though the sections on the influence of Vitruvius are extremely interesting, many important objections to the Fludd drawings raised by recent contributors to the controversy remain unanswered (e.g. what degree of faith can be placed on the accuracy of the German engravers used to ornamenting designs? and how much weight can be placed on the five entrances basic to the argument when only one of the memory theatres shows five doors?). Minor contributions to our knowledge of Shakespeare's theatre and the conditions under which players performed have been unusually numerous. The activities of members of a company of English instrumentalists in Den-

mark in the 1580s have been documented;[5] an allusion to the sign of the Globe has been detected in the Induction to *Antonio and Mellida*;[6] an emendation has been proposed for *Bussy D'Ambois* V, iii, 55 which relieves us of the necessity of regarding the 'arras' and 'canapie' of the Elizabethan stage as identical;[7] Salisbury's relations with the Blackfriars' company have been examined;[8] and Giulio de Medici's reactions to a performance on 23 July 1621 have been recorded.[9] The transition from the Renaissance theatre to the Protean career of the corpus in performance is effected by an essay on staging by Adolph L. Soens,[10] furnishing us with clues to the way in which scenes in *Romeo and Juliet* may originally have been produced. Soens demonstrates that contrasting styles of fencing, Spanish and Italian, are employed by Tybalt and Mercutio respectively and describes the way in which their fight and Mercutio's death should be conducted. Valuable insights into late seventeenth-century adaptations, productions and editions have been afforded by essays from W. W. Bernhardt on the rationale behind Dryden's adaptation of

[1] 'Calantha's Dance in *The Broken Heart*', *ibid.*, CCXIV (1969), 294–5.
[2] 'Ludowick Carlell: An Echo of Webster', *ibid.*, 288.
[3] 'A Source for Shirley's *The Contention of Ajax and Ulysses*', *ibid.*, CCXV (1970), 217.
[4] Routledge and Kegan Paul, 1969.
[5] Gunnar Sjögren, 'Thomas Bull and other "English Instrumentalists" in Denmark in the 1580s', *Shakespeare Survey 22* (Cambridge, 1969), 119–24.
[6] Ejner J. Jensen, 'A New Allusion To The Sign Of The Globe Theater', *Shakespeare Quarterly*, XXI (1970), 95–7.
[7] Evert Sprinchorn, '"Wrapt In A Canapie"', *Theatre Notebook*, XXIV (1969–70), 36–7.
[8] Robert M. Wren, 'Salisbury And The Blackfriars Theatre', *ibid.*, XXIII (1968–9), 103–9.
[9] Murray F. Markland, 'Two Italian Glimpses of the English Theatre', *Theatre Research*, X (1969–70), 32–6.
[10] 'Tybalt's Spanish Fencing in *Romeo and Juliet*', *Shakespeare Quarterly*, XX (1969), 121–7.

Troilus and Cressida,[1] Christopher Spencer on the implications of Davenant's borrowings from *Macbeth* in the first scene of *The Rivals*,[2] John Edmunds on Shadwell's creation of a 'satirical tragedy' from *Timon of Athens* and *Le Misanthrope*,[3] Robert J. Fehrenbach on the performance dates of *The Tempest* in the 1677–8 theatre season,[4] and John W. Velz on the Restoration quartos of *Julius Caesar*.[5] Eighteenth-century interpretations, though more meagerly documented, are fittingly represented by Robert Wilks's Hamlet (discussed by E. Pearlman),[6] while Akihiro Yamada's account of a fragmentary version of *1 Henry IV*[7] provides an interesting footnote to the adaptations of the period. Conveniently bridging an unusually wide gap between the theatrical practices of the early eighteenth and late nineteenth centuries is an amusing record[8] of Australian theatricals *c.* 1790 to post 1870. Two interesting points emerge from this poignant record – the persistency with which actors continued to produce a remarkably wide range of Shakespearian plays under the most trying conditions, and the way in which the antipodian theatre reversed the practice of the Globe by featuring women in men's roles. Early twentieth-century productions have been the subject of two *Theatre Research* articles. Lise-Lone Marker[9] has provided us with a detailed account of David Belasco's *The Merchant of Venice* (1922), in which pictorial fidelity was carried to its ultimate extreme (impressing Stanislavsky), and Hugh Hunt[10] has discussed Granville-Barker's work at the Savoy Theatre 1912–14, stressing his achievement of a 'stylized form of naturalism' forming, at its best, 'a scholarly contribution to the understanding of Shakespeare's play'. Modern productions have received their due share of critical notice. Gareth Lloyd Evans[11] has reviewed the 1968 Stratford season with his usual polish (some interesting comments here upon the possible effects of the

'quantitative assurance and qualitative dubiety' of Stratford audiences on productions); Robert W. Speaight[12] has passed charitable judgement upon Stratford, Chichester and The National Theatre 1969; Arnold Edinborough,[13] emphasising the necessity for firm direction, has contrasted a successful *Measure for Measure* at Canada's Stratford with an 'eccentric and degrading' *Hamlet*; Mildred C. Kuner[14] has criticised a performance of the same play at the New York Shakespeare Festival on the same grounds; Peter D. Smith[15] has celebrated *Hamlet* and *Henry V* at Stratford, Connecticut;

[1] 'Shakespeare's *Troilus and Cressida* and Dryden's *Truth Found Too Late*', *ibid.*, 129–41.

[2] '*Macbeth* and Davenant's *The Rivals*', *ibid.*, 225–9.

[3] '*Timon of Athens* blended with *Le Misanthrope*: Shadwell's Recipe for Satirical Tragedy', *The Modern Language Review*, LXIV (1969), 500–7.

[4] 'Performance Dates of *The Tempest* in the 1677–78 Theatrical Season', *Notes and Queries*, CCXV (1970), 217–18.

[5] '"Pirate Hills" and the Quartos of *Julius Caesar*', *The Papers of the Bibliographical Society of America*, LXIII (1969), 177–93.

[6] 'The Hamlet Of Robert Wilks', *Theatre Notebook*, XXIV (1969–70), 125–33.

[7] 'An Eighteenth-Century Stage Adaptation Of The Falstaff Part In *The First Part Of Henry IV*', *Shakespeare Quarterly*, XXI (1970), 103–4.

[8] Eric Irvin, 'Shakespeare in the Early Sydney Theatre', *Shakespeare Survey 22* (Cambridge, 1969), 125–33.

[9] 'Shakespeare and Naturalism: David Belasco produces *The Merchant of Venice*', *Theatre Research*, X (1969–70), 17–32.

[10] 'Granville-Barker's Shakespearean Productions', *ibid.*, 44–9.

[11] 'The Reason Why: The Royal Shakespeare Season 1968 Reviewed', *Shakespeare Survey 22* (Cambridge, 1969), 135–44.

[12] 'Shakespeare in Britain', *Shakespeare Quarterly*, XX (1969), 435–41.

[13] 'The Director's Role at Canada's Stratford', *ibid.*, 443–6.

[14] 'The New York Shakespeare Festival, 1969', *ibid.*, 449–54.

[15] 'The 1969 Season at Stratford, Connecticut', *ibid.*, 447–50.

J. H. Crouch[1] has commented on the difficulties raised by the dust at Colorado; Robert Ornstein[2] has recorded a disappointing Great Lakes Festival; Homer D. Swander[3] has lamented the urge to adapt apparently still in force in San Diego; and Betty Bandel[4] has described commendable efforts to remain faithful to Shakespeare's text at the University of Vermont.

Charles H. Shattuck's supplement to *The Shakespeare Prompt Books*[5] (items of particular note include J. P. Kemble's *The Tempest* and Charles Kean's *A Midsummer-Night's Dream*) provides a useful link between production history and the evolution of Shakespearian scholarship – studies of which multiply annually. This year's earliest critical commentary on a Shakespearian play comes in the form of an allusion to *Antony and Cleopatra* in a blackletter pamphlet of 1614, which, though testifying to the impact of the play, reflects adversely on the understanding of the commentator in its radical confusion of both persons and action.[6] Seventeenth-century enthusiasm of a more judicious kind is recorded by John Freehafer[7] in a discussion of the first published expression of Shakespeare idolatry (1640), while eighteenth-century scholarship is represented by the re-publication of three items of outstanding interest, Charles Gildon's *The Life of Mr. Thomas Betterton* (1710),[8] Edmond Malone's *An Inquiry into the Authenticity of Certain Miscellaneous Papers and Legal Instruments*,[9] Malone's devastating exposure of Ireland's Shakespeare forgeries, and the replying *An Investigation of Mr. Malone's Claim to the Character of Scholar, or Critic*,[10] by Samuel Ireland, valuable in 'its exemplification of the very attitudes and methodologies of antiquarian scholarship which Malone himself was helping to obviate' (editor). Essays on one neglected Shakespearian and one unneglectable one effect the transition from the eighteenth century to the twentieth. 'Charles Lamb, Shakespeare, and

Early Nineteenth-Century Theater'[11] argues the case for regarding Lamb as a Shakespearian critic of 'some stature', while 'George Bernard Shaw on Shakespearian Music and the Actor'[12] considers, in less polemic vein, Shaw's insistence that 'only through mastery of...the unmatched verbal music...can Shakespeare be truly understood'. Three collections of critical essays bring us as near to the present time as it is proper for this review to approach. Anne Ridler's World's Classics selection of Shakespearian criticism post 1935 has been re-issued as an Oxford Paperback;[13] Helen Gardner has edited a collection of studies by F. P. Wilson[14] (neither editor nor author requires recommendation here); and Richard Hosley, Arthur C. Kirsch and John W. Velz[15] have been concerned in a

---

[1] 'The Colorado Shakespeare Festival – 1969', *ibid.*, 455–8.

[2] 'The Great Lakes Shakespeare Festival', *ibid.*, 459–61.

[3] 'Shakespeare at the "Old Globe" San Diego', *ibid.*, 463–7.

[4] 'The Champlain Shakespeare Festival', *ibid.*, 469–72.

[5] 'The Shakespeare Promptbooks: First Supplement', *Theatre Notebook*, XXIV (1969–70), 5–17.

[6] Reginald Saner, 'How Pompey's Honor Struck a Contemporary', *Shakespeare Quarterly*, XX (1969), 117–20.

[7] 'Leonard Digges, Ben Jonson, and the Beginning of Shakespeare Idolatry', *ibid.*, XXI (1970), 63–75.

[8] Ed. Arthur Freeman, Eighteenth Century Shakespeare No. 4 (Frank Cass & Co., 1970).

[9] Ed. Arthur Freeman, Eighteenth Century Shakespeare No. 22 (Frank Cass & Co., 1970).

[10] Ed. Arthur Freeman, Eighteenth Century Shakespeare No. 24 (Frank Cass & Co., 1970).

[11] By John I. Ades, *Publications of the Modern Language Association of America*, LXXXV (1970), 514–26.

[12] By Charles Haywood, *Shakespeare Quarterly*, XX (1969), 417–26.

[13] *Shakespeare Criticism 1935–1960* (Oxford University Press, 1970).

[14] *Shakespearian And Other Studies* (Clarendon Press, Oxford, 1969).

[15] *Studies In Shakespeare, Bibliography, and Theater* (The Shakespeare Association Of America, New York, 1969).

similar act of homage to the scholarship of James G. McManaway (papers date from 1934 to 1967 and include Professor McManaway's erudite contributions to *Shakespeare Survey*'s 'Textual Studies' review section). A bibliographical work began this paragraph and two others, purporting to provide a rational guide to Shakespeare scholarship, conclude it. Unfortunately there is little about the first, Waveney R. N. Payne's *A Shakespeare Bibliography*,[1] that can be commended. Elementary and technical works are jumbled together without distinction, the allocation of material to sections is highly irrational (cf. the appearance of Chambers's *William Shakespeare* in the 'Literary Criticism: General Works' section), inaccuracies abound (cf. items 36, 400, 467, etc.), paperback editions escape notice (item 17), and the inclusion of some items is indefensible (one wonders, for example, what place Louis B. Wright's *The Folger Library* – 'reports from the Director...brief news sheets...visitors to the library, and other events' – has in a Shakespeare bibliography). All in all, a tribute to the ecclecticism of the Shakespeare Library of Birmingham rather than the scholarship of Miss Payne. *Shakespeare: A Reading Guide* by Stanley Wells, however, admirably fulfils its purpose.[2]

The translation of the corpus continues to be both discussed and promoted. V. E. Stack[3] has compared three French prose translations of *Antony and Cleopatra* made between 1859 and 1942, and commented upon the kind of problems encountered; Álvaro Custodio[4] has translated *Hamlet* into Spanish, equipping the play with full critical commentary in the same language; and Rouben Zarian[5] has traced Armenian interest in Shakespeare from the seventeenth century to its culmination in the translations of Houhannes Massehian, and the performances of Petros Adamian.[6]

Three very different items must serve to epitomise the incalculable and unclassifiable influence of Shakespeare's work on subsequent creative artists. The first, by Sacvan Bercovitch,[7] discerns a straightforward echo of *The Merchant of Venice* in Hawthorne's *The Marble Faun*; the second, by A. M. Gibbs,[8] finds, more subtly, that *The Rape of Lucrece* was 'stirring in Yeats' memory' during the composition of 'The Second Coming', and the third, by Charles Haywood,[9] describes the process whereby 'the most popular author on the American stage' became the object of 'unabashed hilarity' in the hands of the Negro minstrelmen, a hilarity which found expression not only in direct parody but in such pertinent comments on scholarly methodology as:

Let us examine de wherfore and de whatall ob poetry ob which dere are t'ree kinds – lyric, dramatic, and epidemic. De last form we shall examine fust. Epidemic poetry is divided into t'ree parts – de epoch, de epicure and de epitaph. De last form we shall examine fust, because it is so monumental. We must always look up to the epitaph. It towers above us.

It does indeed.

[1] The Library Association, 1969.

[2] English Association (1967).

[3] 'Shakespeare in Translation', *English*, XVIII (1969), 53–6.

[4] Edición Bilingüe (Ediciones Teatro Clásico De México, Mexico, 1968). The same writer has also produced a comparative study of the work of Lope de Vega, Calderón and Shakespeare (*Lope-Calderón y Shakespeare*, Ediciones Teatro Clasico De México, Mexico, 1969).

[5] *Shakespeare and the Armenians*, trans. Haig Voskerchian (Armenian Society for Friendship and Cultural Relations with Foreign Countries, Yerevan, 1969).

[6] Armenian interest in the dramatist is also demonstrated by *Shakespearakan, An Armenian Yearbook of Shakespeare II* (Yerevan, 1967).

[7] 'Miriam as Shylock: An Echo from Shakespeare in Hawthorne's *Marble Faun*', *Forum For Modern Language Studies*, v (1969), 385–7.

[8] 'The "Rough Beasts" of Yeats and Shakespeare', *Notes and Queries*, CCXV (1970), 48–9.

[9] 'Negro Minstrelsy And Shakespearean Burlesque', *Folklore and Society, Essays In Honor Of B. A. Botkin* (Folklore Associates, Hatboro, Pennsylvania, 1966).

© LEAH SCRAGG 1971

3. TEXTUAL STUDIES

reviewed by RICHARD PROUDFOOT

The publication of the Norton facsimile of the First Folio, edited by Charlton Hinman,[1] is the culminating achievement of many years of devoted labour by the editor and by earlier investigators of the printing of the Folio. In a real sense this is the first edition of *the* First Folio, of a book representing as nearly as is possible the ideal copy of the Folio as Isaac Jaggard and Edward Blount intended to publish it. Where extant copies of the Folio may vary in formes corrected at press, this facsimile presents every variant forme in its latest or most fully corrected state[2] and in addition it reproduces each page from the most legible exemplar to be found among thirty of the best copies of the Folio in the Folger Shakespeare Library. Editorial matter is limited to the marginal printing of through line numbers (as advocated by McKerrow) which will provide a new standard system of numbering for the Folio plays and to the supplying of cross-references to the conventional act, scene and line numbering at the foot of each page. The facsimile is followed by an appendix of fourteen plates illustrating the cancelland and cancel settings of the last page of *Romeo and Juliet* and the first of *Troilus and Cressida*, two of the extant proof-sheets, together with the corrected state of the pages involved and three selected pages in uncorrected and corrected states.

Professor Hinman's introduction gives a brief account of the value and authority of the Folio as a source of the text of Shakespeare's plays, followed by a description of the printing and proof-reading of the Folio itself and of the aims and methods of the facsimile. His dual emphasis on the unsurpassed importance of the Folio as the basis for Shakespeare's text and on the extent to which its authority is vitiated by the frailties of compositors and proof-readers is none the less important for being familiar. A useful feature is the listing of all the press-corrections which affect substantive readings, together with a note of the compositor in each case. Seen in one place, this evidence goes far to justify pessimism about the proofing, especially about the unfortunate effect of compositor *E* on Folio *Hamlet*, *Othello* and *King Lear*. Even in so excellent a facsimile there are few letters and points which are illegible or unclear, presumably because they are so in the original: a list of these readings would not be very long and would add the finishing touch to what must remain the definitive Folio facsimile.

The high quality of reproduction sets the Norton facsimile in a class apart, but even the cruder results afforded by Xerox processes can provide useful texts. The Scolar Press have added to their Shakespeare volumes the three early texts of *Hamlet*, the Quartos of 1603 and 1604/5 and the Folio (the last arranged on the page in single columns approximating to the layout of the Quartos).[3] All three reproduce copies in the British Museum,[4] missing leaves from the Quartos being supplied from the Huntington copy of Q1 and the Trinity College, Cambridge, copy of Q2. Q1 fares best, both in reproduction and editing. Three pages of Q2, wholly legible in the original, are not so in the facsimile, and the list of readings designed to make good this weakness is unreliable in detail, omitting the comma at the end of l. 36 on M2, which is clear in the original. The Folio text gives the most heavily corrected page in *Hamlet*, 2p5 v, in its uncorrected state without

[1] W. W. Norton: Paul Hamlyn, 1968.
[2] Except p. 656.
[3] Menston, 1969.
[4] BM shelf-marks: C.34.k.1; C.34.k.2; C.39. i.12.

mentioning the fact or listing the sixteen readings involved. There are good arguments for including uncorrected formes in a facsimile,[1] but in any case readers should be informed of the state of the text in the copy chosen for reproduction.

The problems of editing facsimiles are further exemplified by the costly *Eighteenth Century Shakespeare* series published by Frank Cass under the general editorship of Arthur Freeman. As reading texts of some important early writings on Shakespeare, especially on the editing of his plays, these volumes will fill a need, but they are not entirely faithful to their originals in non-textual matters. Signatures are missing from several pages of the two specimen volumes received for review.[2] More serious doubts affect the choice of the editions to be reproduced. Thomas Edwards's *Canons of Criticism* is reproduced from the seventh edition of 1765, itself a reprint of the sixth edition of 1758, which was the last to incorporate revisions by Edwards, who died in 1757. Not only does the 1765 edition introduce misprints, but it alters the page numbers of the main text while retaining those of the sixth edition in its reprint of the index. As the book consists chiefly of comments on particular passages and as only the index enables the reader to trace in it all the scattered references to a given play, the choice of 1765 rather than 1758 as the text to reproduce is hard to account for except on grounds of expediency: it is the commoner book and a copy was obtainable to be dismantled for photography.

F. P. Wilson's magisterial survey of the growth of the bibliographical approach to the text of Shakespeare was first published in *The Bibliographical Society, 1892–1942: Studies in Retrospect*.[3] 'Shakespeare and the New Bibliography' was by far the longest and most exhaustive paper in that collection and is now appropriately reprinted as a book in its own right.[4] The text has been revised by Helen Gardner to incorporate extensive annotations made by Wilson about 1948: the editor has wisely refrained from attempting to bring the essay up to date but has added footnote references to more recent work. Inevitably these references sometimes call Wilson's conclusions in question, particularly in the section on the printing of the Folio, where Willoughby's work, on which he necessarily relied, has been superseded by Hinman's. Elsewhere, though some questions have been answered (we no longer invoke shorthand to account for the Quarto text of *Lear*) as many remain open (the debate about the 'copy' for Folio *Richard III* and *Othello* shows no signs of drying up). In the section on Textual Criticism a reference might happily have been added to Dover Wilson's eventual adoption, in the 1954 revision of his New Shakespeare *Hamlet*, of Q2's 'browes' at III, iii, 5, a reading championed by F. P. Wilson.[5] The breadth of treatment and balance of judgement of this essay make it doubly regrettable that its author found no occasion to revise it between 1948 and 1963, a period of great activity in the study of Shakespeare's text. Readers wishing to supplement Wilson's survey may, however, turn to another reprint. J. G. McManaway's *Studies in Shakespeare, Bibliography and Theater*[6] ends with a series of substantial excerpts from his annual *Shakespeare Survey* reviews of Textual Studies for the years 1948 to 1965,

---

[1] *The Library*, 5th series, VII (1952), 272.

[2] Joseph Ritson, *Cursory Criticisms on the Edition of Shakespeare Published by Edmond Malone, 1792* (1969), G2, K2 unsigned; Edmond Malone, *A Letter to the Rev. Richard Farmer, D.D., 1792* (1969), B1, B2 unsigned; Thomas Edwards, *The Canons of Criticism, 1765* (1970), O2, O4, T1, X2, Z3 unsigned.

[3] Edited by F. C. Francis (The Bibliograpnical Society, London, 1945).

[4] Edited by Helen Gardner (The Clarendon Press, Oxford, 1970).

[5] P. 103, n. 1.

[6] The Shakespeare Association of America, New York, 1969.

years which saw the publication, for instance, of the later volumes of the New Cambridge Shakespeare, Alice Walker's *Textual Problems of the First Folio*, Greg's *The Shakespeare First Folio*, Bowers's *On Editing Shakespeare and the Elizabethan Dramatists* and Hinman's *The Printing and Proof-Reading of the First Folio of Shakespeare*. As resident Shakespearian at the Folger Shakespeare Library, McManaway had a particular interest in Hinman's work, which was only made possible by Folger's collection of seventy-nine Folios: this reprint fittingly closes with his 1968 review of the Norton facsimile.

A further six volumes of the Oxford Shakespeare Concordances[1] cover the last six of the comedies in Folio order, using the Folio text except for *The Merchant of Venice*, which is concorded from the Heyes Quarto of 1600. The main obstacle to easy use of the concordances is now removed with the publication of the Norton facsimile, to whose through line numbers they are geared, even when a Quarto text is used. One feature not noted in last year's review is the inclusion in the introductions of details of the distribution of work between compositors. If any students of Shakespeare remain sceptical about the findings of compositor analyses, they will find the spelling evidence laid out graphically, for instance, in the concordance to *The Winter's Tale*, where the work of *A* and *B* is clearly distinguished by such pairs of spellings as *here/heere* and *young/yong*. But of course the real significance of the record of spellings in the concordances is that *all* the spellings in a given text are now readily accessible for analysis.

Editions of Shakespeare published this year include a paperback reprint of J. M. Nosworthy's New Arden *Cymbeline*, reset to incorporate revisions made in 1960.[2] *All's Well that Ends Well*[3] and *Timon of Athens*[4] join the New Penguins, the equivalent American Shakespeare is now published in England as

The Complete Pelican Shakespeare,[5] and an old-spelling *Twelfth Night* is among the first titles in the Fountainwell Drama Texts.[6] All are essentially popular editions, but they offer their readers Shakespeare in various guises. S. Musgrove's *Twelfth Night* combines the text and apparatus of a scholarly critical edition with an introduction and commentary mainly designed for non-specialist readers. Though a carefully edited old-spelling text of Shakespeare is a long-felt want, this edition seems to fall between two stools. Can the same reader need both an introductory critical introduction and a list of accidentals altered? Or can he need to be told that 'maugre' means *despite*, and not that 'I' means *ay*, 'and' *if* or 'whether' *whither*? Much fuller annotation of the difficulties arising from old spelling, and old punctuation, would be needed to make this text truly useful to, for example, undergraduate readers. The most interesting new suggestion comes in the textual introduction. Rejecting the view that the play shows signs of revision, the editor draws attention to details in II, iii, especially Maria's descriptive comments on Malvolio and the 'embryo of a delicious comic idea', that Sir Andrew should challenge Malvolio, at ll.113–17, which may indicate 'that this scene, or part of it, was written very early in the play's composition, before Shakespeare had settled all the details of the plot'.

Of course, the suggestion that Shakespeare

[1] *Oxford Shakespeare Concordances*, edited by Dr T. H. Howard-Hill: *The Merchant of Venice*; *As You Like It*; *The Taming of the Shrew*; *All's Well That Ends Well*; *Twelfth Night*; *The Winter's Tale* (Oxford University Press, 1969).

[2] Methuen, 1969.

[3] Edited by Barbara Everett (Penguin Books, Harmondsworth, 1970).

[4] Edited by G. R. Hibbard (Penguin Books, Harmondsworth, 1970).

[5] General editor, Alfred Harbage (Allen Lane, The Penguin Press, 1969).

[6] Edited by S. Musgrove (Oliver and Boyd, Edinburgh, 1969).

may not always have written the scenes of a play in the order in which they appear in the finished work is not in itself new. It has been particularly valuable in discussions of such anomalies as the various speech prefixes used for Dogberry and Verges in the Quarto of *Much Ado* or the two incompatible valuations of a talent in *Timon*. G. R. Hibbard accepts a view of *Timon* which admits of some degree of irregularity in its composition, seeing it as unfinished, at least in the manuscript which served as copy for the Folio, which he takes to have been 'a rough draft which had never been thoroughly revised and prepared for use in the theatre'. The pervasive minor inconsistencies in the Folio text, particularly in the spelling of proper names, bear out the impression given by the play of 'something that was tinkered about with, probably over a period of time, because it was recalcitrant and refused to come out'. Although he finds the Folio text remarkably good in the circumstances, he proposes seven new readings, of which at least three seem likely to win widespread acceptance: ''Tis honour with worst lands to be at odds' (III, v, 117) for Folio 'most lands'; the transposition of 'not' from l. 74 to l. 75 in IV, iii, to read 'If thou wilt promise...If thou dost not perform', to the benefit of sense and metre alike; and 'those milk-paps/That, through the window, bared, bore at men's eyes' (IV, iii, 116–17), where 'bared' is an emendation of 'barne' far more powerfully in the spirit of Timon's disgust than Johnson's widely-accepted conjecture, 'window-bars'. The critical introduction usefully defines the peculiar quality of the play without removing it from the tragic genre, though stressing its lack of 'the strenuousness that is so characteristic of Shakespearian tragedy in general', and its affinity with fable and parable.

Barbara Everett sees the main problem of *All's Well* as one of tone and supplies in her introduction and commentary a sensitive and penetrating analysis of the play's stylistic range, which controls its exploration of the difficulties of conducting a natural life in a courtly world. She identifies one main obstacle in the path of many readers of this 'serious comedy' by pointing out that 'though "romantic", the play is strikingly unfantastic' and suggests that its structure can be the better understood by analogy not only with its conventional partner, *Measure for Measure*, but also with *The Winter's Tale*, whose synthesis *All's Well* interestingly anticipates. Her list of further reading might have found room for Brian Vickers's analysis of the rhetoric of the play's important prose scenes in his *The Artistry of Shakespeare's Prose*. Though the text is basically conservative, it retains a considerable number of traditional readings, making a special plea for the Folio's 'gentle *Astringer*' in v, i. Attractive new readings are adopted at I, i, 51, 'have't' for 'haue—', and at IV, ii, 38, 'I see that men make vows in such a flame' for 'I see that men make rope's in such a scarre', which has the merit of making very good sense, though it is not self-evidently the only solution of the crux and may be picking the wrong words to alter – Daniel's 'may rope's in such a snare' seems at least as possible and requires a less elaborate series of compositorial misreadings.

The Complete Pelican Shakespeare, prepared by a galaxy of American Shakespearians under the general editorship of Professor Alfred Harbage, gives a more permanent form to a series already highly reputed in North America, by bringing together in one volume thirty-eight editions of separate works, first published between 1956 and 1967. Comprehensive preliminaries are added in the form of general introductory essays on such topics as 'The Intellectual and Political Background', 'Shakespeare's Theatre' and 'The Original Texts', together with a reduced facsimile of the opening pages of the First Folio. The introductions provide an orthodox and conservative view of topics necessary to be understood by any serious reader of Shakespeare. Where many contributors are involved inconsistencies and duplications are bound to occur, but they are few, as are the minor omissions and errors. The discussion of acting styles should have made some reference to the prevalent habit of doubling in small parts and the figures in the table on p. 31 need verifying. C. Walter Hodges has contributed six clear and pleasing illustrations, ranging in subject from Church Street, Stratford, in Shakespeare's schooldays to the interior of an Elizabethan printing house, a scene richly emblematic of one direction of Shakespeare studies in our century.

The texts are presented chronologically within five groups, comedies, histories, tragedies, romances and poems: *Troilus and Cressida* appears among the tragedies, *Pericles* and *Cymbeline* among the romances. The apocryphal poems are included, but neither the Shakespearian parts of *Sir Thomas More* nor *The Two Noble Kinsmen*, although the introductory discussion of the canon accepts his authorship, even inclining to the view that his hand is also detectable in *King Edward III* and in the additions to *The Spanish Tragedy* printed in 1602. Undoubtedly most readers will find this arrangement of the plays convenient and coherent: it avoids the vexed questions of the overall chronology while presenting each play in a clear context of the development of Shakespeare's art. Equally agreeable is the book's typography, which achieves the difficult feat of fitting a great deal of text into the page without any appearance of crowding or any loss of clarity. The novel system of line numbering will suit new readers better than old: only those lines are numbered which contain points requiring annotation, the annotations being located at the foot of the text page. As a result,

gaps in numbering of a dozen or fifteen lines are not uncommon, while elsewhere the margin bristles with numbers. It is less clear that the uniformity of tone and length found in the introductions to the plays suits a collected edition as well as separate volumes. Many general points are too often repeated and the scrupulous avoidance of scholarly documentation, designed to avoid intimidating the unacademic reader, sometimes makes it hard to establish the basic facts about a given play without reading an extended critical essay on it. English readers may jib at an occasional reminder that this edition of our national poet was prepared by Americans for Americans, such as the references, by the editor of *Romeo and Juliet*, to 'the Library of Oxford University' and to 'Dorsetshire'. More serious exception may be taken to the same editor's account of his play as 'difficult to interpret... in Aristotelian terms, since the parents are really the ones who have the "tragic flaw" and suffer the results of their folly', or to the description of Polydore Vergil as a 'Romanist' (presumably a misprint for 'Humanist') in the introduction to *King John*. In fairness, it must be added that the best of the introductions, Harbage's own to *King Lear*, for example, or Richard Wilbur's to the *Poems*, are masterly in their selection and arrangement of material and that in general they maintain a critical orthodoxy which avoids staleness as successfully as eccentricity.

The texts are conservative, relying on their basic texts to an extent which implies a greater faith in their detail than Hinman's view of the Folio, mentioned above, would seem to justify. Future readers of Shakespeare may find such caution as characteristic of our age as over-confident emendation was of the eighteenth century, but of the two extremes it is the less insidious, though it may give rise to some strange assumptions about Elizabethan idiom and prosody.

Writing in 1966 of 'Today's Shakespeare Texts and Tomorrow's', Professor Bowers instanced several readings which, in his view, should no longer appear in a properly edited Shakespeare:

Hamlet's flesh, for instance, will become *too, too sullied*, not *solid*. Cordelia's love will become *more ponderous* and not *more richer*, and so on. As an easier problem, the last vestiges of indefensible bad-quarto readings in plays like *Richard III* and *Romeo and Juliet* will be weeded out. In the future we shall no longer read *spy* for *see* in *Richard* or *name* for *word* in *Romeo and Juliet* on the basis of assumed literary superiority when the physical, bibliographical facts make the odds about a thousand to one against their correctness.[1]

The Pelican editors score three out of four on this test: Juliet's *name* is retained, but is felt to need extended defence by the general editor in his introduction.[2] Usually, the editors may be applauded for adhering to principles enunciated by Malone in 1792: 'I began by ascertaining what were the authentick copies. I then formed my text upon those copies; from which I never knowingly deviated without apprizing the reader by a note.' This edition finds room within its single volume for remarkably full textual apparatus, though here, as elsewhere, its origin shows in wide differences of scale and procedure between editors. Only a minority give the sources of emendations accepted, and the usual practice of restricting collations to departures from the basic text is oddly abandoned in the interest of rejected variants from the Quarto text of *Lear*, but not for similar readings from Quarto *Othello* or from Folio *Troilus*. It is hard to see why the general introduction ends with a list of selected cruxes, with full collations of early texts and major attempts at emendation. These details are virtually meaningless outside the context of a full discussion of the text of the play in question. The intention of the list seems, sadly, to be to invite each reader to

exercise his skill as an editor, but in fact it does no more than to assert that not all the readings in Shakespeare can be regarded as settled. The texts seem to have been checked with care, but a few misprints have inevitably got through: the present reviewer can contribute two in *Titus Andronicus*, *piece* for *pierce* at IV, iii, 12, and *witness* for *witnesses* at V, iii, 78. The apparatus seems less reliable, if a spot-check on the earlier acts of *Coriolanus* is representative. Departures from the Folio are not collated at I, i, 87, stale] scale; I, iii, 41, contemning.] *Contenning*,; II, ii, 170, speech prefix, CORIOLANUS] Com.; and III, ii, 21, taxings] things. Misprints further reduce the reliability of these collations: the Folio reads 'Titus' not 'Lartius' at I, v, 3 s.d., 'Ouerture' not 'Ouverture' at I, ix, 46, and 'Cumalijs' not 'Cumalius' at III, iii, 136 s.d.

The editing of Shakespeare is the subject of two articles in the current issue of *Studies in Bibliography*. John A. Hart[3] invites us to reconsider the conventional denigration of Pope as an editor of Shakespeare. His contention that Pope has been unfairly underrated by later scholars with different editorial aims and assumptions is well, if narrowly, supported by two main lines of argument. The first is that some of his erroneous glosses and etymologies are in agreement with the best authorities available to him, notably Nathaniel Bailey's *Dictionary* of 1721. The second is that Pope's care in consulting early editions can be shown to have been greater than has sometimes been alleged, although it was not his practice to leave evidence of it in the form of full collations. Three texts provide the evidence, *King Lear*, *Hamlet* and *Antony and Cleopatra*. Pope's omission from his edited text of some passages of *Lear* found only in the Quarto might seem

[1] *Studies in Bibliography*, XIX (1966), 64.
[2] P. 45.
[3] 'Pope as Scholar-Editor', *Studies in Bibliography*, XXIII (1970), 45–59.

to argue his failure to notice them, but his use of the Quarto seems rather to have been deliberately limited to the correcting or supplementing of the Folio text where he found it in error or seriously inadequate. His knowledge of the Quarto text is demonstrated by his adoption of readings from it which Rowe had rejected. Similarly in *Hamlet* Quarto readings (taken from Q3 or Q5) are sometimes preferred to Folio readings accepted by Rowe, while in acts II and III of *Antony*, no less than forty-nine readings in Pope's text represent a return from Rowe to the Folio, not only implying careful collation, at least of these two acts, but arguing from their nature Pope's superior critical sensibility. They include the reinstatement of the following four Folio readings in II, ii: 'give' for 'beg' at l. 88; 'fame' for 'Frame' at l. 193; 'yarely' for 'yearly' at l. 247; and 'stale' for 'steal' at l. 274 (the last being of particular interest as 'steal' is the reading of all editions from the Second Folio to Rowe). Thus Pope's care as an editor is to some extent vindicated, though it remains clear that his aim was not 'to reproduce the historical text of Shakespeare' but 'to examine all the available material so that he could select the "best" of it for the entertainment and edification of his age'.

Jürgen Schäfer[1] concentrates his attention on a group of twenty-two proper names in Shakespeare's plays which either have historical associations outside the plays or are significant in themselves. He shows that recent editors of modernised texts have been thoroughly inconsistent in handling these names and argues that they should all be modernised on the grounds that no consistent Elizabethan form exists and that 'the principle of full modernization, once embraced, has to be applied without exception since it is the only method, paradoxically enough, that is able to reflect the Shakespearian meaning within the new context'. His case seems sound and provides good reason for reading 'Marseilles' rather than

'Marcellus' in *All's Well* (unlike the New Penguin editor); 'Mote' for 'Moth' in *Love's Labour's Lost*; 'Lance' for 'Launce' in *The Two Gentlemen of Verona*; and 'Lancelet' for 'Launcelet' in *The Merchant of Venice*. The list of historical names could, with advantage, have been extended to embrace, for instance, 'Innogen', 'Glendour' and 'Bullingbrooke'.

Editors of Shakespeare will also note with interest the first fruits of two large-scale bibliographical investigations, the one, by J. A. Lavin, of Elizabethan printers' ornaments, the other, by W. Craig Ferguson,[2] of pica roman founts used in England between 1590 and 1610. Lavin's account of 'John Danter's Ornament Stock'[3] involves him in a discussion of the printing of the First Quarto of *Romeo and Juliet*, 1597. He rejects the view of H. R. Hoppe that Danter's shop was raided during the printing of this book and points out that the fact that sheets E–K were printed in Edward Allde's shop implies no such exceptional circumstances, as the division of books between two printing houses for simultaneous setting was a normal practice and one in which Danter engaged for a number of other books, including both Greene's *Groatsworth of Wit* and Chettle's *Kind-Heart's Dream*, which he shared with John Wolfe in 1592.

Also in *Studies in Bibliography*, Clifford Leech,[4] in the role of general editor of the Revels Plays, gives practical advice to young editors of Elizabethan and Jacobean drama. It is a surprise to find in the pages of this journal an account of editing which lays so little stress on bibliographical techniques: indeed Professor Bowers, on this occasion Professor Leech's editor, takes him to task for using the term 'copy-text' in speaking of modernised editions

[1] 'The Orthography of Proper Names in Modern-Spelling Editions of Shakespeare', *ibid.*, 1–19.
[2] 'Thomas Creede's Pica Roman', *ibid.*, 148–53.
[3] *Ibid.*, 21–44.
[4] 'On Editing One's First Play', *ibid.*, 61–70.

and substitutes 'basic copy'. The uses and abuses of the vexed term 'copy-text' are likewise the subject of a note by G. T. Tanselle,[1] who attempts to reassert Greg's definition of it and to resist a growing tendency to use it as equivalent to 'printer's copy'. Greg's own classic statement on the subject, 'The Rationale of Copy-Text' (1949) is reprinted, together with Bowers's 'Current Theories of Copy-Text', in a collection of papers on *Bibliography and Textual Criticism*.[2] H. F. Brooks, joint general editor of the New Arden Shakespeare, makes an eloquent plea for the dignity of the editor's task on the occasion of the seventieth birthday of J. H. P. Pafford.[3] Drawing on wide experience in several periods, Professor Brooks provides a refreshing reminder that editing texts is a literary endeavour, and one that demands humanity as well as method: for him, as for Dr Johnson, 'nothing is a trifle by which his author is obscured'.

John Barton's adaptation of Shakespeare's earliest histories as it was played with great applause by the Royal Shakespeare Company at Stratford in 1964 is now published under its apt title of *The Wars of the Roses*.[4] It is presented, modestly, as 'the record of a specific production' for which it was held practically necessary to reduce to three plays the three parts of *Henry VI* and *Richard III*. The success of the production in the theatre and, later, on television, is already history: 'How must it have joyed brave Talbot...that he should triumph again' before an audience of 'more people than had ever seen the plays in their whole lifetime's history'. Few, if any, previous adaptors of Shakespeare can have indicated so precisely the nature and extent of their revisions: words, lines, speeches, and even whole pages of italic distinguish the hand of John Barton from that of William Shakespeare. These additions are in general serviceable, if anonymous. One may question the need for so extensive rewriting, but its lapses from a

possible idiom are not frequent and usually occur where Barton has attempted a poetic flight: for instance, *cankers* in Shakespeare eat buds rather than defacing flowers.[5] Granted the assumptions of the producer, Peter Hall, the adaptation is eminently workmanlike, clarifying the multiple action of *Henry VI* for an audience ignorant of the chronicles, naming characters unnamed by Shakespeare as often as the metre will admit their names and paring down rhetorical utterance in favour of pointed speech and vigorous action. It is here, of course, that the fundamental incongruity of the present publication becomes obtrusive. Shakespeare's *Henry VI* and *Richard III* are supremely plays of verbal, rhetorical exuberance and intelligence: to adapt them for a twentieth-century directors' and designers' theatre is to create a new work, valid in itself, but palely reflected in the printed words of its scenario. Time and again in the introduction to this text, reference is made to visual effects, especially to the set which dominated the Stratford stage. It seems a pity that none of the photographs included after the text shows this set and that the stage directions are limited to the briefest statement of entrances, exits and indispensable business. As a record of this particular production the text alone, without a fuller account of what happened on stage, leaves one unhappily aware of how much less words count for in the theatre today than they did in the 1590s.

Liisa Dahl's monograph on *Nominal Style in the Shakespearean Soliloquy*[6] brings heavy linguistic guns to bear on a small target and

[1] 'The Meaning of Copy-Text: A Further Note', *ibid.*, 191–6.

[2] Edited by O. M. Brack Jr and W. Barnes (University of Chicago Press, London, 1969).

[3] *Librarianship and Literature: Essays in Honour of Jack Pafford*, edited by A. T. Milne (Athlone Press, 1970).

[4] British Broadcasting Corporation, 1970.

[5] Pp. 19–20.

[6] *Annales Universitatis Turkuensis*, ser. B, tom. 112 (Turku, 1969).

reaches the reassuring conclusion that Shakespeare's developing use of nominal and partly nominal constructions in soliloquies reflects a progressive increase in introspection on the part of his soliloquists. It is surprising that such a linguistic study should still choose as its basis the Globe text of Shakespeare.

Eighteenth-century scholars are the subjects of two notes. Donald A. Low[1] draws attention to the preservation of William Mason's commonplace book in York Minster Library and prints from it his suggestions for several disputed points in Shakespeare's text. These were made in a letter to Malone, dated 26 May 1792. Mason defends several readings rejected by Malone in his edition: Folio 'unteemable' (*All's Well*, I, iii, 197); 'remorse' (*Othello*, III, iii, 472) and 'seat' (*Macbeth*, I, vi, 1) and also Q1 'chear' (*A Midsummer Night's Dream*, II, i, 101). He also argues against the view that the Player's speech in *Hamlet* (II, ii, 446 ff.) was written to ridicule the play from which it was alleged to have been taken. R. L. Wildman[2] reports the presence in the Folger Shakespeare Library of Maurice Morgann's copy of Theobald's 1733 edition of Shakespeare, containing manuscript notes on *The Tempest* and *A Midsummer Night's Dream* which may suggest that Morgann projected an edition of his own.

Other notes relating to particular plays follow. H. F. Brooks[3] discusses the major crux at *A Midsummer Night's Dream*, V, i, 208. He proposes that the Q1 reading 'Moon vsed' is a misreading of 'mure rased' in the autograph manuscript used as copy and that Q2's 'morall downe' results from a botched attempt to emend, without authority, to 'wall downe'. The Folio's 'morall downe' should not, therefore, be the point of departure for emendation, so that the usual editorial 'mural downe' and 'mure all downe' must be ruled out. Emendation must start from the Q1 error and 'mure rased' meets the double requirement of pro-

viding the right sense and making the compositor's error comprehensible. Norman Nathan[4] cites scripture in defence of the form 'Abram' rather than 'Abraham' at *Merchant of Venice*, I, iii, 73 and 161, while conceding that no modern editor has thought otherwise than he does. Prince Hal's soliloquy at *1 Henry IV*, I, ii, 188, is disintegrated by A. G. Gross,[5] who finds lines 197–200 inconsistent with the rest of the speech and proposes the view that these four lines represent the whole speech in a revised form written after the completion of part 1, but erroneously printed in the middle of the speech in the Quarto, though intended to replace it. Granted some obscurity in the speech's line of thought, this solution seems unduly extreme, and the four lines on their own hardly carry enough weight to constitute Hal's only important confidence to the audience. James J. MacKenzie[6] argues that the Folio stage direction for Ophelia's last exit, '*Exeunt Ophelia*', should read '*Exeunt Ophelia and Queene*', and points out that stage practice has anticipated his suggestion. W. P. Williams[7] adduces fresh circumstantial evidence in support of annotated quarto copy for Folio *Othello*, arguing from the employment on *Othello* of compositor *E*, whose inexperience seems to have discouraged Jaggard from letting him work from manuscript copy. He makes the further point that the care with which proofs were read for quire 2v (which contains most of the matter added to the text in the Folio) reflects the exceptional difficulty of the copy for these pages, set by compositor *B*, in which the annotation of the Quarto must have been

[1] *Notes and Queries*, n.s. XVII (1970), 309–12.
[2] *Ibid.*, 125.
[3] *Ibid.*, 125–7.
[4] *Ibid.*, 127–8.
[5] *English Miscellany*, XVIII (1967), 49–52.
[6] *Notes and Queries*, n.s. XVII (1970), 129–30.
[7] 'The F1 *Othello* Copy-Text', *Papers of the Bibliographical Society of America*, LXIII (1969), 23–5.

heaviest and least easily legible. J. B. Winterton[1] considers the stage directions of *King Lear*, IV, vii, in the Quarto and in the Folio and recommends an arrangement of the scene to avoid inconsistent action and words on the part of the Gentleman whose role in the Folio text subsumes that of the Quarto's Doctor. This Gentleman's entry should be delayed until l. 21, when he should come on with the King. E. B. Lyle[2] refers to Davenant's adaptation of *Macbeth* and to Middleton's *The Witch* in support of his claim that there may be grounds for assigning the speeches headed '1' in the Folio at IV, i, 62–76 and 125–32, to Hecate rather than to the first Witch. The effect would be to increase Hecate's role in the scene and specifically to associate her with the apparitions, to which she has previously alluded in III, v.

[1] *Notes and Queries*, n.s. XVII (1970), 133–4.
[2] 'The Speech-Heading "1" in Act IV, Scene 1, of the Folio Text of *Macbeth*', *The Library*, 5th Series, XXV (1970), 150–1.

© RICHARD PROUDFOOT 1971

INDEX

INDEX

INDEX